I0795765

IMAGES
of America

WOODSTOCK
1860–1970

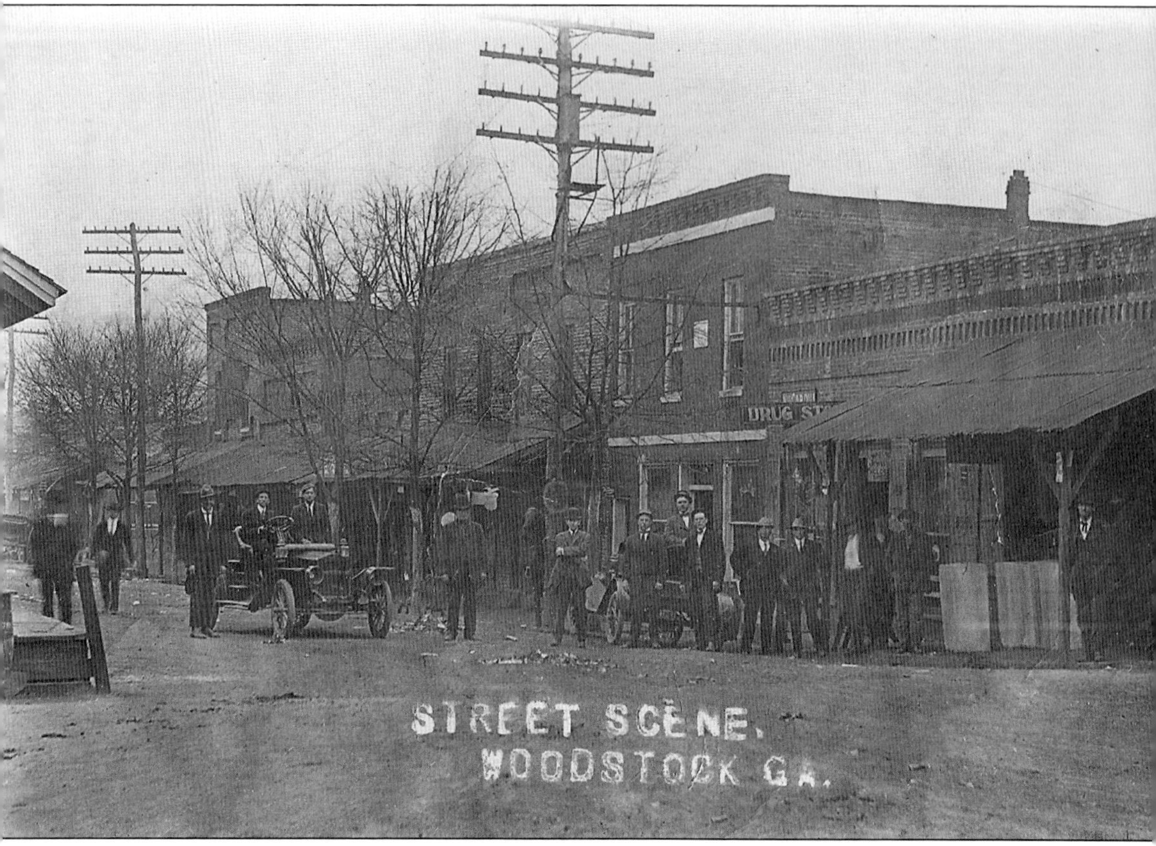

WOODSTOCK, 1911. This street scene in 1911 of Woodstock depicts the prosperous small town it had become from successful farming. After the Cherokees were immigrated to Oklahoma, Woodstock was settled by farmers. The population was sparse, but as homesteads grew and prospered, a small agriculture community grew to a town with general stores, blacksmiths, mills, and livery stables. With the help of the railroad line in 1879, trading and communication improved and helped grow the town. (Courtesy of Preservation Woodstock, Inc.)

ON THE COVER: Linton Dean (seated middle row center), the proprietor of Dean Drug Store, is pictured with local Woodstock men in front of his store in 1910. The drugstore sold a wide variety of items from patent medicines to house paint, auto tires, and gasoline. The store also served as a bus stop and later where residents paid their utility bills in the 1960s. The store had always been a local meeting place to catch up on local news and socialize. (Courtesy of Preservation Woodstock, Inc.)

IMAGES
of America

WOODSTOCK 1860–1970

Felicia S. Whitmore

ARCADIA
PUBLISHING

ISBN 978-0-7385-5425-9

Published by Arcadia Publishing
Charleston, South Carolina

Printed in the United States of America

Library of Congress Control Number: 2008922973

For all general information contact Arcadia Publishing at:
Telephone 843-853-2070
Fax 843-853-0044
E-mail sales@arcadiapublishing.com
For customer service and orders:
Toll-Free 1-888-313-2665

Visit us on the Internet at www.arcadiapublishing.com

This book is dedicated to Juanita Hughes. This book would not be possible without her help and historical expertise of Woodstock. Her enthusiasm and knowledge helps keep the history of Woodstock alive.

Contents

Acknowledgments

My friend Juanita Hughes approached me with the idea of publishing another history book about Woodstock, a photographic history. The previous history of Woodstock in 1997, *Georgia's Woodstock: A Centennial Tribute*, celebrated Woodstock's centennial.

With Juanita's help, I contacted and solicited help from current and former Woodstock residents. Many did not hesitate to provide photographs and information about themselves, relatives, churches, schools, and businesses. This book would not be possible without their help. This is their book; I put their history into words.

Several of the photographs from 1930 came from glass-plate negative images. They were donated to the Woodstock Centennial Commission (now Preservation Woodstock, Inc.) by the Jim Dawson family. The wet-plate process was introduced in 1851, sometimes referred to as the collodion process. It was the first widely used photographic process that resulted in a negative image on a transparent photographic medium. Due to the process and equipment used, these photographs may appear hazy and slightly out of focus on the edges.

Introduction

Before 1835, Georgia was part of the Cherokee Indian Territory. The Treaty of 1835 between the Cherokees and the United States outlined the movement of Native Americans out of Georgia. By May 24, 1838, the Cherokee Territory was officially taken over by the State of Georgia and the Cherokees were forced into Oklahoma.

After the Cherokees were immigrated to Oklahoma, Woodstock was settled by farmers. The population was sparse, but as homesteads grew and prospered, a small agriculture community grew to a town with general stores, blacksmiths, mills, and livery stables. With the help of the railroad line in 1879, trading and communication improved and helped grow the town. In 1897, the town was granted a city charter.

Cotton and slavery were the wealth of Georgia before the Civil War. In 1860, there were 33 cotton mills in Georgia employing about 2,800 workers. Railroads and banks, the two institutions that were most helpful for the marketing of cotton, received government aid.

By the 1890s, Woodstock was said to be shipping 2,000 bales of cotton yearly. This figure was larger than shipments made by any town of comparable size in the area. A number of Woodstock's developers were influential in introducing innovative farming methods to the county.

A significant business heavily influenced the early community. Little River Mills, which was located on Little River, one of the largest tributaries of the Etowah River, began as a gristmill probably in the late 1830s. Land records prove that a gristmill existed in 1842. In the early 1870s, the mill produced yarn until the early 1900s, when the mill produced cotton rope.

The mill changed owners several times, and in 1883, James A. Atherton purchased the mill and formed a partnership with Elias A. Fincher, who owned and operated Shoal Creek Cotton Mill in Pickens County. By the next year, the mill was producing 576 spindles of cotton. In 1897, the mill property consisted of 100 acres.

John Dorn purchased the land and mill in 1903 and replaced the wood structure with brick. Dorn lived on the property with his family. The mill community existed on both sides of Little River.

In 1928, Dorn sold the mill and property to Appalachian Development Company, who sold it to Georgia Power. Joe and Smith Johnston leased the mill and operated it from 1928 to 1949. During its last 20 years of operation, the mill continued to produce rope for plow lines or wound it into large coils weighing about 59 pounds for well rope and other purposes. The mill employed 20–30 workers who lived in the mill village of seven houses along the river.

Cotton rope was produced from lower-grade cotton. Cotton bales were dropped from a chute from the warehouse onto the mill floor. The bales were fed into a machine that decompressed the cotton in fluffy masses. The cotton was then fed into the picker machines that cleaned the cotton and formed sheets rolled onto metal cylinders.

Townspeople and the farm community continued to be self-sustaining and removed from city life during the 1920s and 1930s. Their lifestyles and economy bore little resemblance to those of other towns or cities. They were content with their daily routines and enjoyed their independence.

News was distributed by word of mouth at the train depot, where passengers and goods were unloaded. The depot was a bustling place when the train stopped to unload. Local residents and farmers gathered on Main Street to meet and greet friends. People sat along the platform waiting for the train, which arrived exactly on time.

Farm owners who benefited from their cotton crops turned their land over to tenants and moved to town. They desired to live in town to be a part of the community and the activities of town life. Those who lived in town kept out-buildings on their property and maintained gardens to provide fruit and vegetables for the family. Homes situated on several acres kept woodsheds, cribs, hen houses, and toolsheds.

By 1906, Woodstock had a thriving downtown business district. The Bank of Woodstock began business in 1905, and Dean Drug Store opened in 1906 and sold items such as patent medicines, rock candy, sarsaparilla, chewing tobacco, kerosene, coffee, sugar, cigars, and Coca-Cola. Several general stores opened on Main Street to accommodate the thriving community.

Cotton was king in the 1920s. By the 1930s and with the drastic effects of the Depression, the cotton industry faded. The decline of the cotton industry in the area greatly affected Woodstock. With the invasion of the boll weevil (a beetle whose larvae fed on the silky fibers inside the cotton bolls), the establishment of a large industrial development in Marietta, and the creation of a broiler industry in the county, the labor force began to decline. The cotton labor force was leaving the industry.

The six or seven cotton warehouses along the railroad remained empty most of the year until the harvest. Farmers would then flock to Main Street to cash in their harvest. "What will you carry me for this year?" the farmer would ask the merchant.

Prior to the 1940s, most families in the Woodstock area raised their own poultry. Later, when the Depression left many cotton farmers broke, some farmers joined the poultry industry to raise chickens in larger quantities to sell.

Farmers were accustomed to and familiar with traditional farming and not with organized business or industry. When the boll weevil swept through the cotton crops, farmers looked to a new source of income. South Georgia farmers switched their efforts to growing peanuts and tobacco. North Georgia farmers switched to raising chickens.

Many profited from this new venture. However, as local poultry farmers learned, they had to compete with the larger growers and had to compete for help with other industries that were locating near Woodstock. Local Woodstock poultry farmers eventually fell out of the market. During the late 1960s, most chicken houses were abandoned and used as utility sheds.

Woodstock experienced city growth not only in population but in city services and businesses. Between 1950 and 1960, the population grew from 545 to 726. In the 1950s, Woodstock employed a deputy marshal and night watchman for $25 per month, and the town had its first water system with 125 customers. The water was obtained from the existing drilled well at the rear of the bank. The one well produced 26 gallons of water a minute. The city purchased a 1939 La France fire engine for $2,100. Woodstock residents had their first dial phone in 1956. Residents used the Glendale exchange. It was soon discovered that local callers could be reached by dialing only the last four digits of the phone number.

Also in the 1950s, the city converted city hall (the depot) into the firehouse where the fire engine would be kept. Storefronts on Main Street were remodeled in 1961, and street names were established in town. Woodstock and Acworth were added to the Atlanta Metropolitan Telephone Service Plan in 1962. A medical clinic opened in August 1962, as did the first hospital in Woodstock, the space-age 22-bed Cherokee Atomedic Hospital.

As the decades passed, Woodstock became a booming bedroom community, an expansion of the Atlanta metropolitan area. Subdivisions were developed to accommodate the increasing population, and cotton warehouses were torn down to make room for businesses on Main Street.

Today downtown Woodstock is a mixture of new shops such as a florist, antique shops, and a drugstore. Storefronts still have the old look about them. Many of the old homes have been restored.

The Towne Lake community, which was once the Thousand Acre Woods, drew families to relocate to south Cherokee County. Additional businesses were established to meet the needs of the new community. Thousand Acre Woods was leased by a paper company for timber used as pulpwood. Nearby residents had used the woods for hunting.

Many families have moved to Cherokee County because of the relatively low taxes and lower population than other metro-Atlanta counties.

However, longtime Woodstock residents say the extreme traffic only increased dramatically over the past 15 years. They say Woodstock has remained the small close-knit community that it had been for over 100 years.

A pivotal point in the change of Highway 92 was the removal of the Old Dixie Inn, which was replaced with a gas station, the establishment of McDonald's and Hardees, the opening of Wal-Mart, and the opening of the Dixie Speedway. Woodstock has emerged as an extension of Atlanta.

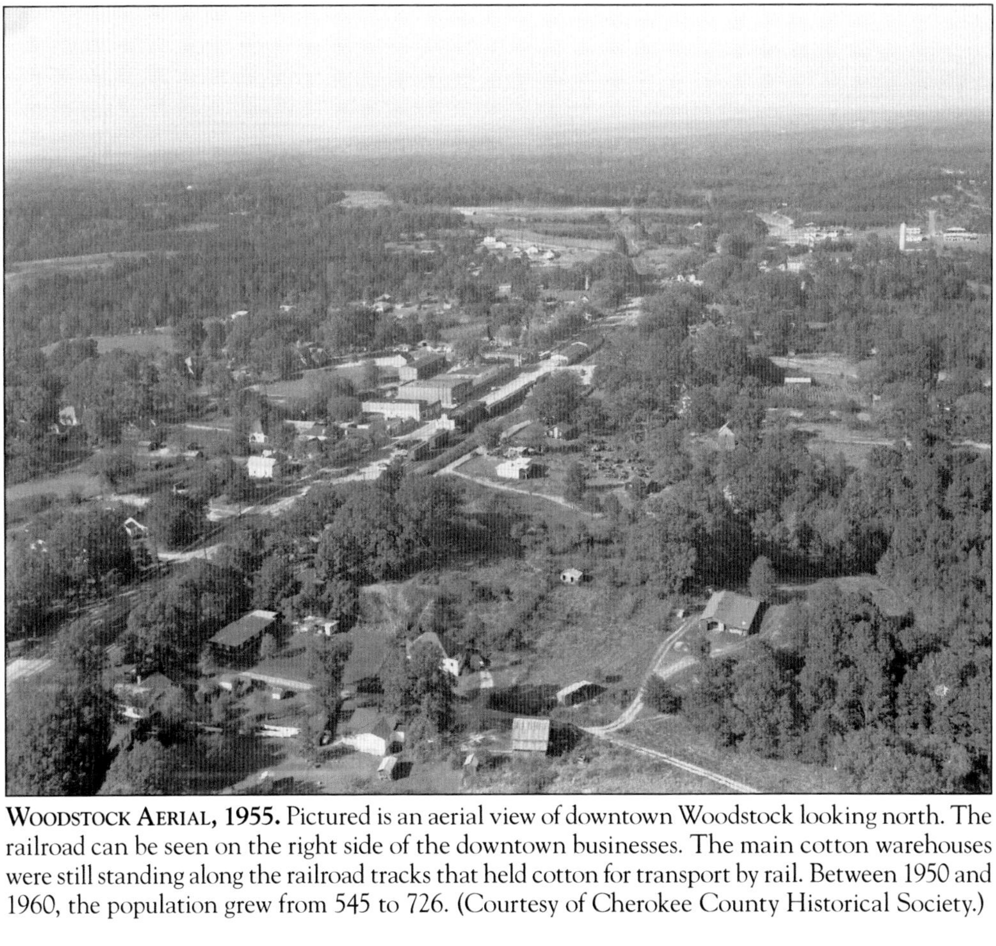

WOODSTOCK AERIAL, 1955. Pictured is an aerial view of downtown Woodstock looking north. The railroad can be seen on the right side of the downtown businesses. The main cotton warehouses were still standing along the railroad tracks that held cotton for transport by rail. Between 1950 and 1960, the population grew from 545 to 726. (Courtesy of Cherokee County Historical Society.)

One

War Veterans

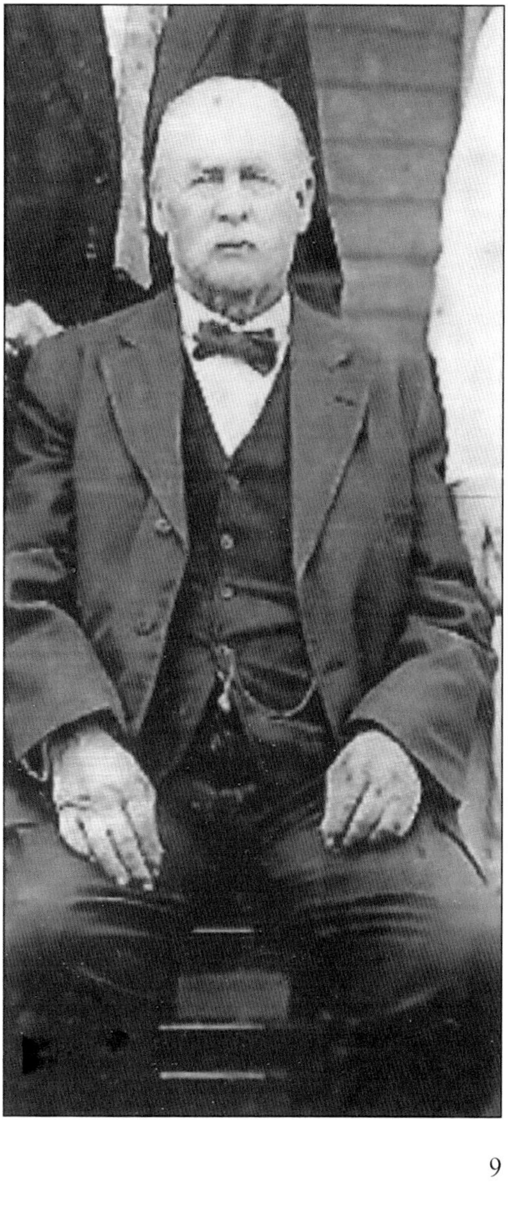

George Christopher Whitmire, 1908. Born in 1844 in Forsyth County, Whitmire served in the Confederate army in Company I, 38th Infantry. He was captured in Strasburg, Virginia, on August 19, 1864. He was released at Point Lookout, Maryland, on June 22, 1865. His son, Thomas Albert Whitmire, managed a dry goods/grocery store on Main Street, Woodstock, in the 1920s. (Courtesy of John Whitmire.)

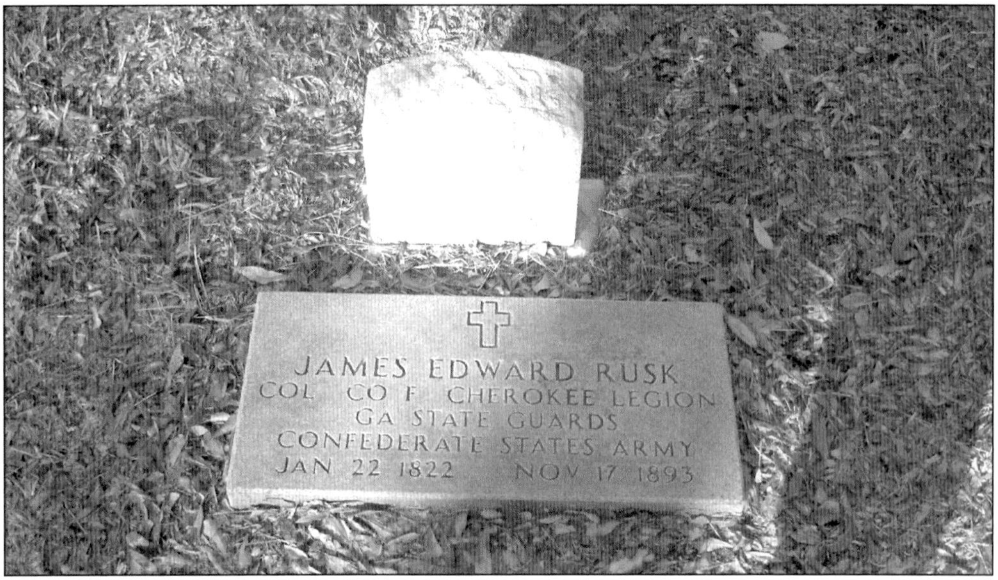

Col. James Edward Rusk, Cherokee Legion. Colonel Rusk (1822–1893) served in the Cherokee Legion, Georgia State Guards in the Confederate army. Rusk fought with the Cherokee Light Artillery, endured the hardships of Vicksburg, and was captured on July 4, 1863. After an exchange, the unit participated in the campaigns of the Army of Tennessee from Missionary Ridge to Bentonville. Rusk settled on a farm east of Woodstock and later served as senator in 1886–1887. His father was David Rusk, who settled in Woodstock in 1831. His grandson was Secretary of State Dean Rusk, who was born in Woodstock. (Courtesy of Felicia Whitmore.)

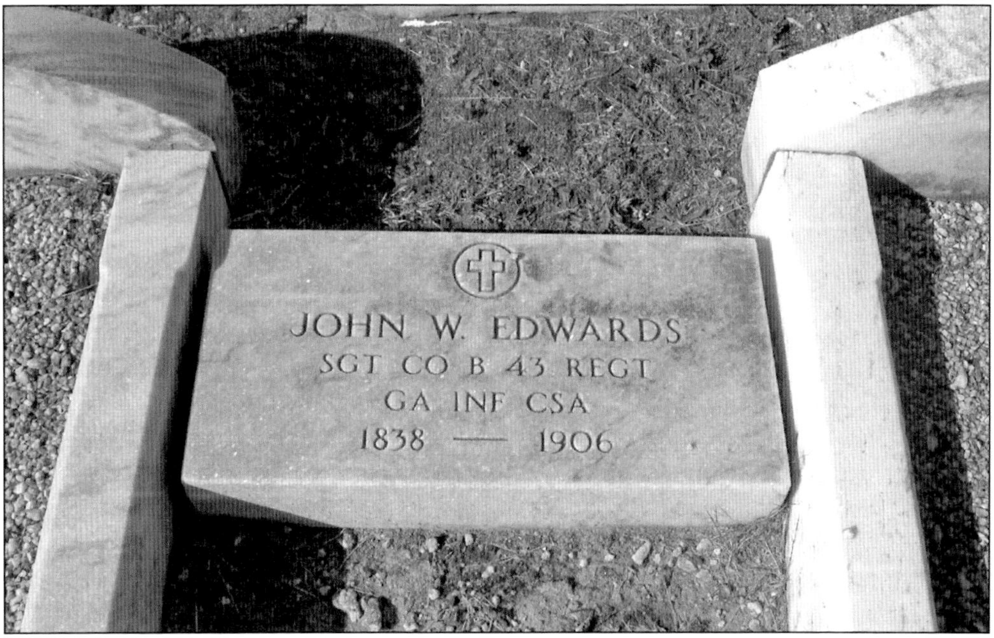

John W. Edwards, Sergeant of Company B, 43rd Regiment, Georgia Infantry. Edwards and the unit moved to Tennessee, then to Mississippi, and fought conflicts at Chickasaw Bayou and Champion's Hill. Edwards and the 43rd Regiment were captured in Vicksburg. (Courtesy of Felicia Whitmore.)

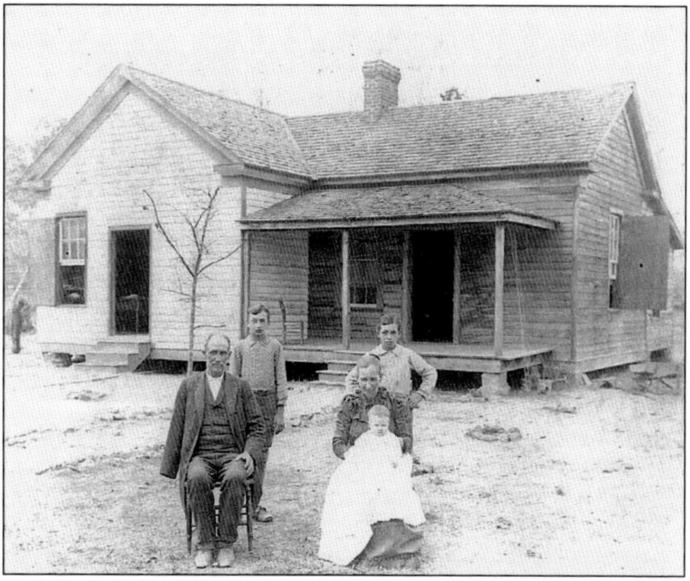

EDWARDS FARM, ARNOLD MILL ROAD, 1894. From left to right are John W. Edwards, whose grave is pictured on the previous page, Claude E. Chandler, Walter Chandler, Amanda Edwards, and Eva Edwards (baby). The Edwards family lived on an 80-acre farm on Arnold Mill Road. In 1910, the family moved to town on Elm Street in a new home. Walter, pictured behind his mother, continued to work on his mother's farm in his later years. (Courtesy of Mae Dobbs.)

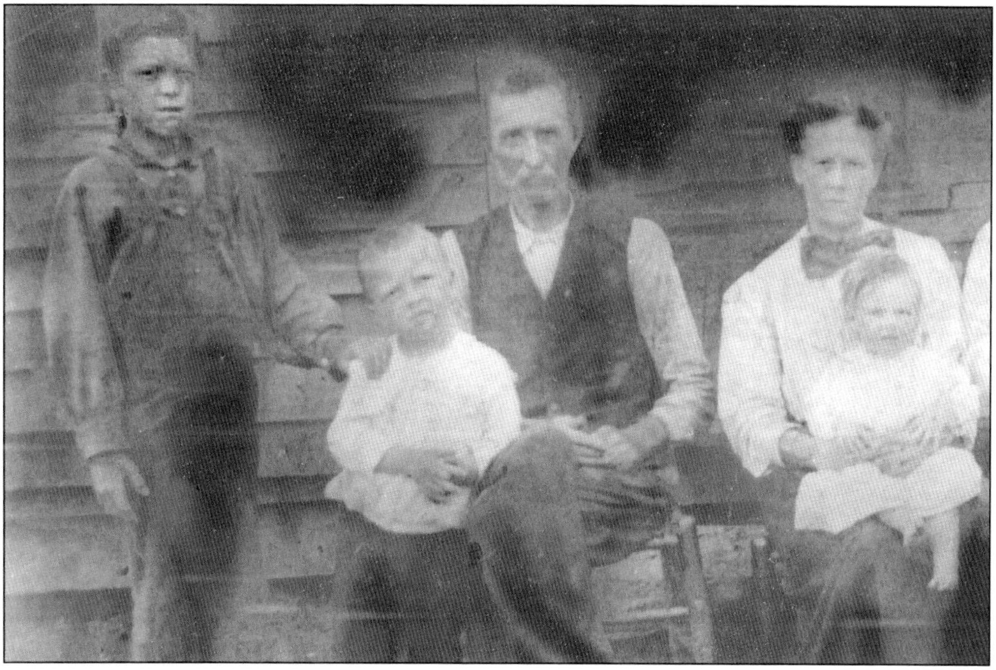

JOHN GRIMES, PRIVATE, COMPANY A, ROSWELL BATTALION, GEORGIA CAVALRY, C. 1915. Grimes was 15 years old when he fought with Company A, Roswell Battalion, in the Georgia Cavalry. The battalion was organized on June 28, 1863, to protect areas north of Atlanta to the Alabama and Tennessee lines. Most soldiers served under Maj. G. W. Cunningham at Roswell Factories. On December 31, 1864, Roswell Battalion combined with other battalions and served with the Army of Tennessee with Gen. Joseph Wheeler's cavalry. John Grimes was 66 years old when his son Newt was born in 1910. His mother was 25. Pictured are, from left to right, John's stepson Calvin Parker, Newt Grimes, John Grimes, Lula, and baby Lina. The Grimes family lived on the Hal Dean farm, where John Grimes farmed. (Courtesy of Mary Ann Parker Eubanks and Jeanette Parker McArthur.)

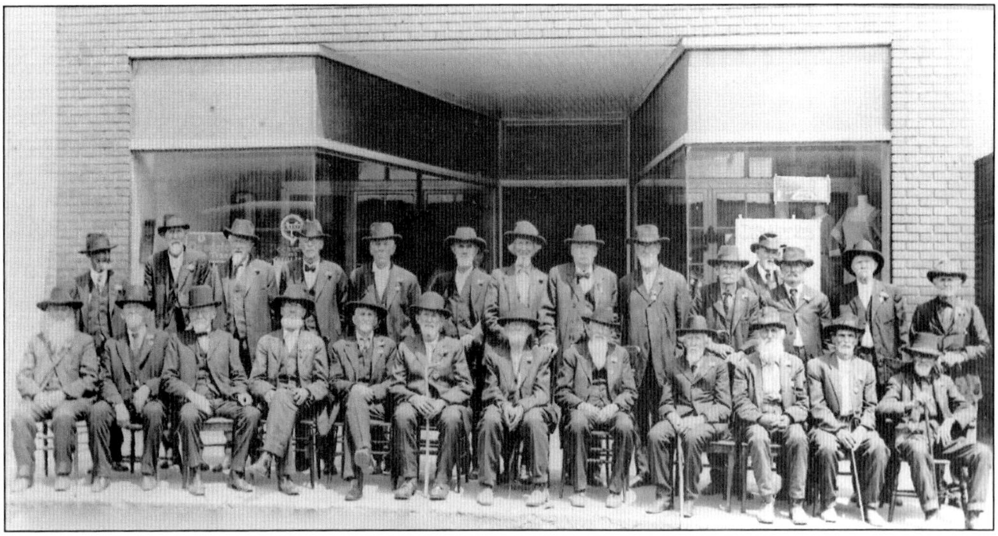

Civil War Soldiers Reunion, Canton, April 26, 1923. Pictured from left to right are (first row) ? Abercrombie, J. W. McAfee, B. Burch, Truman Knox, ? Lindsey, George Watson, Joseph Wilister, W. T. McCollum, A. B. Coggins, Benson Knox, Jasper Richardson, and ? Allred; (second row) Elias Fincher, Henry Steel, David Smith, Shault Coker, H. Sanford Goss, W. F. Chamblee, Joe Knox, George Whitmire, Henry Edwards, ? Attaway, L. B. Hughes (man behind the row), Jim Hulsey, George Washington Tippens, and Jessi Gramling. (Courtesy of Cherokee County Historical Society.)

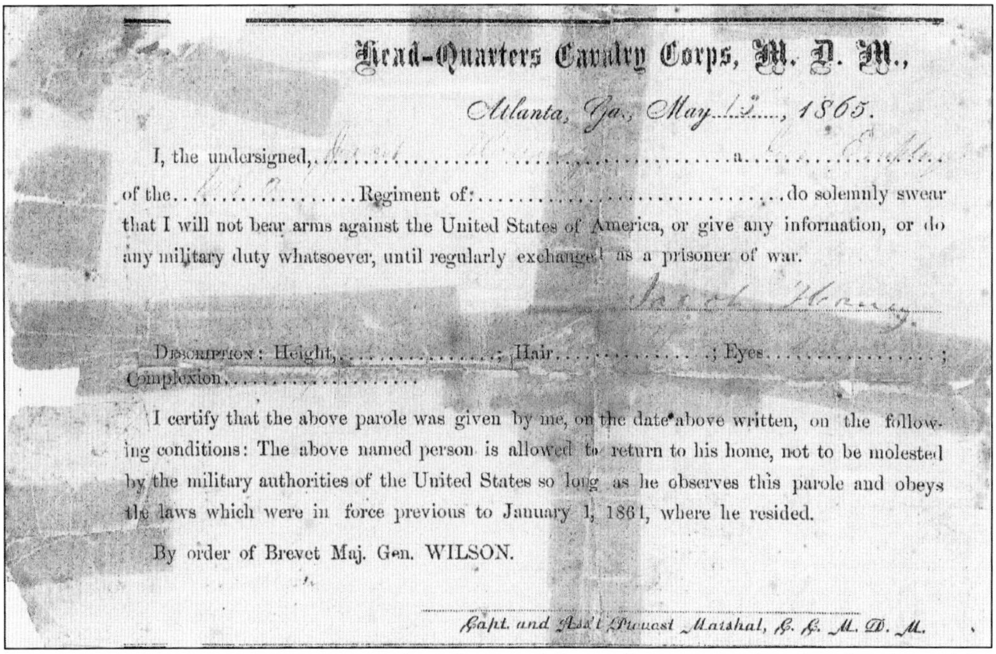

Head-Quarters Cavalry Corps, M. D. M.,

Atlanta, Ga., May 1[illegible], 1865.

I, the undersigned, [illegible] a [illegible]

of the [illegible] Regiment of [illegible] do solemnly swear that I will not bear arms against the United States of America, or give any information, or do any military duty whatsoever, until regularly exchanged as a prisoner of war.

Jacob Haney

Description: Height, ...; Hair ....; Eyes ....; Complexion ....

I certify that the above parole was given by me, on the date above written, on the following conditions: The above named person is allowed to return to his home, not to be molested by the military authorities of the United States so long as he observes this parole and obeys the laws which were in force previous to January 1, 1861, where he resided.

By order of Brevet Maj. Gen. WILSON.

Capt. and Ass't Provost Marshal, C. C. M. D. M.

Parole Oath, Jacob Haney, 1865. When the Confederate forces surrendered at the close of the Civil War in 1865, the men were given paroles or passes permitting them to go home safely. The parole oath was in force while an exchange was being made of war prisoners. Jacob Haney, as a soldier of the Army of the Confederate States, had to swear allegiance to the United States. He carried the document with him the rest of his life. (Courtesy of Virginia Switzer Wald.)

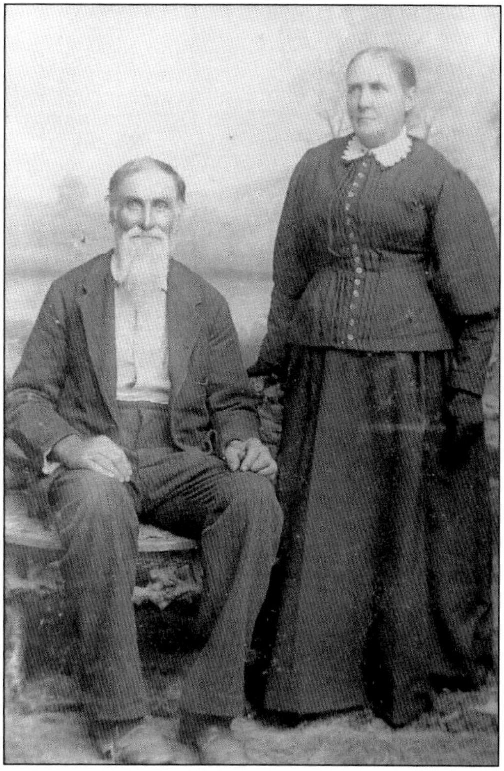

Willis W. Poor, Private, Company B, 43rd Regiment, Georgia Infantry. Pictured with his wife, Rebecca (1837–1924), Poor (1836–1916) was an early settler in Woodstock. Poor and the unit moved to Tennessee, then Mississippi, and fought in conflicts at Chickasaw Bayou and Champion's Hill. Poor and his regiment were captured in Vicksburg. (Courtesy of Jeanne Cosey.)

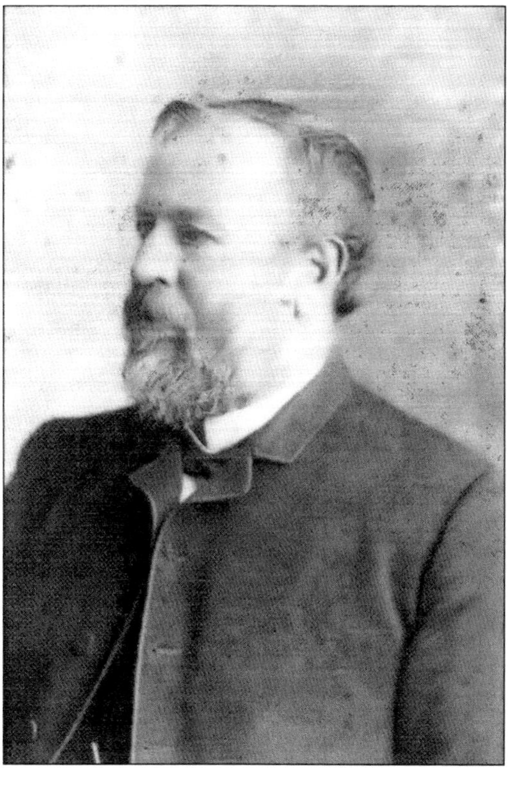

Capt. William Choice Dial Sr., Cobb's Legion. Dial settled in Woodstock from Spartanburg, South Carolina. He was a captain in Cobb's Legion, Georgia, and later served on the Georgia State Legislature. According to Dial's son, Dial was wounded three times during the war. Cobb's Legion was organized by Howell Cobb in 1861 and fought with the Army of Northern Virginia. The unit fought at Cold Harbor and suffered casualties at Brandy Station and Gettysburg. They participated at the Wilderness, Spotsylvania, and Chancellorsville. In 1865, the cavalry unit joined T. M. Logan's brigade, fought in the Carolinas, and surrendered with the Army of Tennessee. (Courtesy of Harold Johnston.)

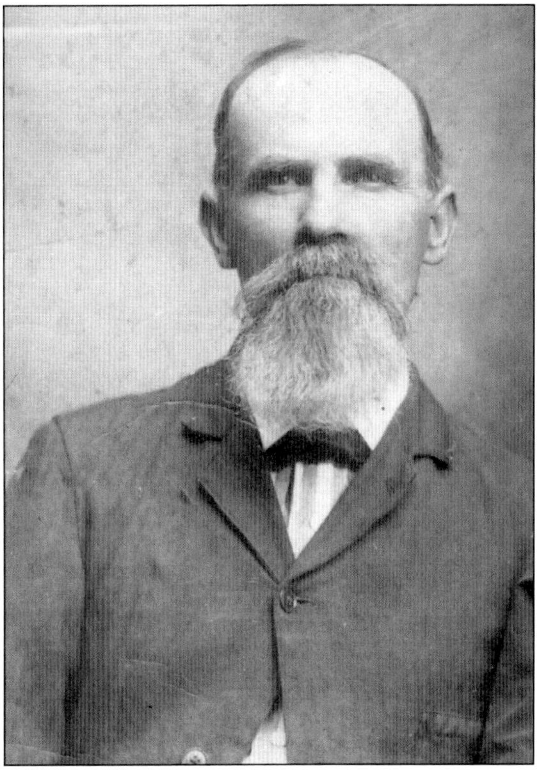

WILEY PARKS DOBBS, PHILLIPS' LEGION, GEORGIA, COMPANY C. Dobbs served in Phillips' Legion, which was organized just before June 1861. The unit of 463 served in Georgia and along the South Carolina coast, then moved to Virginia, where it served under generals Wade Hampton, Benjamin Butler, and Pierce Manning Butler Young. The unit participated in the campaigns of the Army of Northern Virginia from Fredericksburg to Cold Harbor and then helped in the defense of Petersburg. The unit surrendered with less than 50 men in April 1865. (Courtesy of Marilyn Dobbs Morrell.)

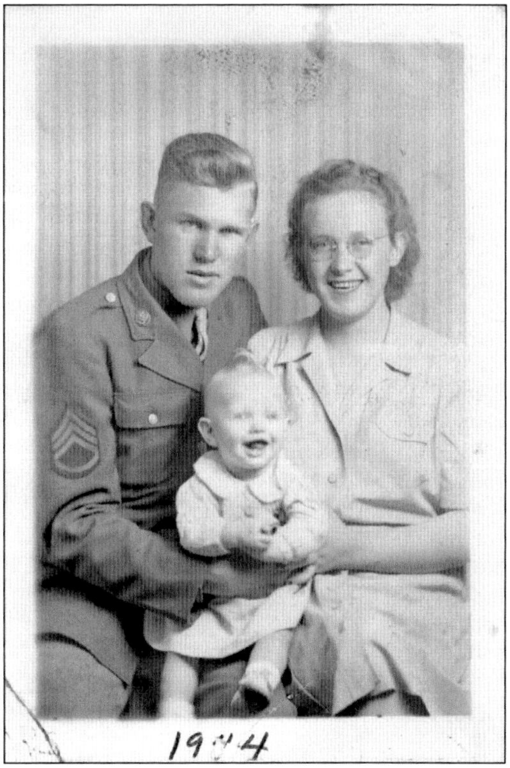

RADFORD STARKE BROOKS, ARMY AIR FORCE, 1944. Brooks is pictured with his wife, Ara Lowe, and daughter Sonya. Brooks was drafted into the Army Air Force in early 1943 and was stationed at Marianna, Florida. He was deployed to overseas duty and participated in the China-Burma-India Campaign. As staff sergeant and crew chief on a C-46 transport plane, he and the crew flew supplies over the Himalayas and China. While Brooks served in China, his youngest brother, Richard, was serving in the war in France. Brooks was awarded the Distinguished Service Medal. Upon completion of his military service, Brooks was given an honorable discharge in 1945 and returned to Woodstock. (Courtesy of Sonya Brooks Dobbs.)

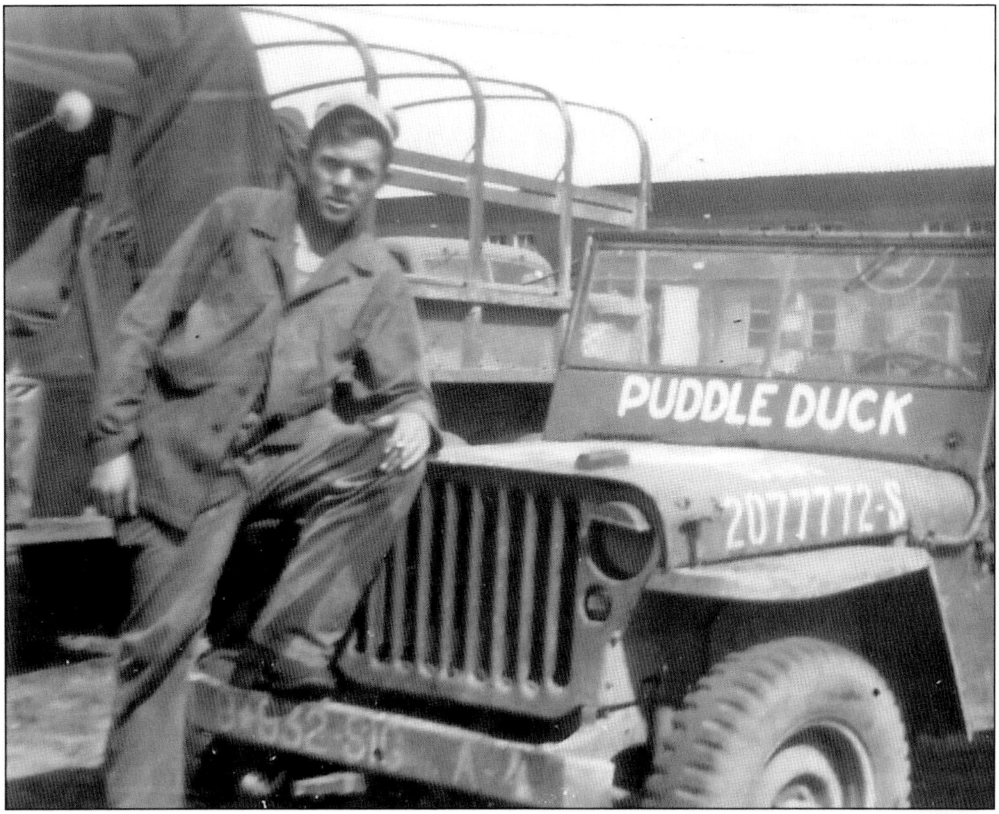

RICHARD BROOKS, 1943. Brooks served in the Civilian Conservation Corps (CCC) prior to World War II and helped build Fort Benning. He joined the Army Air Force in 1943 and was first stationed in England. Soon after, he was deployed to France during the U.S. occupation of France. While driving a military supply truck delivering supplies, he also transported captured German soldiers, most of whom were badly injured. He was honorably discharged in December 1945 and returned to Woodstock and his wife, Lottie. They later had three children, Anthony, Jerry, and Debbie. (Courtesy of Sonya Brooks Dobbs.)

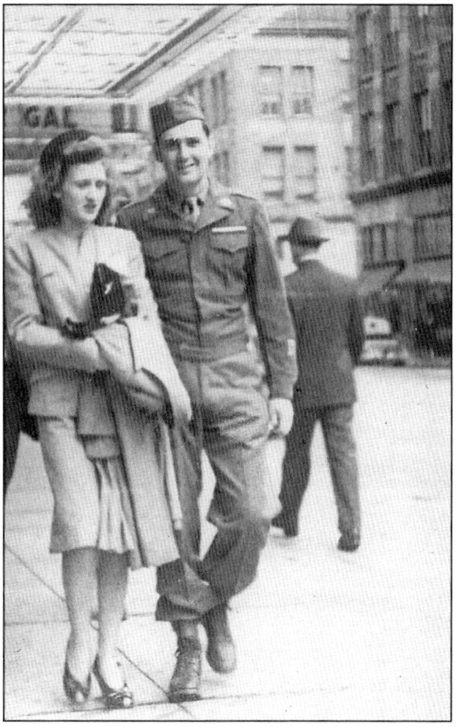

CLAUD BARNES WITH HIS WIFE, RUTH MERRITT, ATLANTA, 1944. Barnes served in the 3rd Army in World War II and was based in England six months before D-Day. Barnes avoided Nazi bullets and capture on Omaha Beach, Normandy, in June 1944, as he and fellow soldiers waded through the English Channel. Barnes was stationed outside Berlin waiting for the Russians to invade when the war finally ended. (Courtesy of Claud Barnes.)

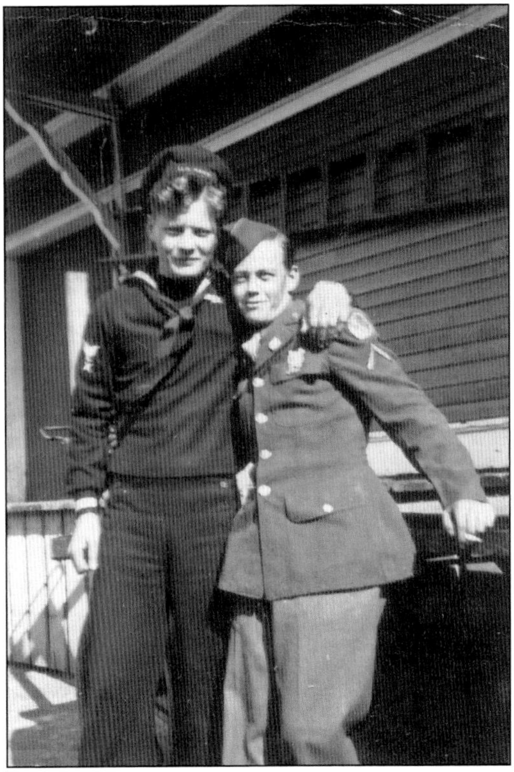

LEROY POOR AND RILEY MEDLEY, 1944. Friends Poor (left) and Medley (right), on leave, pose in front of the depot. Poor and Medley served in World War II in the army; Poor later served in Korea and Vietnam. In World War II, Poor, a 17-year-old gunner's mate third class, was reported missing when his ship, the USS *Rich* (DE-695) was sunk when it encountered a German mine at Utah Beach, Normandy, on June 8, 1944. Poor was one of several rescued from sea. He was later awarded the Purple Heart. Riley Medley later operated Medley's Restaurant on Main Street. (Courtesy of Jeanne Cosey.)

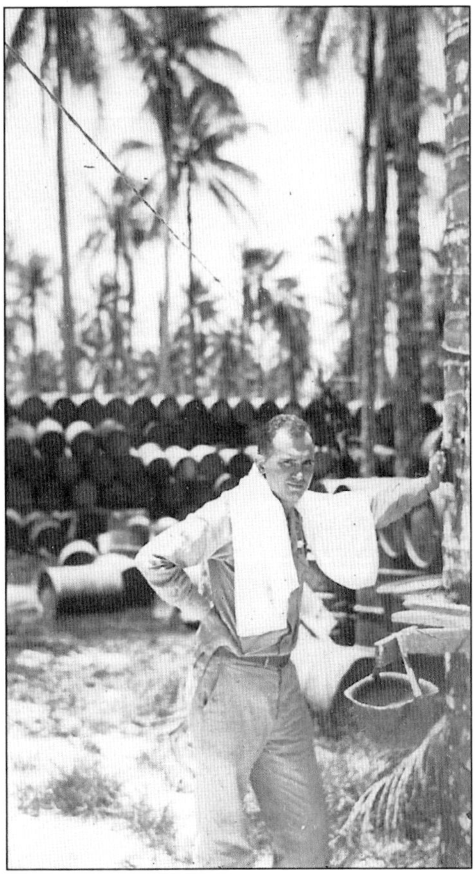

LT. SMITH JOHNSTON JR., PHILIPPINES, 1944. Johnston Jr. served in World War II in the Philippines. Born in 1918, Johnston Jr. attended Emory University and eventually became president of the Bank of Woodstock. Johnston's son Smith Johnston III became a physician to NASA astronauts in Houston, Texas. (Courtesy of Harold Johnston.)

WORLD WAR II VETERAN TRIBUTE, 1944. A senior serviceman presents a folded flag to Ida Rusk Dawson, mother of Bobby Dawson who died at Normandy, at Woodstock Methodist Church. Chior members include, from left to right, (first row) Esther McCollum, Becky Medley, and Vivian Dawson; (second row) Cliffie Johnson and Sara Lee King (hidden beside her). Pictured on the altar are, from left to right, Martha Johnson, E.T. Booth, Hugh Lee Johnston Sr., unidentified, and Smith L. Johnston Sr. (Courtesy of William Johnston.)

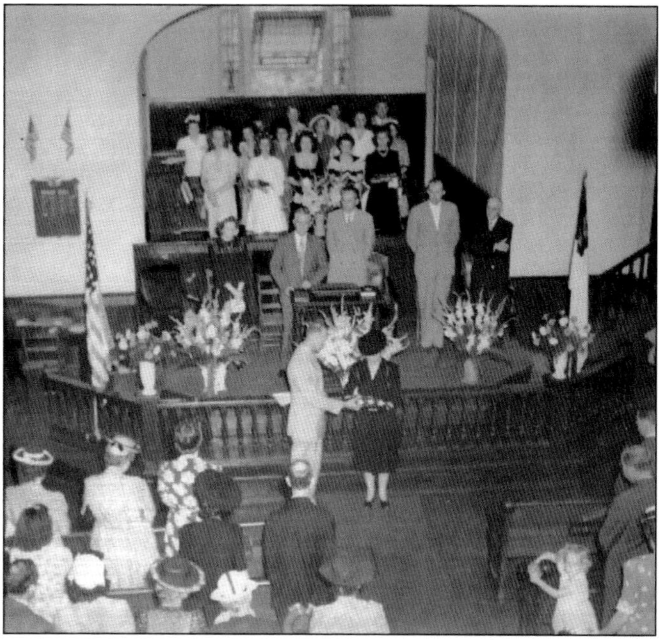

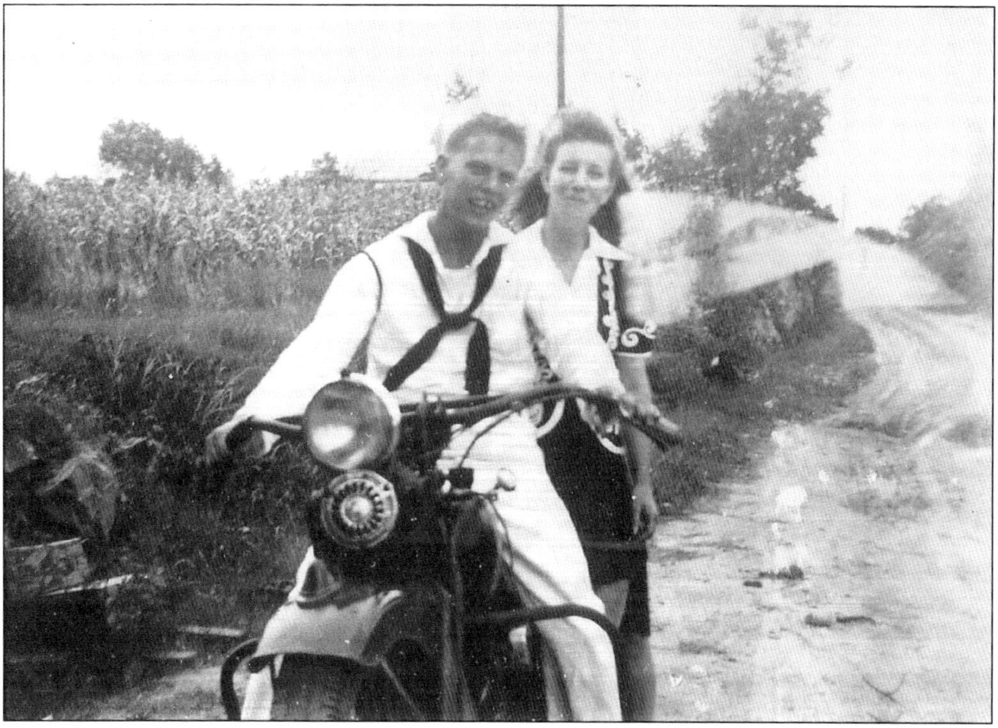

JAMES POOR AND LOLA POORE, 1945. Poor and Poore take a joyride on Poor's motorcycle in 1945. Poor joined the navy after the bombing of Pearl Harbor. He had been in a technical school in Toccoa, Georgia, for a few months at the outbreak of the war. He served on a seaplane tender as an aircraft mechanic in the South Pacific. Of the Poor brothers, James served the longest. After returning home from the war, Poor operated Howell-Poor Company (a grocery) with his father-in-law, Luther Howell. (Courtesy of Jeanne Cosey.)

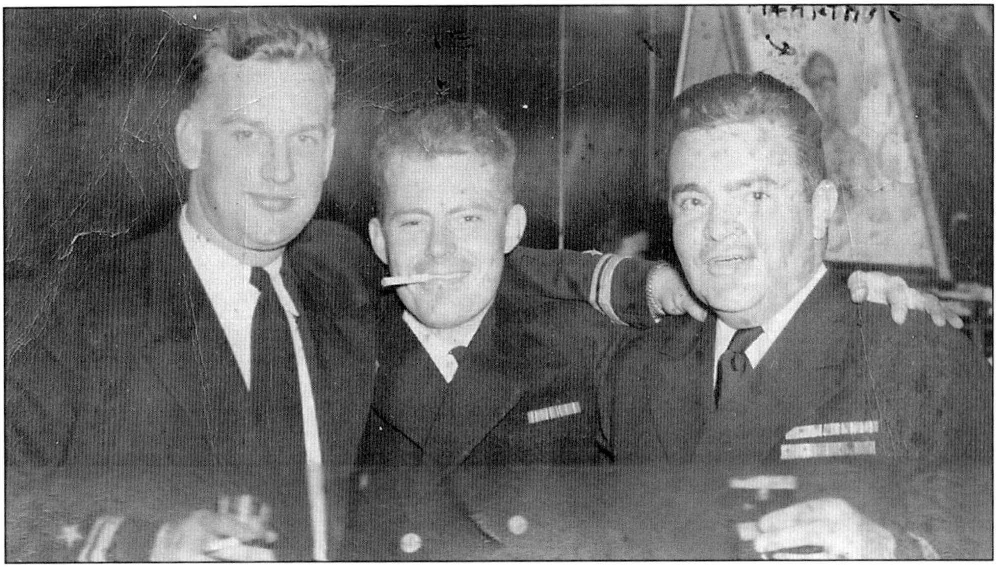

Albert Poor Jr. and Army Friends, World War II. Poor (center) and his army friends take a break from army life in World War II. Poor had taken Navy ROTC at Georgia Tech and within a couple of months was sent to the Naval Academy in Annapolis, Maryland, for basic officer training. He was commissioned an ensign in the navy from the Naval Academy after six months of officer training. He was assigned as an engineer to a destroyer escort, as was his brother Leroy, and he initially served in the Atlantic and around South America. In 1944, his ship was sent to the South Pacific, and he and his brother Leroy happened to meet when their ships were in a China port. (Courtesy of Jeanne Cosey.)

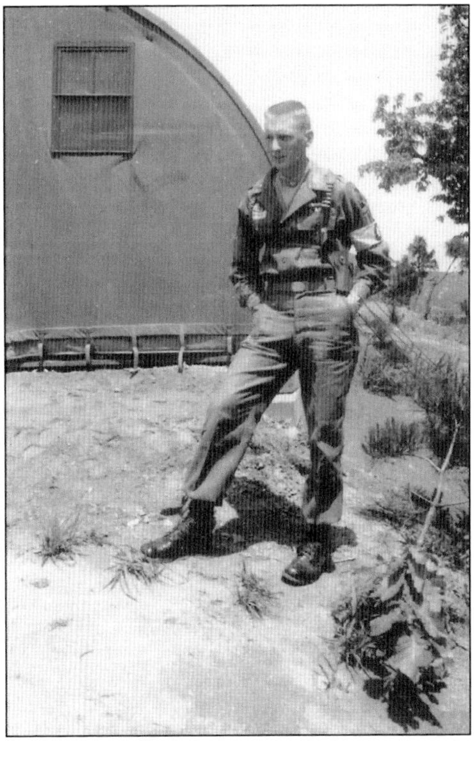

Lt. William Poor, 1954. Poor became a communications officer, 17th Infantry Regiment, 7th Infantry Division, at Camp Kaiser, Korea. Poor also served again in Korea in 1970–1971 and in Vietnam. In the late 1960s, he was stationed in Hawaii. He retired as colonel and became programs and policy division chief for the Office of Army Inspector General at the Pentagon. (Courtesy of Jeanne Cosey.)

Two

Influence of the Railroad

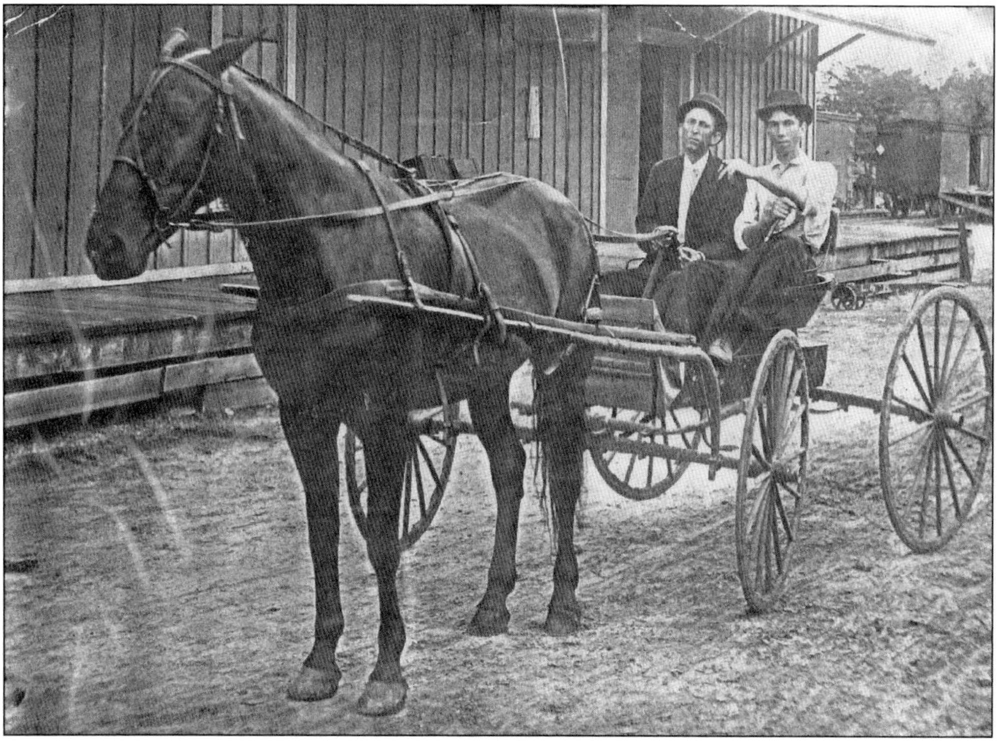

First Woodstock Depot, 1879. Linton Dean (left) and Jim Boring (right) sit in a buggy in front of the first depot. The depot was located on the west side of the tracks, a few feet north of the present depot. The depot was demolished in 1913 after completion of a new depot. The lumber from the depot was used to build the First Church of God north of Woodstock in the Lebanon/TooNigh community. (Courtesy of Alice Dean Felton.)

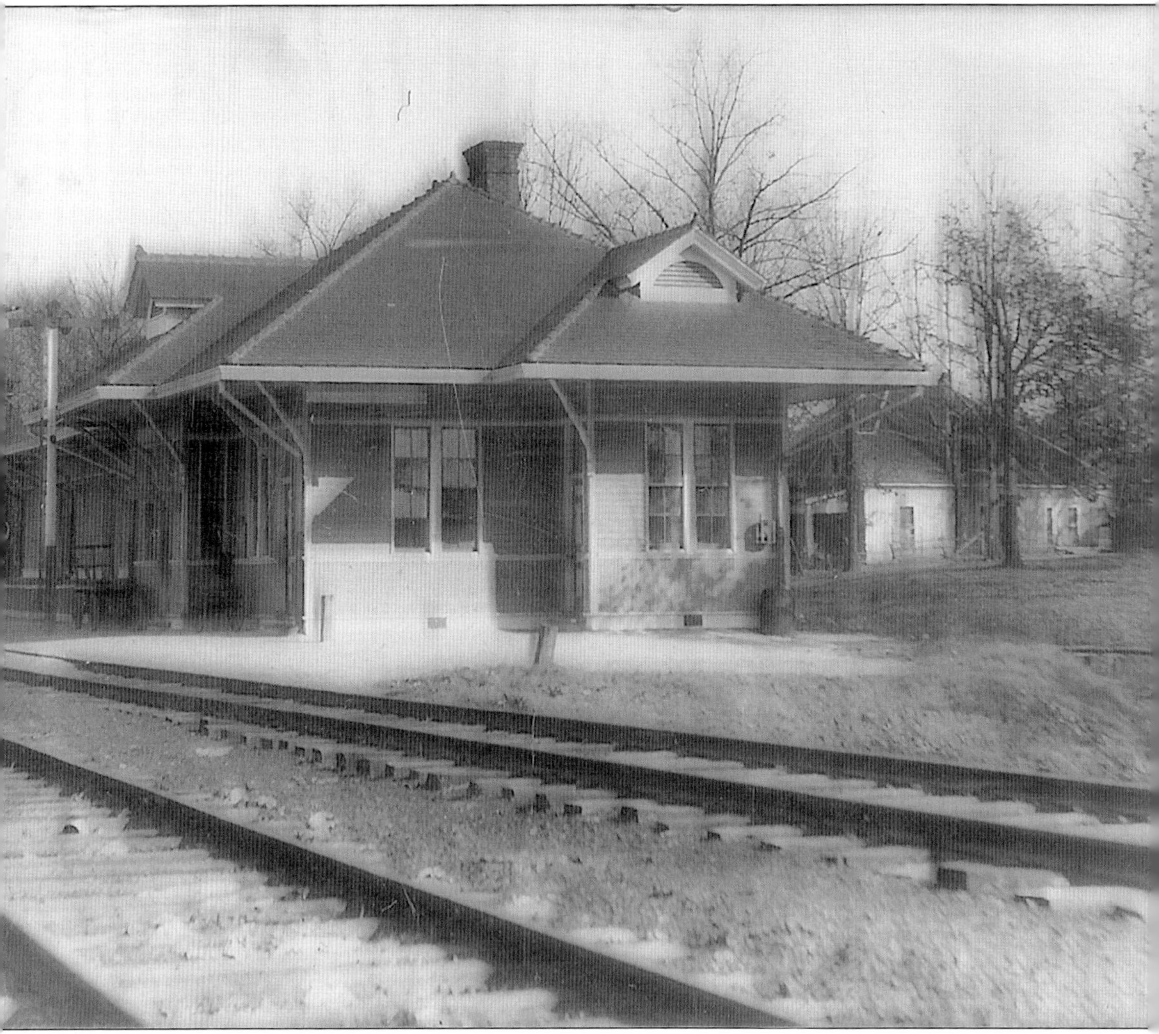

SECOND WOODSTOCK DEPOT, 1912. The Marietta and North Georgia Railroad built a railroad line through Woodstock in 1879, delivering marble, iron, and copper deposits. The original depot was built that year. Both depots were divided into freight and passenger/ticketing sections, with a separate entrance and waiting room for African Americans. (Courtesy of Preservation Woodstock, Inc.)

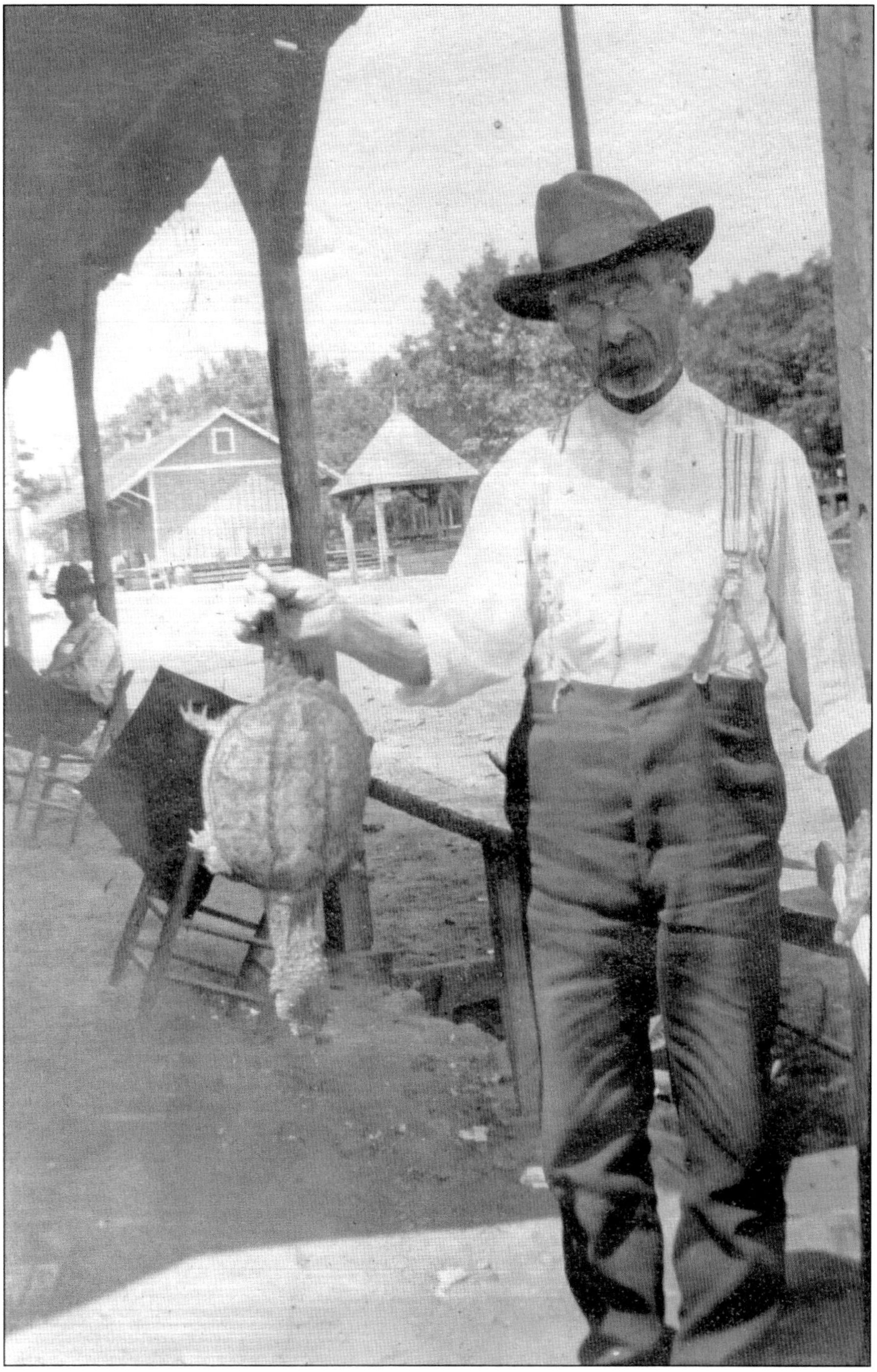

William Posey Dobbs, Store Owner, c. 1910. William Posey Dobbs stands with a turtle near the original train depot, built in 1879 on the west side of the tracks. The current depot, built in 1912, is on the east side. Dobbs (1849–1939) was known to everyone as Uncle Posey. He operated a livery stable and a grocery store located in the current Woodstock Gas building in 1915. (Courtesy of Marilyn Dobbs Morrell.)

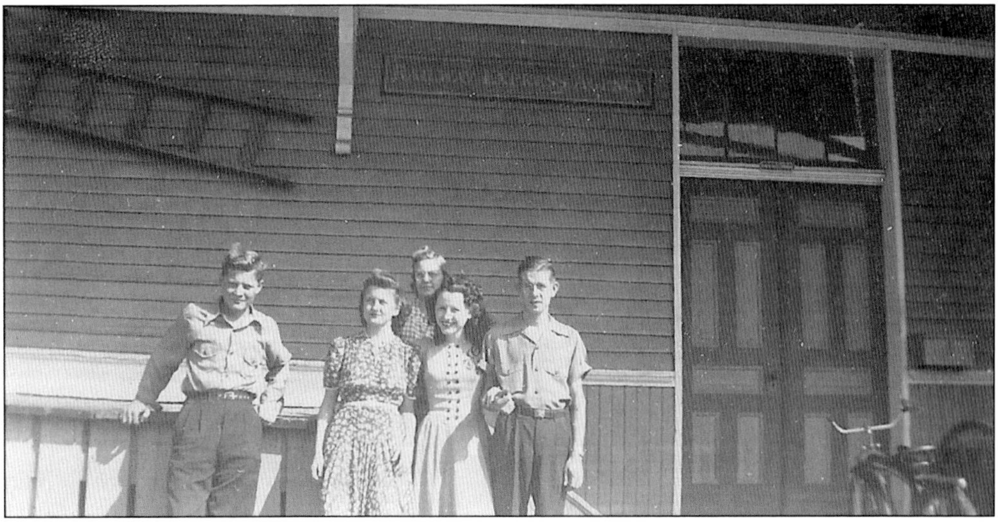

Railroad Express Agency, Woodstock Depot, 1939. From left to right, Leroy Poor, Ann Kemp, Marie Poor, Mary Lois Ingram, and Roy Freeman pose under the Railroad Express Agency sign at the depot. (Courtesy of Jeanne Cosey.)

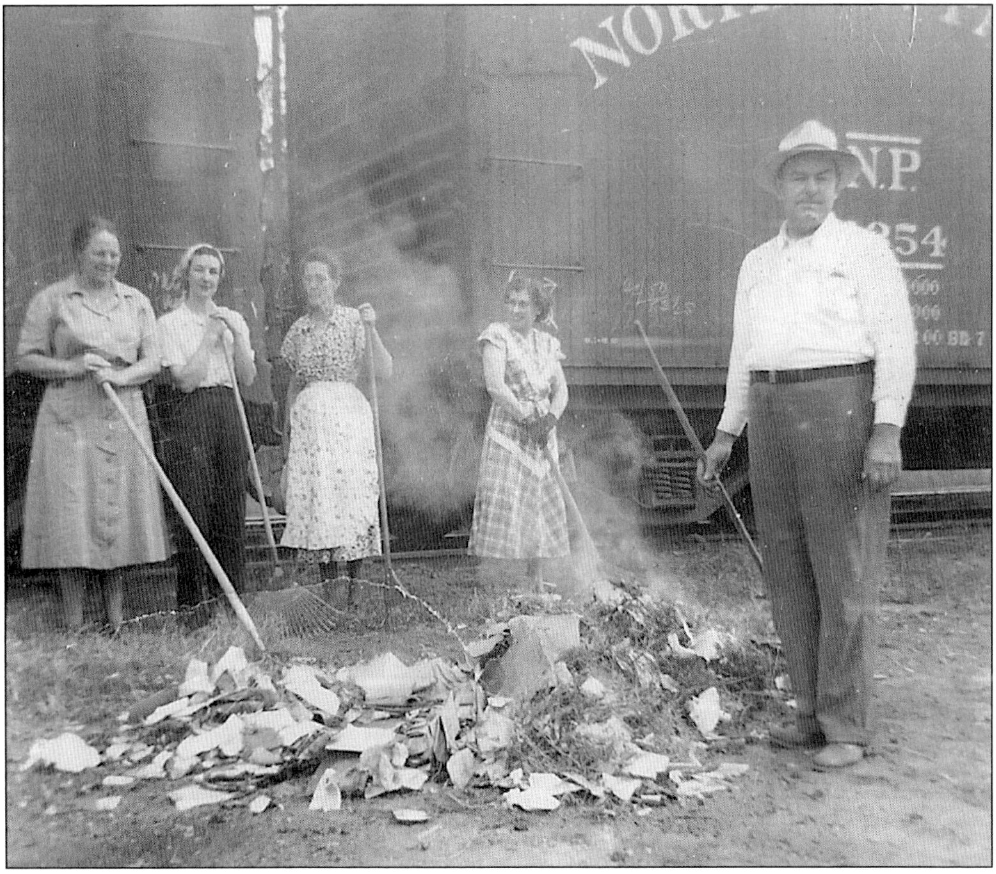

Cleaning Up Along the Train Tracks, Late 1940s. Pictured are, from left to right, Mary Howell, Katie B. Anderson, unidentified, ? Mullinax, and Luther Howell. (Courtesy of Jeanne Cosey.)

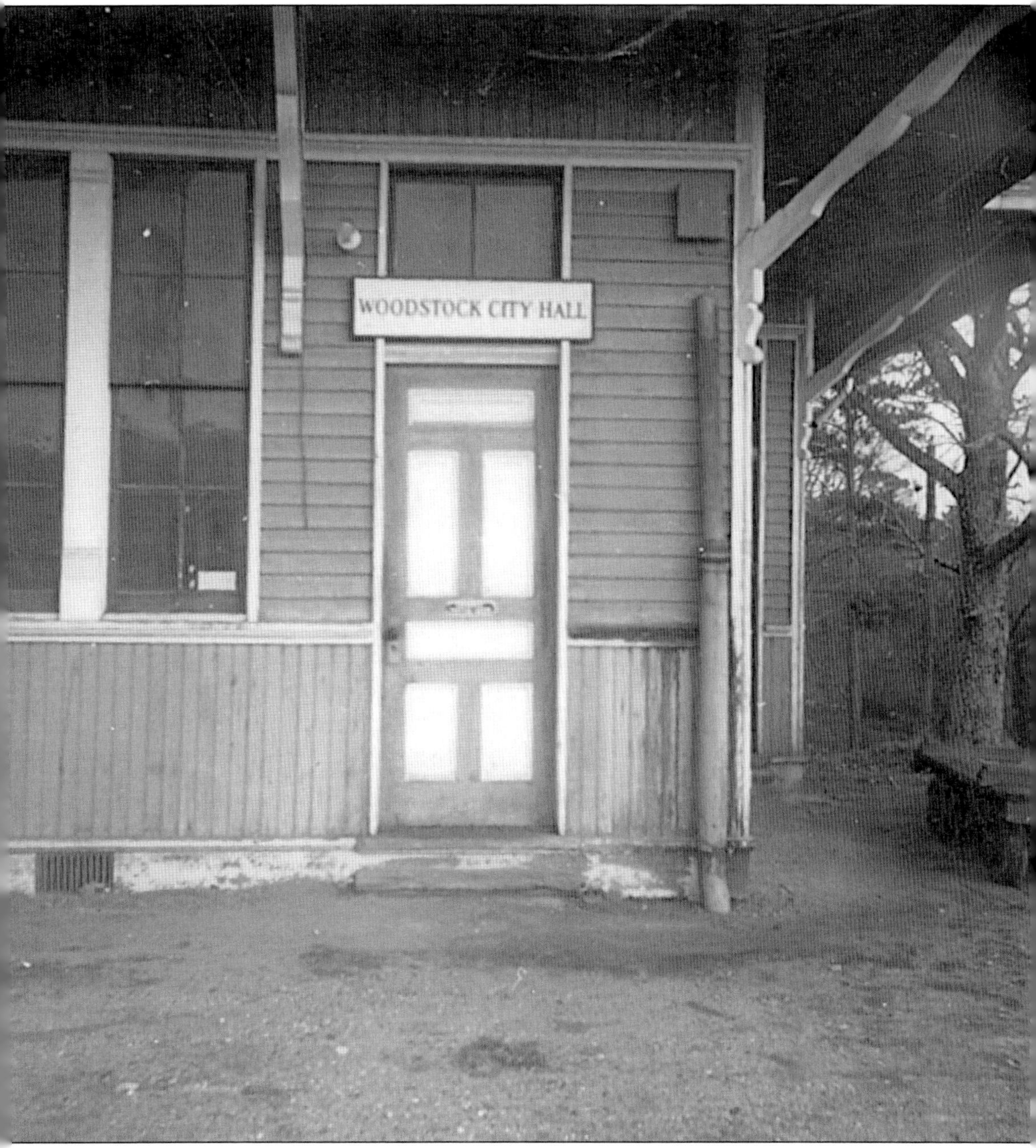

DEPOT AS WOODSTOCK CITY HALL, 1964. The depot served as the city hall, fire department, police department, and community center from 1963 to 1982. The depot was placed on the National Register of Historic Places in the early 1980s. (Courtesy of Woodstock Public Library.)

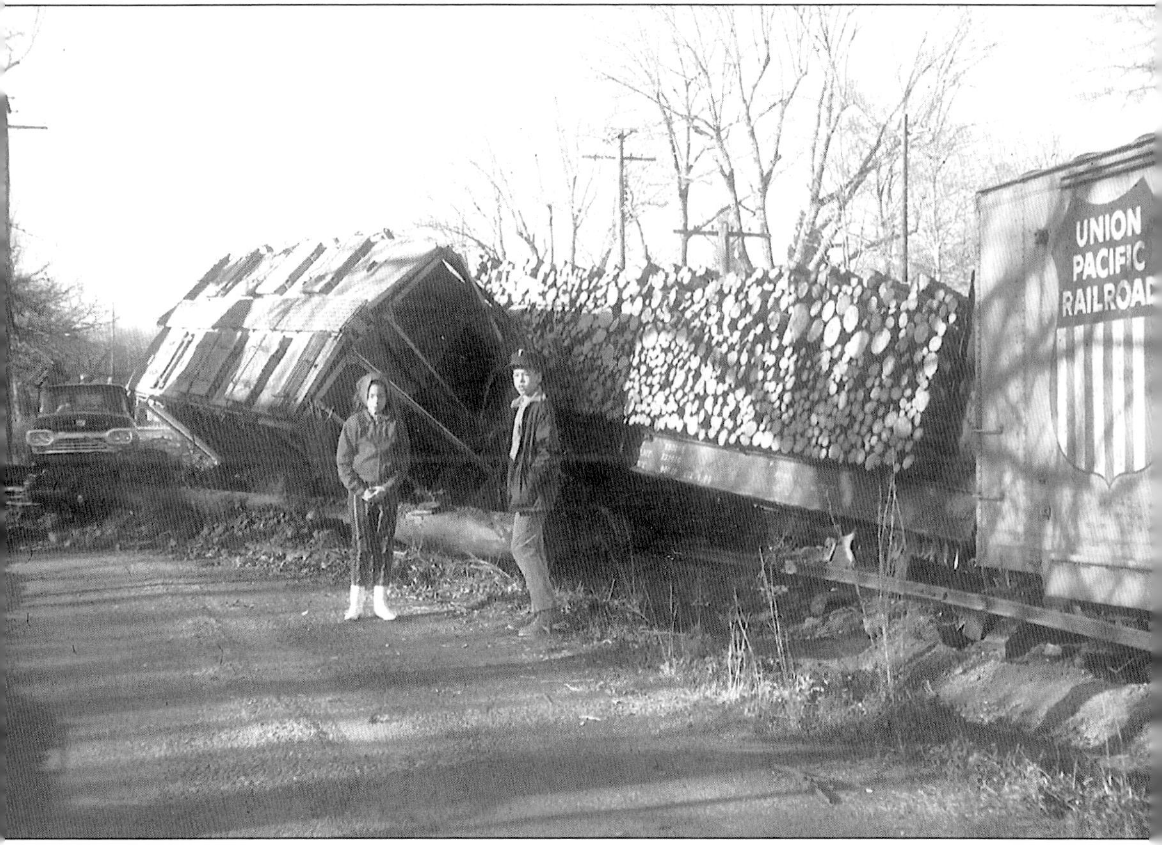

TRAIN CARS DERAILED, 1966. Mary Lou and Sonny Ramsay stand beside derailed train cars loaded with lumber. Logs and lumber spilled onto the road, blocking passage. Passenger trains had stopped passing through Woodstock by 1966. (Courtesy of Sara Frances Dial Ramsay.)

Three

Cotton and Poultry Industry

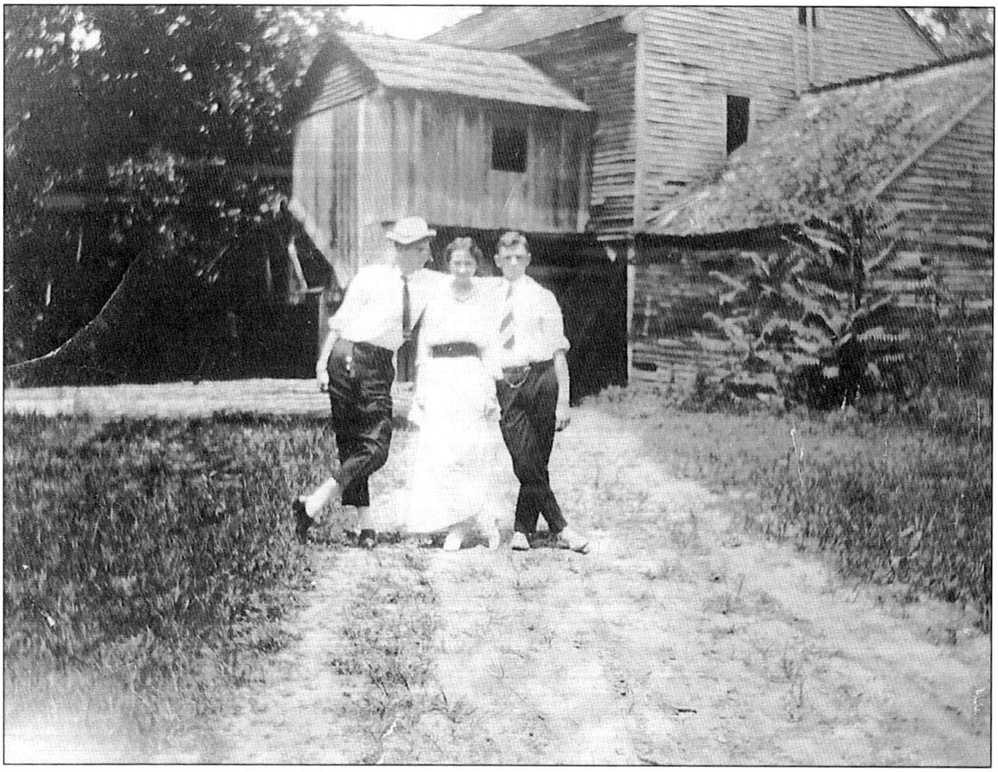

Little River Mills. The mill began as a gristmill in the late 1840s and evolved into a cotton mill and wool yarns mill in the 1870s. Eventually the mill produced rope made from low-grade cotton used for well rope and plow lines. The textile business grew at the turn of the 20th century, and several area mills were established, such as Canton Cotton Mill by R. T. Jones. The Little River Mill building was a wood-frame structure on the north side of the river. A rock dam was built and the river was diverted to where a waterwheel pulled the water and powered the mill machinery. The finished product, 3/8-inch cotton rope, was wound into bales weighing about 40 pounds. The rope was transported to Woodstock by wagon and then by truck and rail. Pictured are, from left to right, Linton Dean, Alice Wellons, and ? Reid. (Courtesy of William and Mary Johnston.)

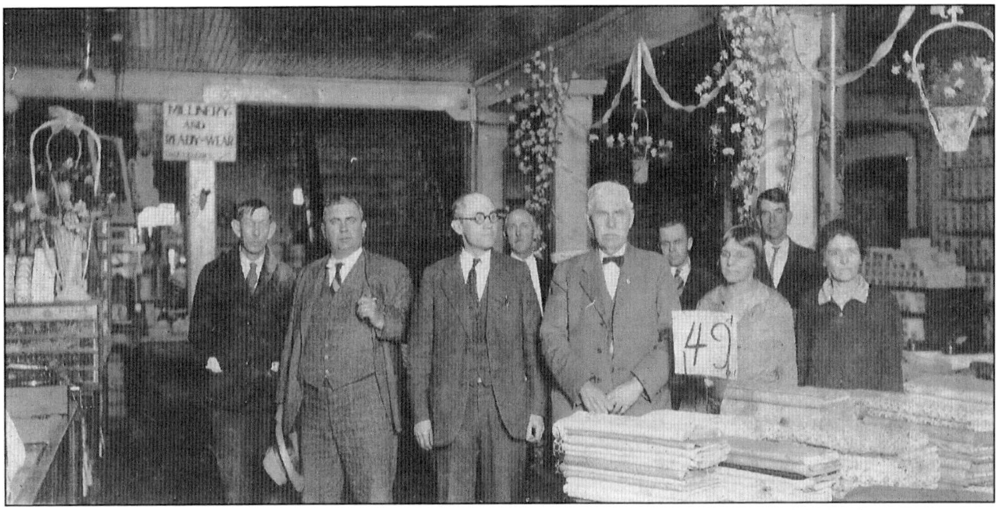

J. H. Johnston Company, Established 1888. J. H. Johnston Company, established in 1888, was the largest general store in town for several decades. Johnston sold dry goods, groceries, hardware, feed, seed, and fertilizer. He offered credit to farmers when he posted the "Credit Season Open" sign in the window. That prompted Johnston to establish a bank later. Stairs led to an upper floor, used as the Masonic Lodge for decades. Pictured in 1930 are, from left to right, Roy Freeman, Joe E. Johnston, Smith L. Johnston, W. Dave Bozeman, J. H. Johnston, Vernon Green, Jessie Robertson, Sam Dawson, and Emma Barnes. (Courtesy of Stanley Johnston.)

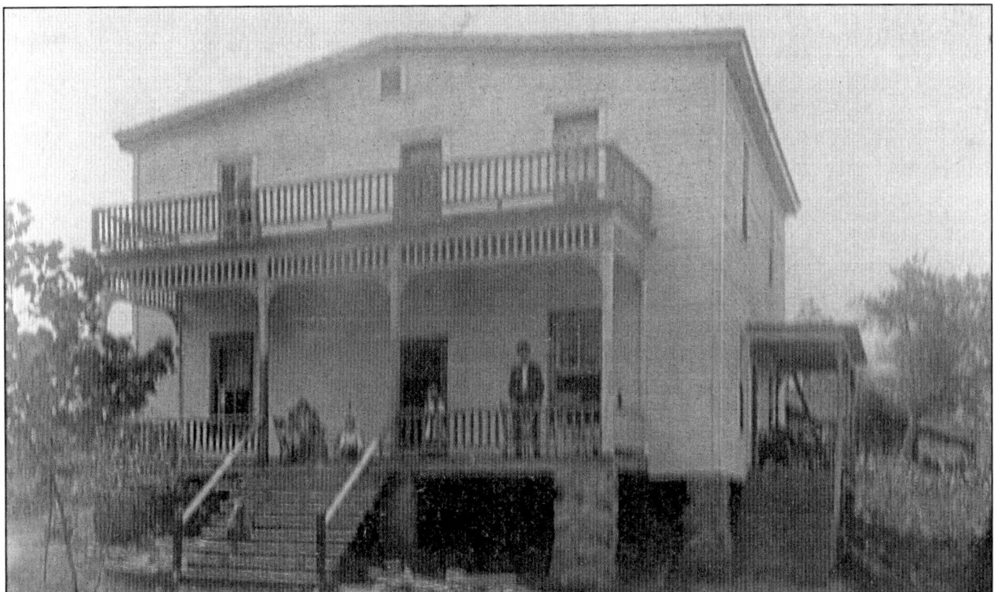

Dorn House, 1903. Leland Dorn, who managed the Rope Mill, lived in this house along the river in the mill village. His father, John Dorn, originally purchased the land and mill in 1903 and replaced the wood structure with brick. The mill community existed on both sides of Little River. John Dorn and his wife, Inez, had six children, and they lived on the mill property. Seven other families worked and lived at the mill, according to census records. Dorn was born in Georgia and was 46 years old in 1910. In 1928, Leland Dorn sold the mill and property to Appalachian Development Company who then sold it to Georgia Power. (Courtesy of Preservation Woodstock, Inc.)

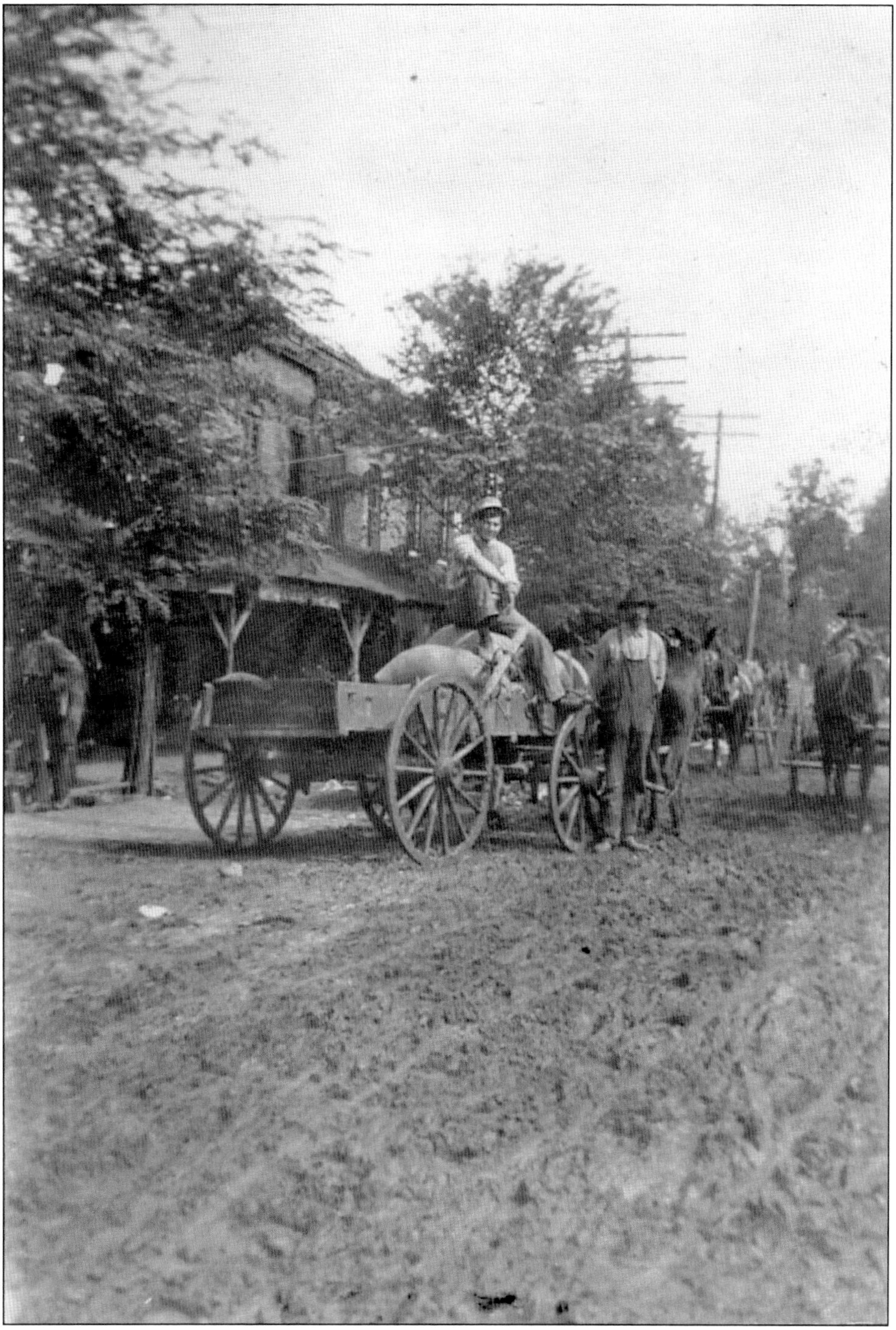

Bringing Harvest to Town, c. 1900. An unidentified farmer poses atop a wagon loaded with cotton he brought to town to sell. William Posey Dobbs, who operated a livery stable, stands next to the wagon. Farmers brought their cotton bales in wagons to the merchants. The merchant would slice the bag of cotton with a knife and pull a wad of cotton to inspect. The merchant graded the cotton and gave a price to the farmer. (Courtesy of Marilyn Dobbs Morrell.)

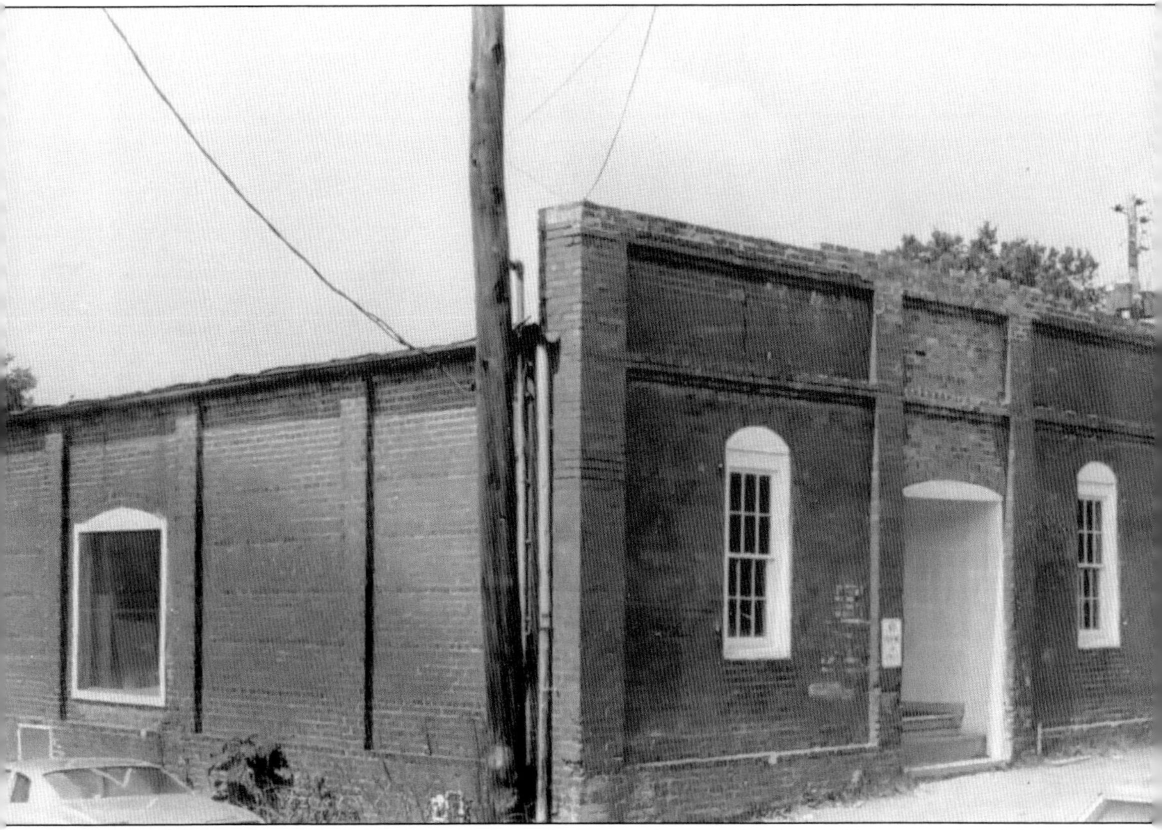

J. H. Johnston Cotton Warehouse, Church Street. In the 1890s, some 2,000 bales of cotton were transported a year by railroad. The last remaining cotton warehouse is currently a business. Johnston owned several cotton warehouses in Woodstock. (Courtesy of Preservation Woodstock, Inc.)

J. H. Johnston Inspecting Cotton Harvest, Early 1930s. During harvest time, farmers lined up on Main Street with wagons piled with cotton to sell. The J. H. Johnston Mercantile Company, established in 1888, offered credit to farmers. Rev. L. L. Burch (left) and J. G. Brooks of Little River Methodist Church pulled their wagon to town for Johnston to inspect. Burch served as pastor from 1933 to 1936. (Courtesy of Harold Johnston.)

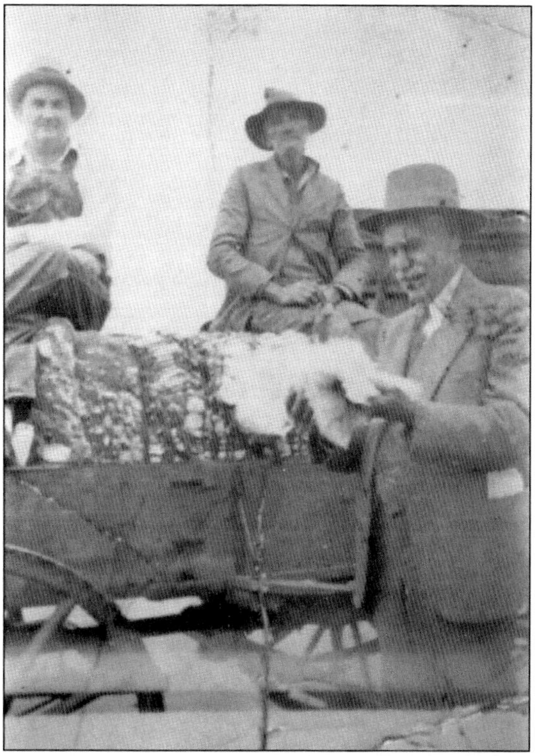

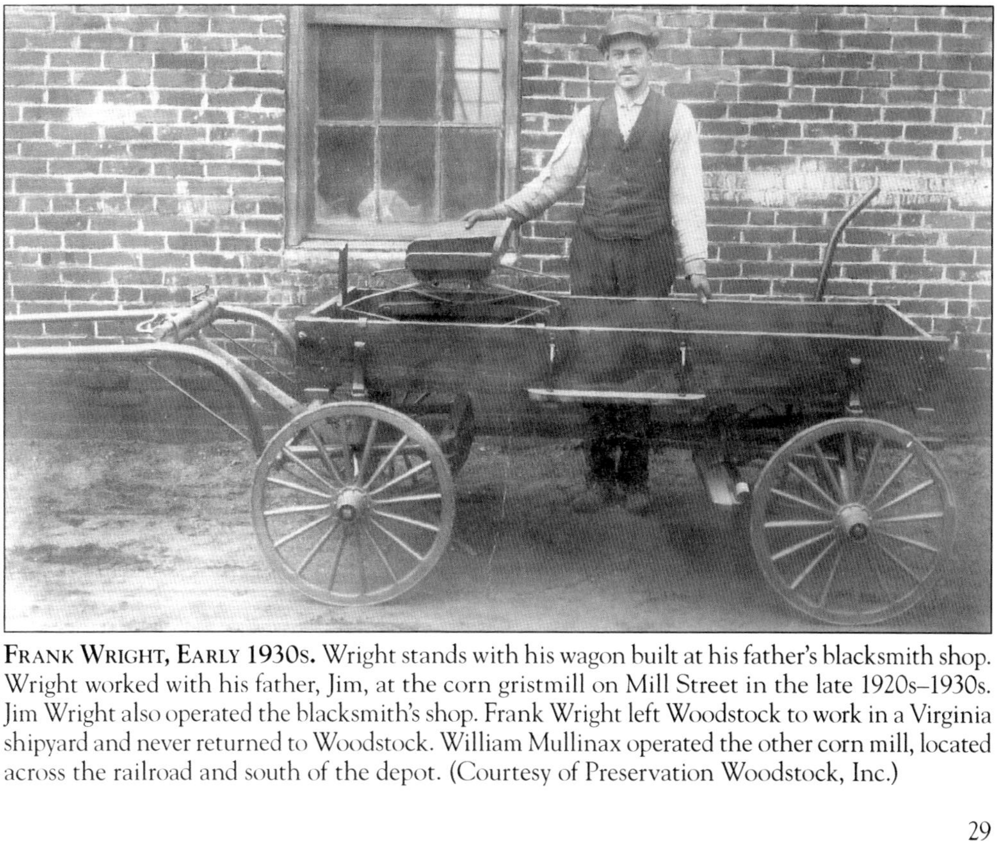

Frank Wright, Early 1930s. Wright stands with his wagon built at his father's blacksmith shop. Wright worked with his father, Jim, at the corn gristmill on Mill Street in the late 1920s–1930s. Jim Wright also operated the blacksmith's shop. Frank Wright left Woodstock to work in a Virginia shipyard and never returned to Woodstock. William Mullinax operated the other corn mill, located across the railroad and south of the depot. (Courtesy of Preservation Woodstock, Inc.)

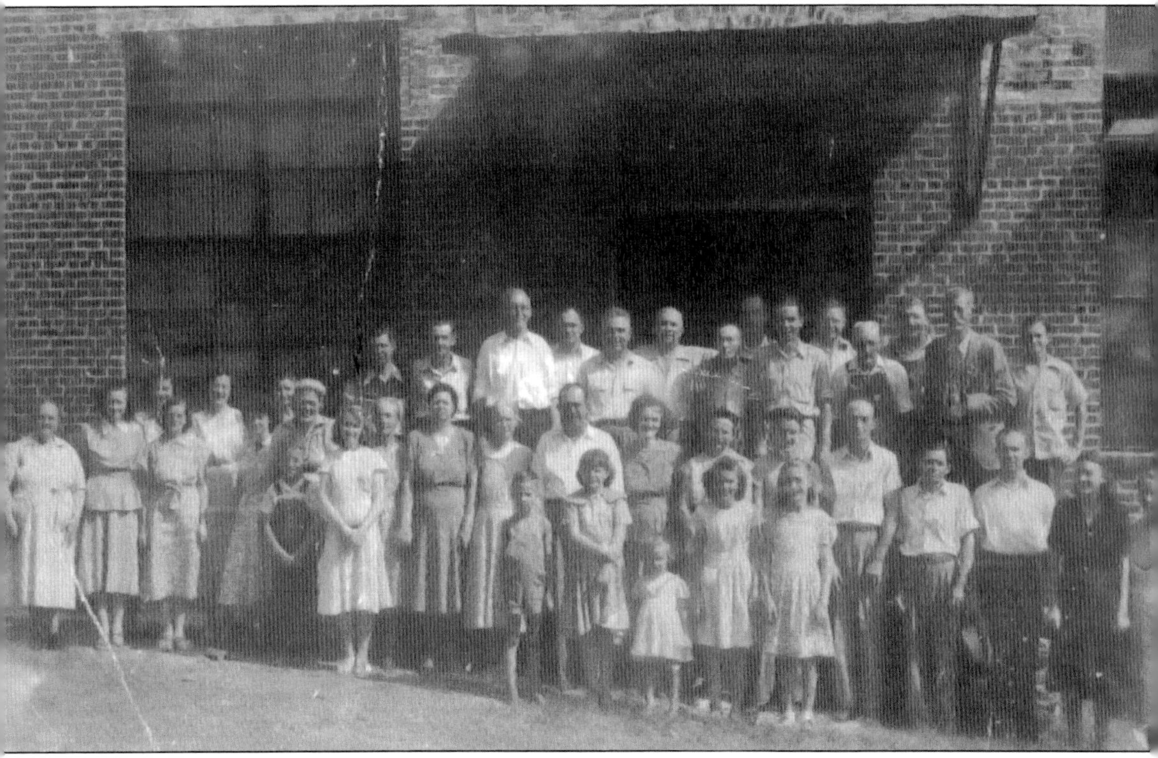

EMPLOYEES AND FAMILY OF ROPE MILL (LITTLE RIVER MILLS/CHEROKEE COTTON MILLS), 1947. Joe Johnston, owner of the mill at the time, closed the mill on September 30, 1949. The next day, employees and families celebrated with a large dinner. Later the remains of the mill were marked by a stone dam and by the factory foundation of stone and brick. From left to right are (first row) Gene Grier, Betty Mize Martin, Joe Dover, Jane Dover Smith, Brenda Sue Booth, Shirley Millwood Mills, and Ruthell Grier Stone; (second row) Bessie Freeman, Fannie Freeman Wilson, Maude Martin, Betty Taylor Wheeler, Lillie Grier, Ida Mae Millwood, Clara Freeman, Love Martin, Cliff Millwood, Parnell Millwood, Ethel Ponder, Lanier "Buster" Ponder, Howard Grier, Leo Taylor, Jasper "Jack" Martin, Irene Grier, and Ruby Taylor; (third row) "Little" Clara Dorn, Mary Ann Dorn, Clara Dorn, Donald Freeman, Odie Freeman, Leland Dorn, Smith Johnston, Claud Hefner, Joe Johnston, William Wilson, Robert S. Millwood, Major Howard, "Uncle" Dean Smith, and Wesley Hendrix; (fourth row) Herbert Millwood, Rev. Gordon Mize, and Sam Millwood. (Courtesy of Stanley Johnston.)

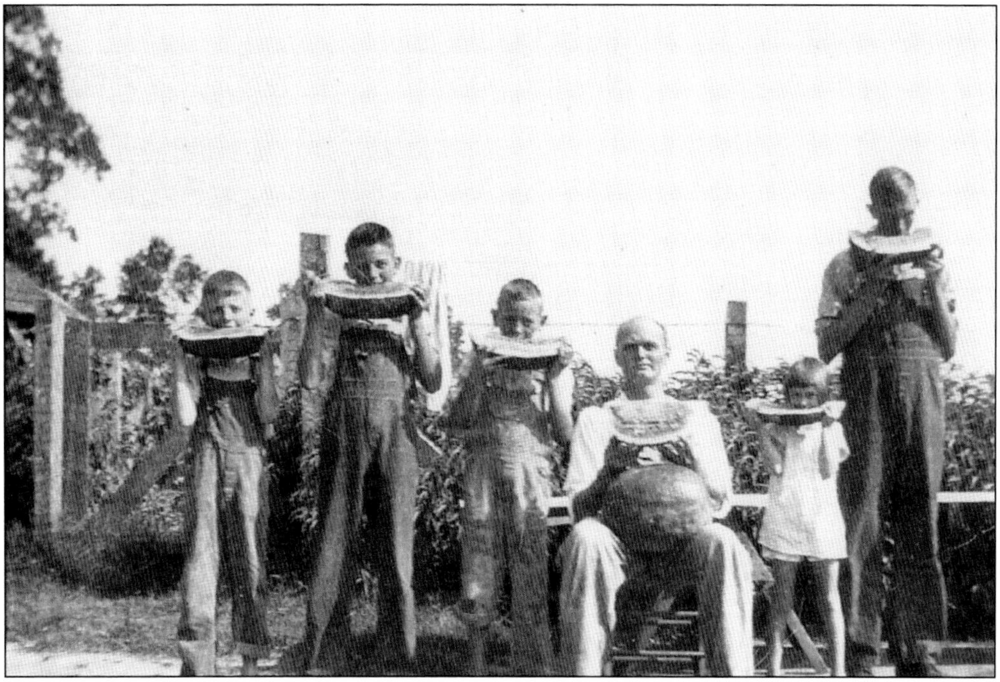

Hames and Cotton Pickers, 1930. Hames (seated), a cotton farmer, and five cotton pickers are pictured taking a break from picking cotton. Workers were paid a penny for one pound of cotton. Hames's home and farm were on the east side of the railroad tracks. (Courtesy of Harold Johnston.)

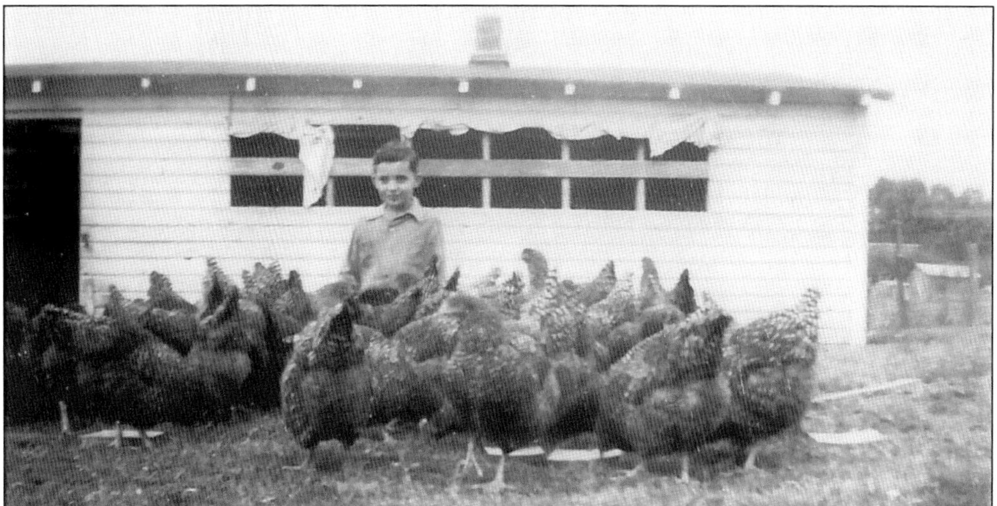

William Johnston Feeding Chickens, 1943. William Johnston is pictured feeding chickens for his father, Smith Johnston. William's brother Smith Johnston Jr. entered the poultry business during World War II. He bought chicks and feed and contracted farmers to raise the chicks. Smith Johnston Jr. and others marketed their poultry business in Atlanta and Canton. He became the president of the Georgia Poultry Federation. None of the processing was done in Woodstock. He got out of the business in 1967 just before the poultry market declined. (Courtesy of William Johnston.)

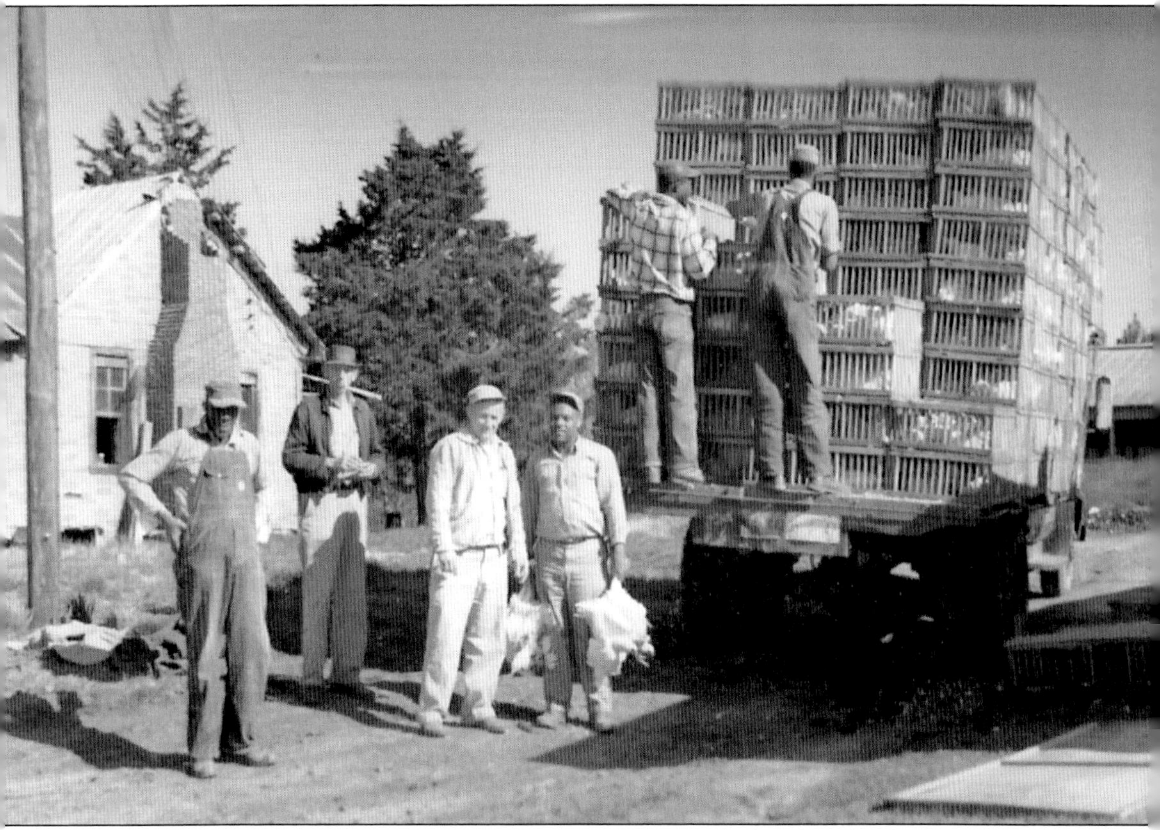

Transporting Chickens for Processing, Late 1940s. The local poultry businesses employed drivers to transport chickens to factories and often to other states. The early broiler houses were cheaply built, usually housing about 500 chickens. A permanent pasture and a period of three years were required before the pasture was ready. The advantages in poultry farming in North Georgia were that the summer nights were usually cool, and most poultry businesses were comprised of small farms. Poultry was a sideline enterprise for some farmers who also had cotton and grain crops. Pictured are, from left to right, Claude Fowler, Ike Wright, Howard Goddard, and Wilkes Foster (holding the chickens), unidentified, and Dude Brownlee. (Courtesy of Stanley Johnston.)

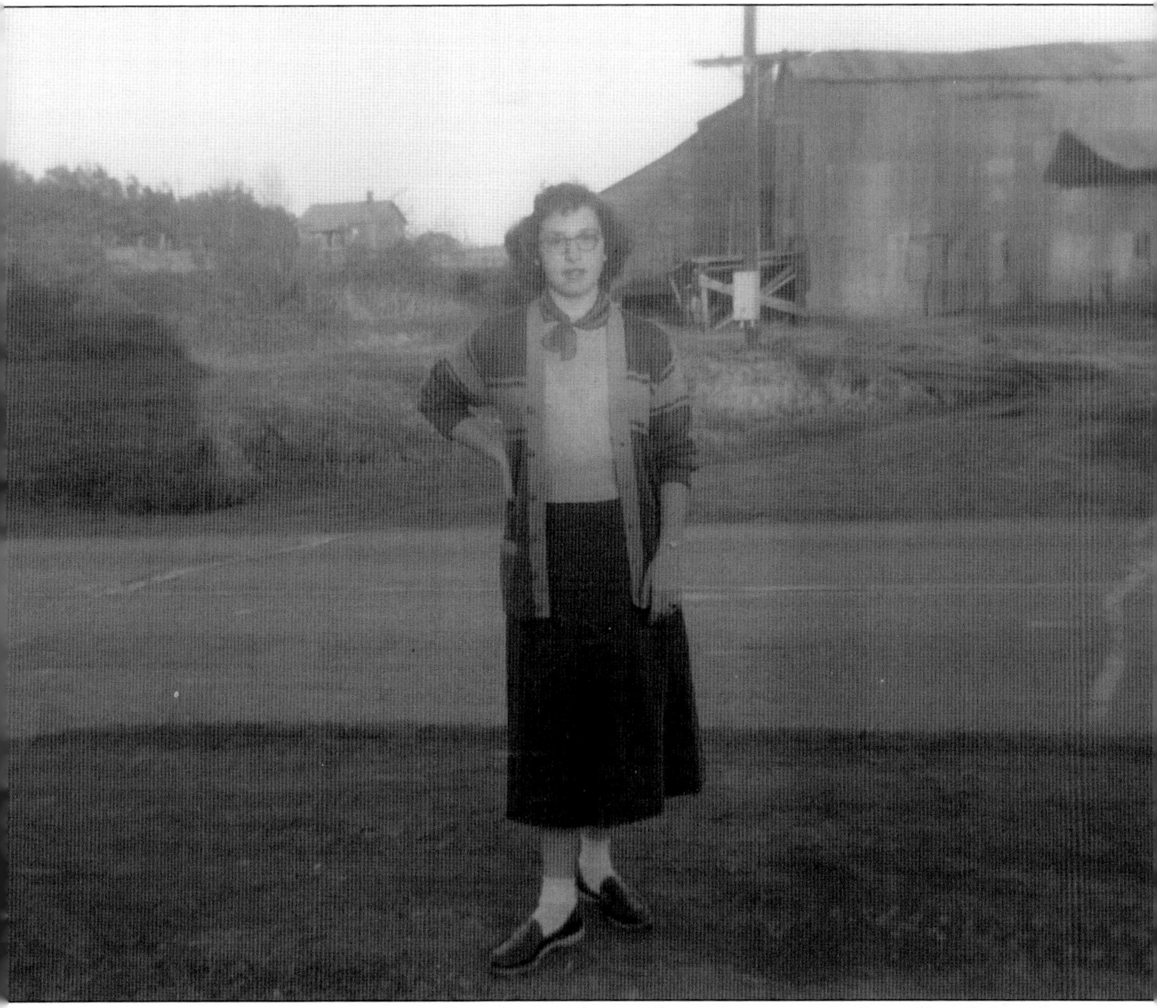

Woodstock Gin, 1950. Jeanette Parker poses in front of a cotton gin near the railroad. Local gins processed cottonseed oil, cottonseed meal, and hulls. The gin separated the cotton seed from the lint, and a press baled the cotton. Machines crushed cotton seed for cottonseed oil. (Courtesy of Jeanette Parker McArthur.)

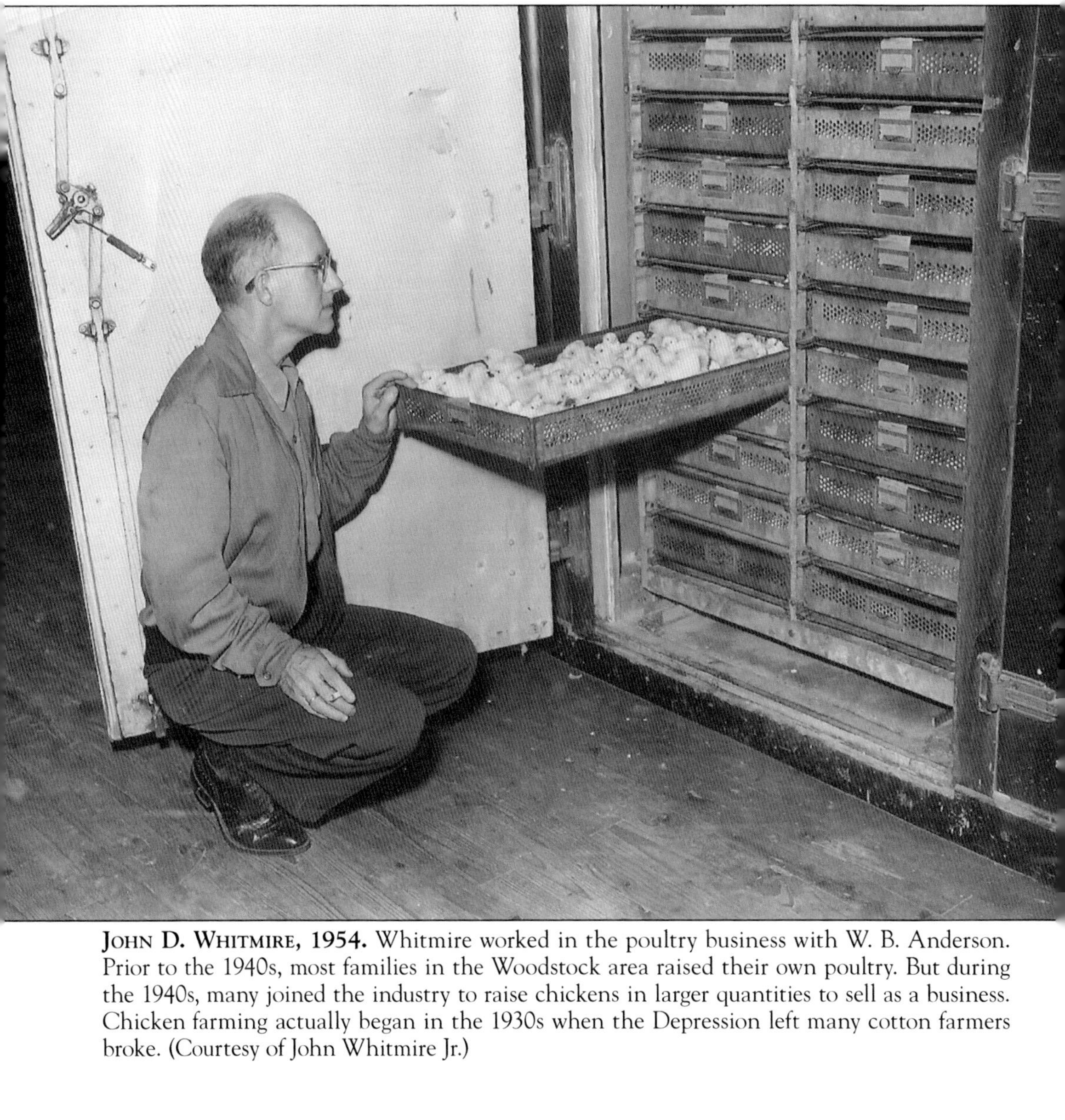

John D. Whitmire, 1954. Whitmire worked in the poultry business with W. B. Anderson. Prior to the 1940s, most families in the Woodstock area raised their own poultry. But during the 1940s, many joined the industry to raise chickens in larger quantities to sell as a business. Chicken farming actually began in the 1930s when the Depression left many cotton farmers broke. (Courtesy of John Whitmire Jr.)

Four

LOCAL MERCHANTS

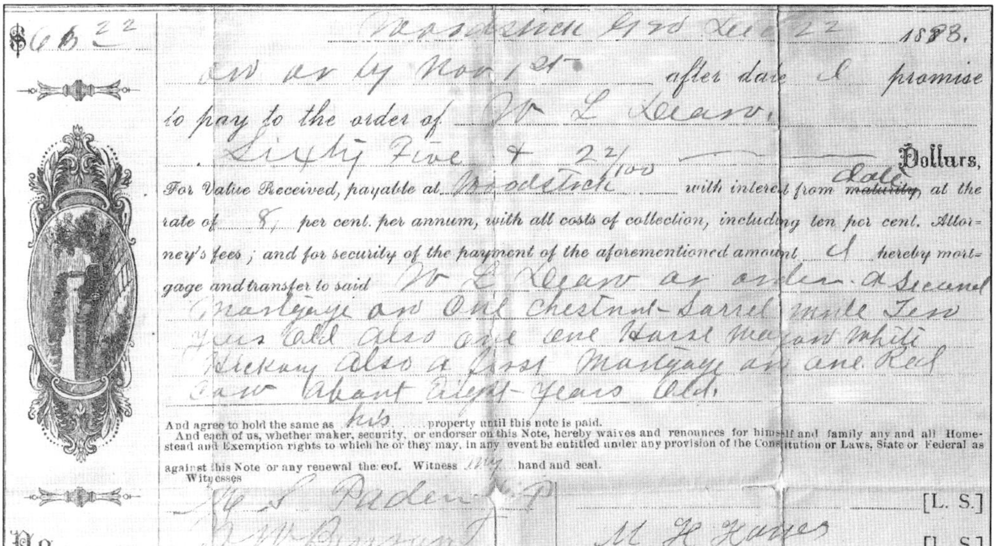

$65 22/

Woodstock Ga Dec 22 1893.

On or by Nov 1st after date I promise to pay to the order of W L Dean,

Sixty Five & 22/100 Dollars,

For Value Received, payable at Woodstock with interest from date at the rate of 8 per cent. per annum, with all costs of collection, including ten per cent. Attorney's fees; and for security of the payment of the aforementioned amount I hereby mortgage and transfer to said W L Dean or order a Second Mortgage on One Chestnut Sorrel mule Ten Years Old Also one one Horse Wagon White Hickory Also a first Mortgage on one Red Cow About Eight Years Old.

And agree to hold the same as his property until this note is paid.

And each of us, whether maker, security, or endorser on this Note, hereby waives and renounces for himself and family any and all Homestead and Exemption rights to which he or they may, in any event be entitled under any provision of the Constitution or Laws, State or Federal as against this Note or any renewal thereof. Witness my hand and seal.

Witnesses

W S Paden [L. S.]

[illegible] M H Hawes [L. S.]

No.

JNO. R. WILKINSON, ATLANTA, GA.

PROMISSORY NOTE FOR PURCHASE OF LIVESTOCK, 1893. The promissory note, dated December 22, 1893, mortgaged a chestnut sorrel 10-year-old male, one white mare, and one red cow about eight years old. All three were mortgaged for $65.22 at eight percent from Dr. W. L. Dean. (Courtesy of Alice Dean Felton.)

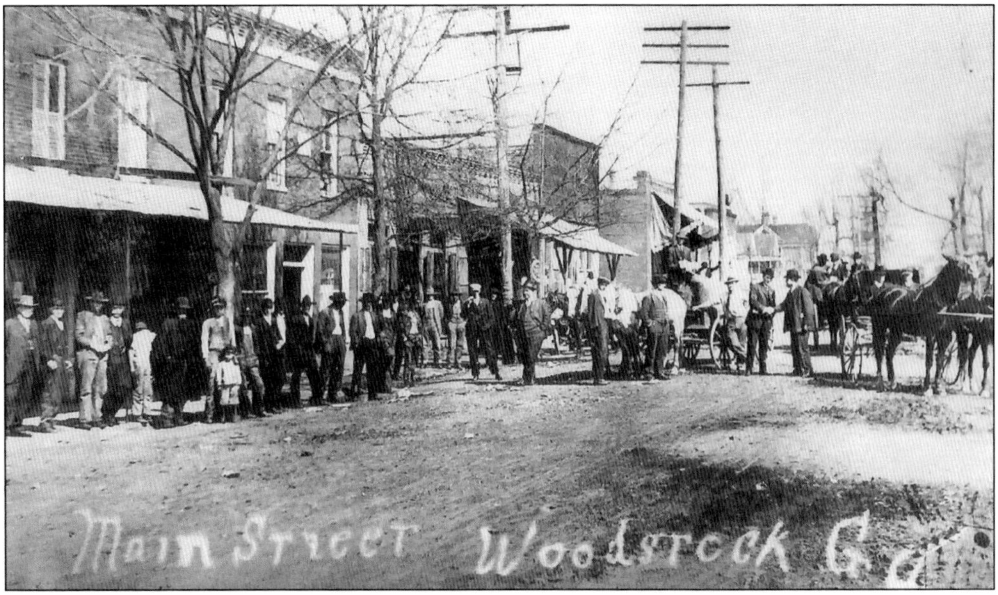

MAIN STREET, WOODSTOCK, 1910. People traversed the area by wagon, buggy, horse, mule, or simply by foot. Eventually, when affordable, most bought used Model T Fords. Traveling in and out of Woodstock became easier when Main Street was paved in 1929. The first streetlights were installed around 1925 when Georgia Railway and Power Company constructed a transmission line east of town. (Courtesy of Alice Dean Felton.)

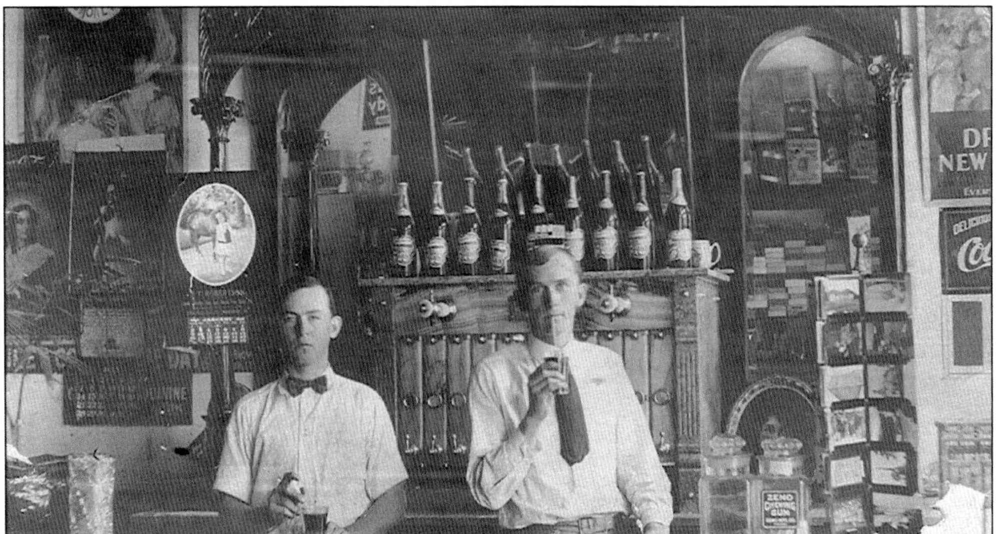

DEAN DRUG STORE, 1906. Linton Albert Dean and his younger brother, William Hugh Dean, take a break at the ornate, mirrored soda fountain, 1910. Opened in 1906 across from the depot, the Dean Drug Store sold items such as patent medicines, rock candy, sarsaparilla, chewing tobacco, kerosene, coffee, sugar, cigars, and Coca-Cola. To prepare for the business venture of opening a drugstore with his father, Linton enrolled in Creighton's Business College in Atlanta. Linton and his father, Dr. William L. Dean, opened the drugstore together, but his father died six months later, leaving the store to Linton. Dean would be the sole proprietor of Dean Drug Store from 1906 until his death at age 95 in 1981. (Courtesy of Alice Dean Felton.)

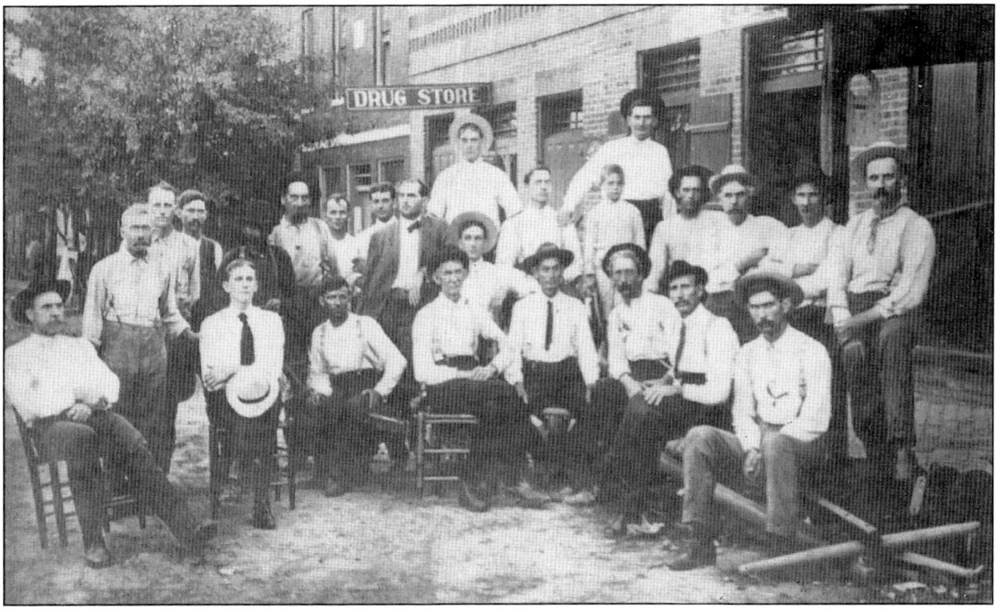

CROWD OUTSIDE DEAN DRUG STORE, 1910. Dean Drug Store sold a wide variety of items from patent medicines to house paint, auto tires, and gasoline. The store also served as a bus stop and later where residents paid their utility bills in the 1960s. The store closed when Linton Dean died in 1981, but the store remains a museum of tins of powders, cigar boxes, and medicines that were once sold there. (Courtesy of Alice Dean Felton.)

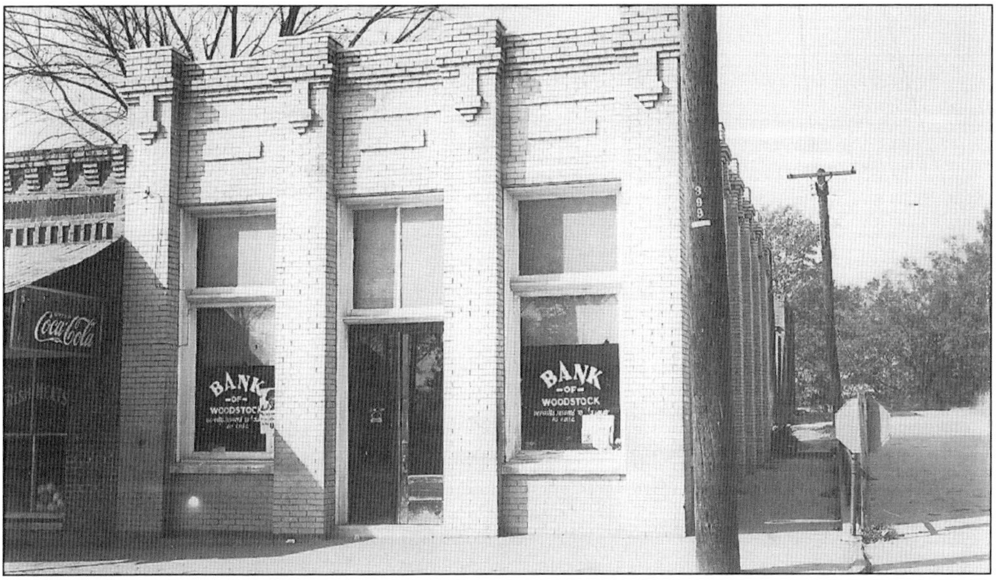

BANK OF WOODSTOCK, ESTABLISHED 1905. The Bank of Woodstock opened for business in 1905 and was the only bank within 10 miles of Woodstock until 1974. It was the second oldest bank in Cherokee County. Prior to 1905, Woodstock residents had to travel to Acworth, Marietta, and Canton to do their banking. Bank of Woodstock's deposits on opening day were $14,000. By 1939, assets grew to $135,000. The bank was deemed sound even in 1932, when President Roosevelt closed all but the strongest banks. The building, later housing the Woodstock Library, still remains on the corner across from the depot. (Courtesy of Stanley Johnston.)

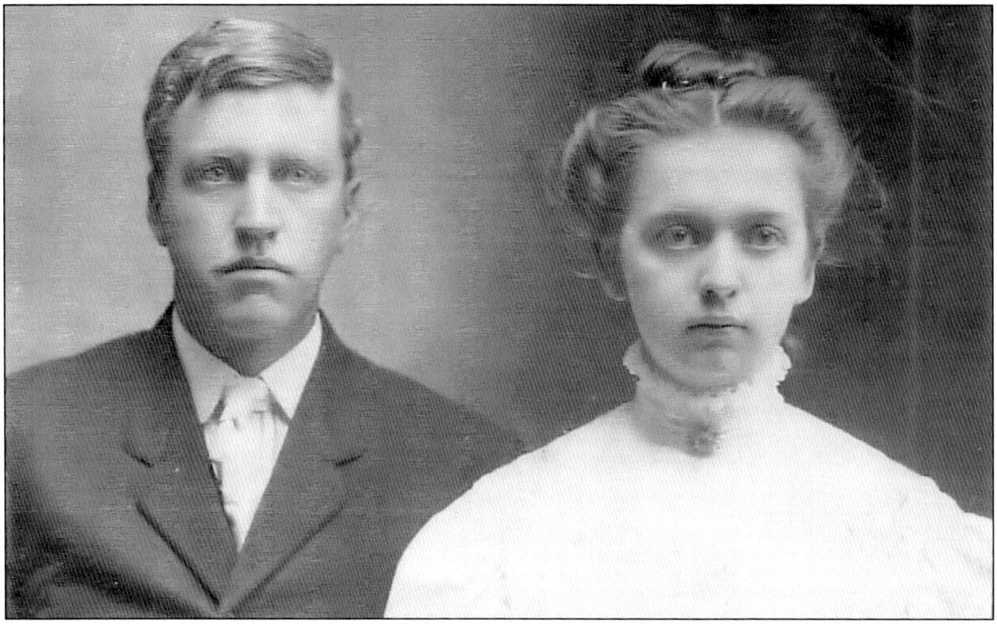

DAVID HANEY AND HIS WIFE, EDNA, 1905. Dave Haney (1878–1930) and W. D. Bozeman (1873–1944) ran a general store on Main Street. Haney-Bozeman General Mercantile Company and Cotton Brokers could not survive the Depression and was forced to close. David Jacob Haney (also a farmer) and Edna Pauline McCleskey married in 1905 and raised seven children: Sara Katherine, Mary Lee, Carrie Pearl, Nancy Elizabeth, David Jacob Jr., Edna Mae, and Jehu Spears. Edna died of cancer six weeks after she turned 40. (Courtesy of Jane Crunkelton.)

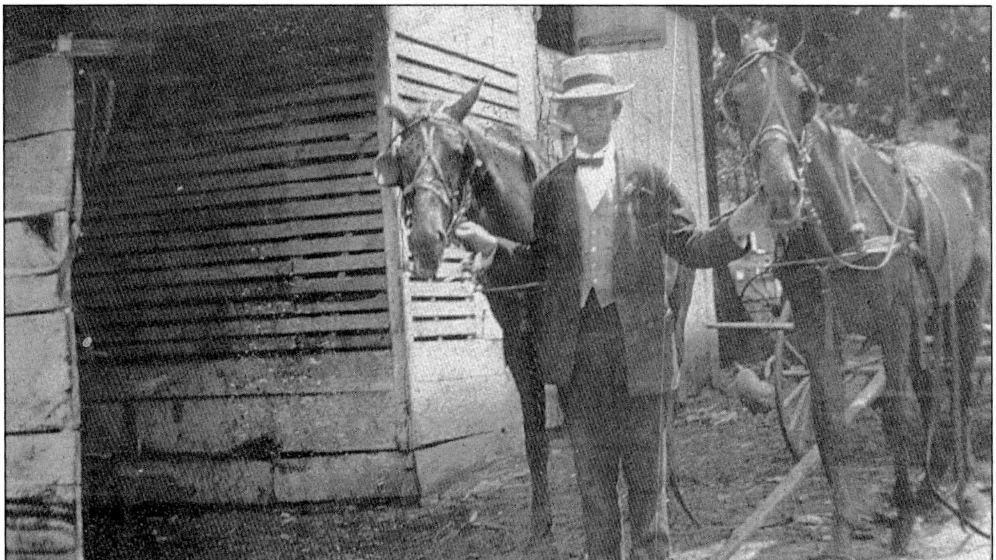

DR. T. J. VAN SANT, C. 1915. Van Sant was still practicing medicine at 85 in 1962, though partially deaf and blind. He had been Woodstock's physician for 55 years. He often made house calls by horse and buggy and by Ford Model T, traveling beyond Woodstock to Canton, Ball Ground, Atlanta, and Tate. During the 1918 flu epidemic, Van Sant spent hours on his feet counting the dead as the undertakers readied the bodies. (Courtesy of Preservation Woodstock, Inc.)

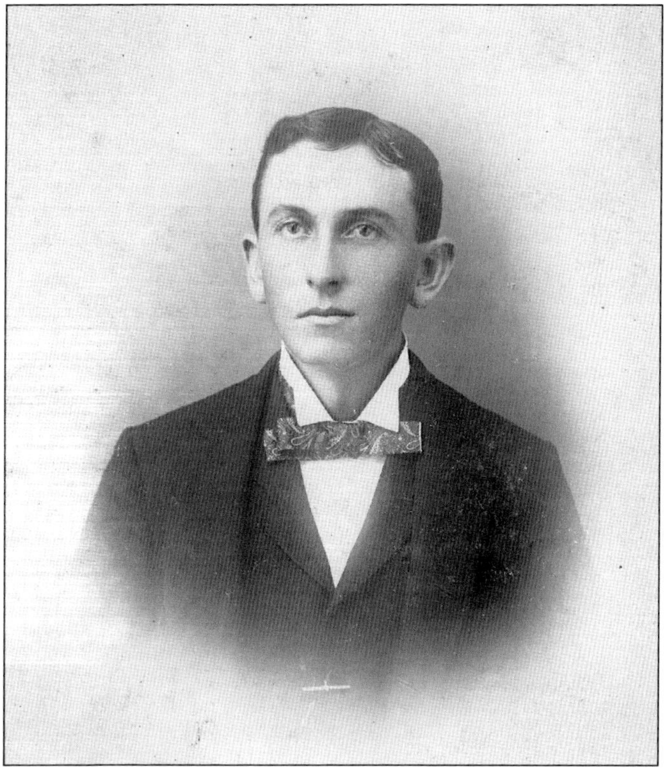

Dr. James R. Boring, c. 1900. Dr. Boring graduated from the Atlanta College of Physicians and Surgeons in 1899 and was licensed to practice medicine that same year. Dr. Boring also served as Woodstock's mayor in 1915. (Courtesy Patty Sellas.)

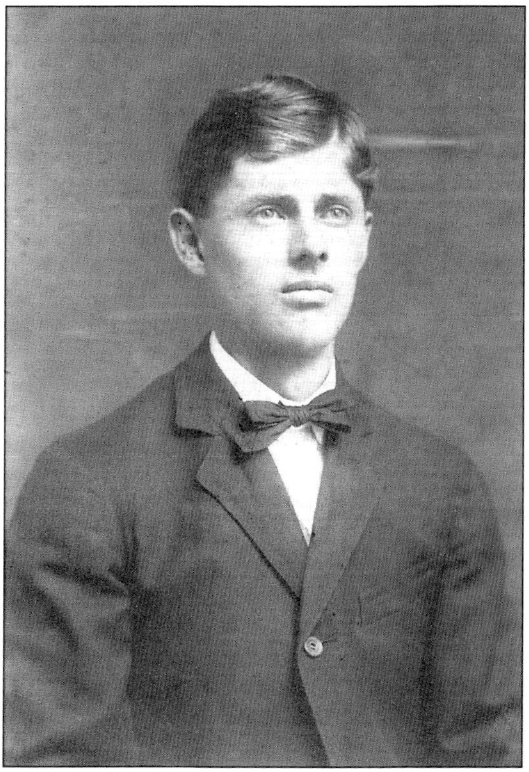

Albert F. Poor, Railroad Machinist. Poor (1885–1956) worked as a foreman in 1905 for the Louisville and Nashville Railroad in Louisville and married Ruby Lee Burton in 1917. They moved to Woodstock in the early 1920s to the Burton farm on Lovingood Road. Poor opened a planing mill in 1928 on Mill Street. The mill building housed a planter, lathe, ripsaw, and other tools used to saw logs for lumber and cross ties for the railroad. He powered his machines by a steam engine. He commuted to Atlanta in the late 1930s to work for Southern Railroad as a machinist. (Courtesy Jeanne Cosey.)

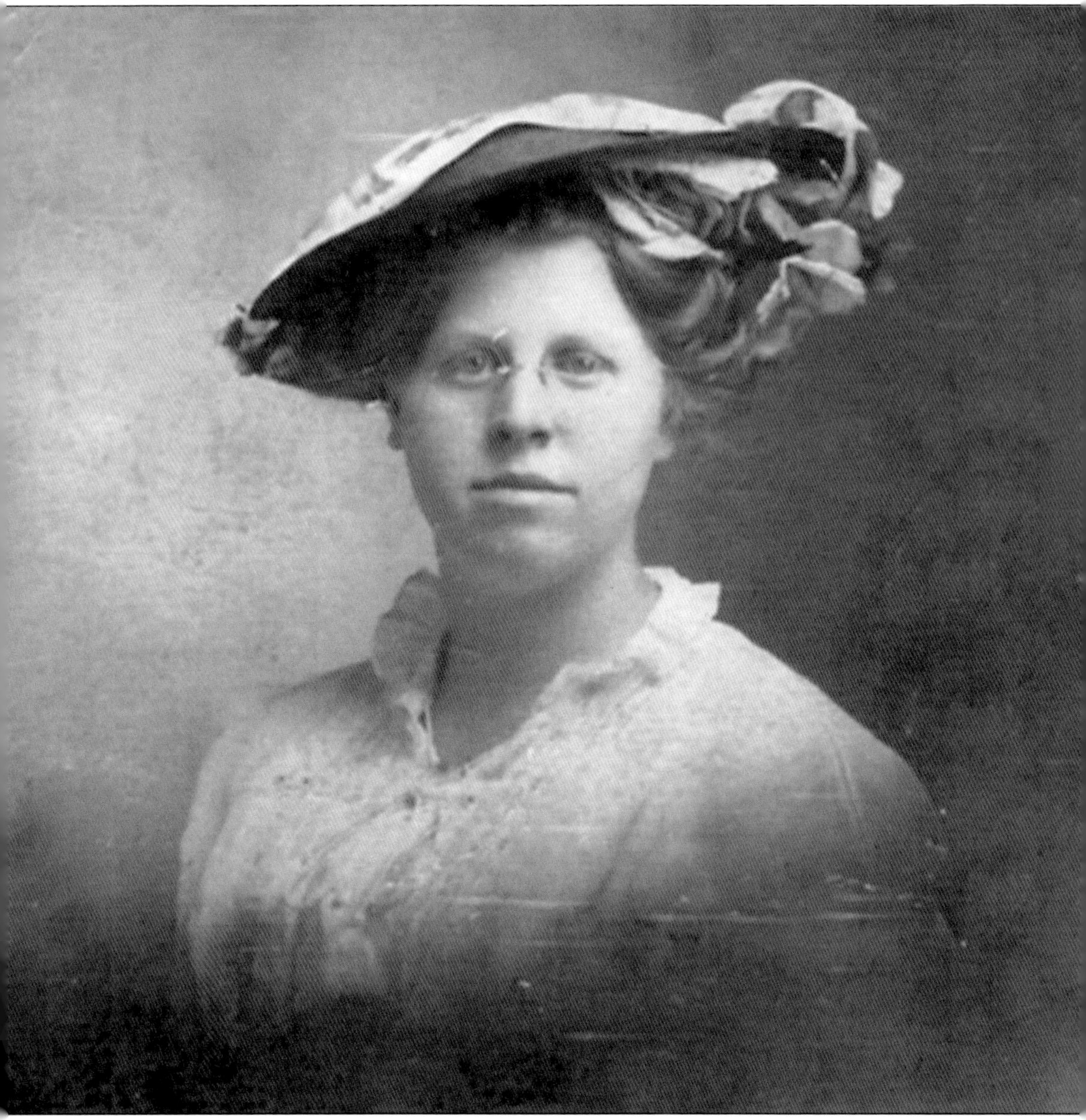

Elizabeth Routh Brooks, Licensed Practical Nurse, c. 1900. Brooks was born in 1893 in Louisiana and moved to the Woodstock area as a young woman with her parents. She met her future husband, James Gilbert Brooks Sr., when she worked as a private nurse for a member of his family. She was a trained nurse who worked primarily in Marietta at the old Marietta Hospital as well as for numerous doctors in Marietta. Brooks delivered many babies and cared for people in the Woodstock area in the early 1900s. People needing her service would transport her to their homes by horse-drawn wagons. For her service, she was usually paid with eggs, chickens, and produce. When she and James married, they moved to the home of James's parents, James Radford Brooks and Martha Elizabeth (McCleskey) Brooks, on Highway 5. They raised all of their children (Gilbert, Radford, Richard, Martha, Allie, and Marie) on their farm. She later retired from professional nursing but provided private nursing until her late 70s. (Courtesy of Patricia Daves Freeman.)

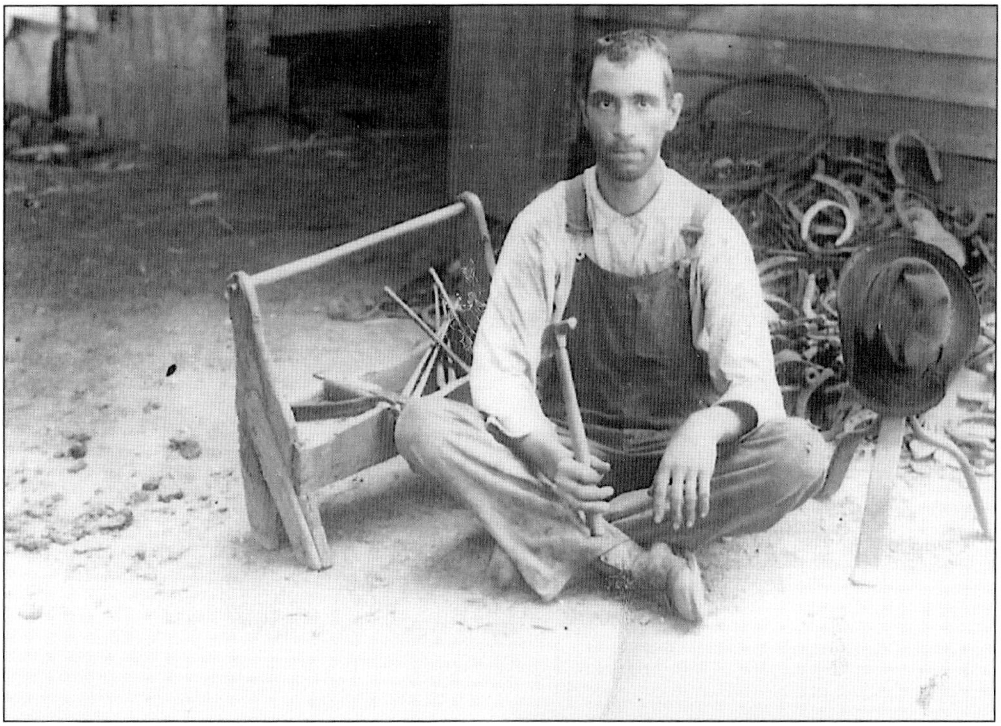

James Isaac Ghorley, Blacksmith, 1920. James ("Jim") Ghorley operated a blacksmith shop on Mill Street. His first shop was located behind the Woodstock Methodist Church. In 1923, Ghorley's brother John moved his family from Keithsburg, Georgia, to Woodstock to help his brother. The shop was known as the Ghorley Brothers Blacksmith Shop. Jim died unexpectedly in 1932, and John continued the business with the help of his young son Oscar. Oscar was drafted into the army in April 1941. (Courtesy of Johnnie Southern.)

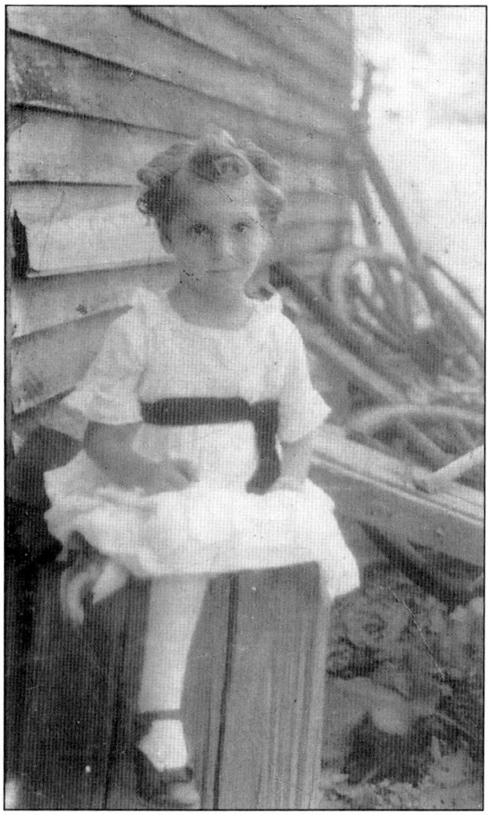

Edna Ghorley, 1922. Edna often watched her father work with iron and handle horses at his blacksmith shop on Mill Street. Born in 1917, Edna lost her father as a teenager. She later married a son of a Civil War veteran, Newt Grimes, attended business school, and worked at the Bell Bomber Plant in World War II. The Grimes were lifelong Woodstock residents. (Courtesy of Johnnie Southern.)

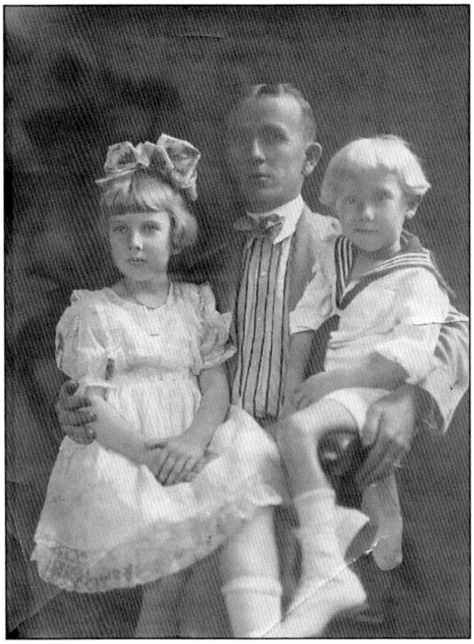

Hubert C. McAfee, Daughter Bertha, and Son Hubert Jr., 1921. Oscar Perkinson and Hubert McAfee co-owned a general mercantile store, built around 1900. The building is currently occupied by the Woodstock Pharmacy. Perkinson and McAfee were cotton brokers as well as salesmen of general merchandise. McAfee was mayor of Woodstock from 1920 to 1921. Cotton buyers such as Perkinson and McAfee were forced to close because of declining cotton prices during the Depression. (Courtesy of Millicent Fox.)

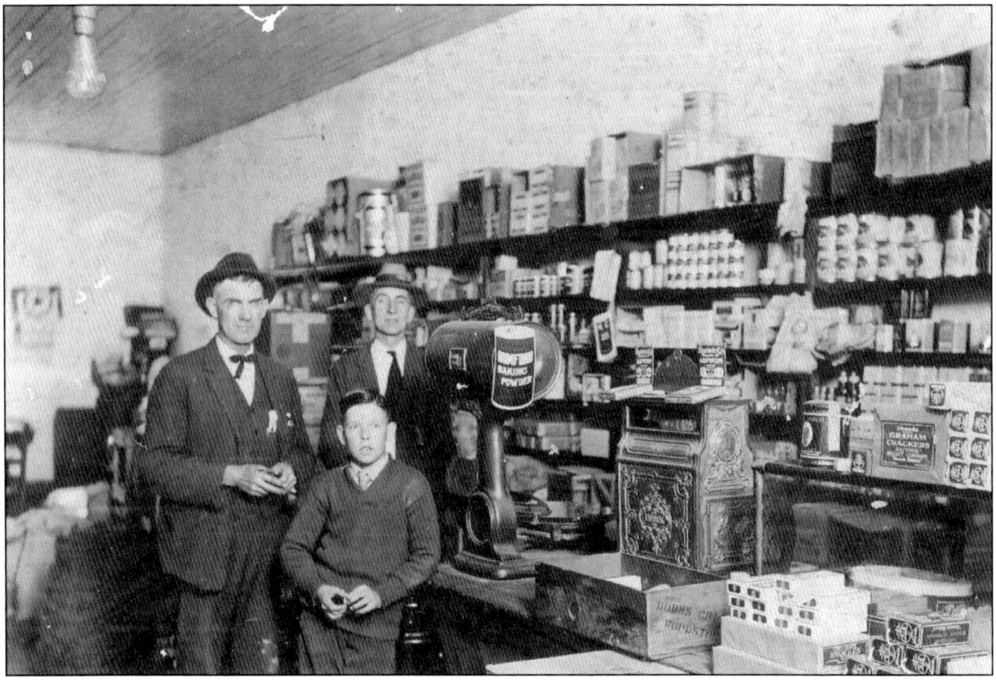

Dobbs Chandler Mercantile, c. 1928. Claude Chandler and Wylie Perry Dobbs Sr. opened a general grocery store in 1905 next door to Dean Drug Store. Dobbs and Chandler built an icehouse behind the store and sold ice that was delivered in 300-pound blocks. They were able to install one of the first ice coolers in Woodstock to keep meat. Chandler's daughter, Maye, later married Dobbs's son, Wylie Jr. Claude Chandler graduated from Reinhardt College in 1910, served as mayor of Woodstock in the 1930s, was the first undertaker in Woodstock, and was a county tax collector. Pictured from left to right are Wylie Dobbs, Claude Chandler, and Ralph Carpenter. (Courtesy of Marilyn Dobbs Morrell.)

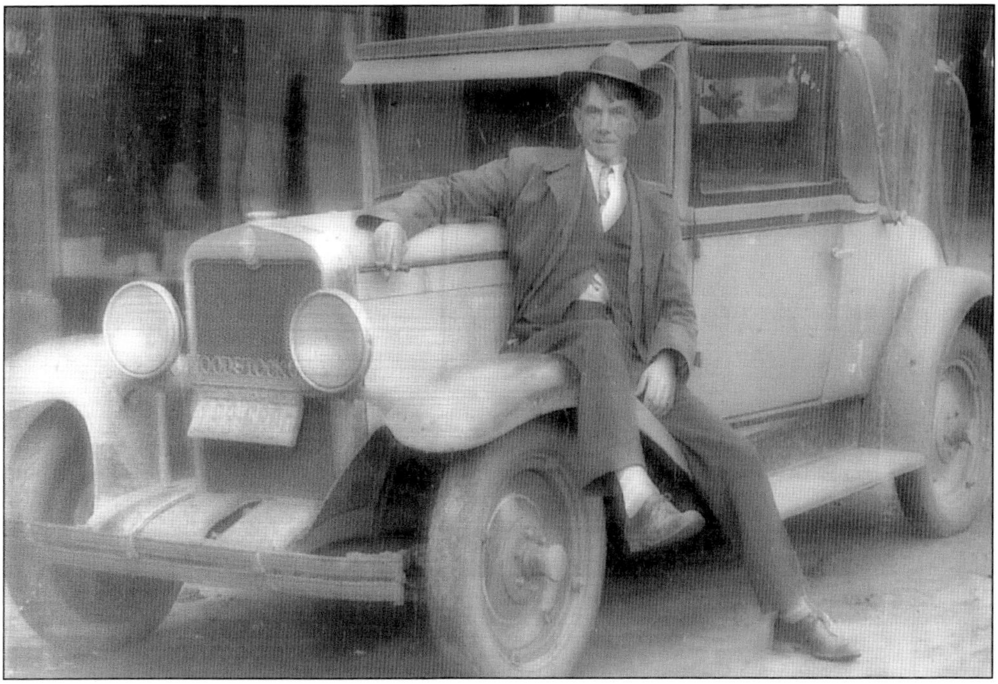

SAM DAWSON AND 1930 MODEL A FORD, 1930. Dawson worked at the J. H. Johnston Company. He was known to be an avid marble shooter who "wore" a cigar most of the time. He eventually owned his own store, Dawson Department Store. (Courtesy of Preservation Woodstock, Inc.)

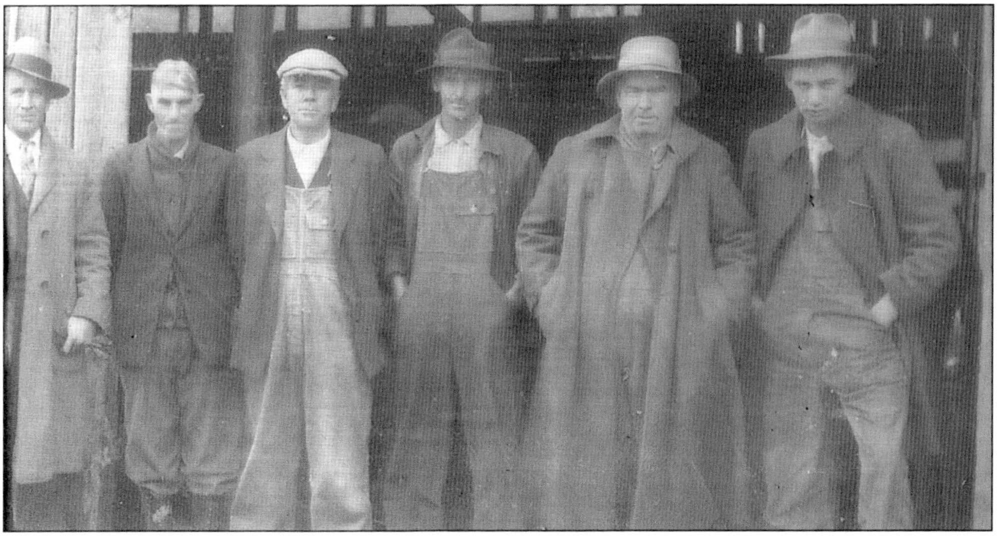

WILL LATIMER'S LIVERY STABLE, 1930. From left to right are Will Latimer, ? Ledford, Harry Latimer, Luke Ledford, ? Ledford, and Ed Ledford. The livery stable sold mules and horses to farmers. Will Latimer and Mutt Austin sold and traded mules and horses to the farmers at the livery stable behind the depot. Livestock arrived in Woodstock by train cars. Most farmers could not afford both a horse and a mule, so the farmer purchased one or the other, usually a mule. Mules were usually given names and were given the job of plowing the rocky soil. Drummers (traveling salesmen), just getting off the train, could rent a buggy and a driver to make their calls in Woodstock. (Courtesy of Preservation Woodstock, Inc.)

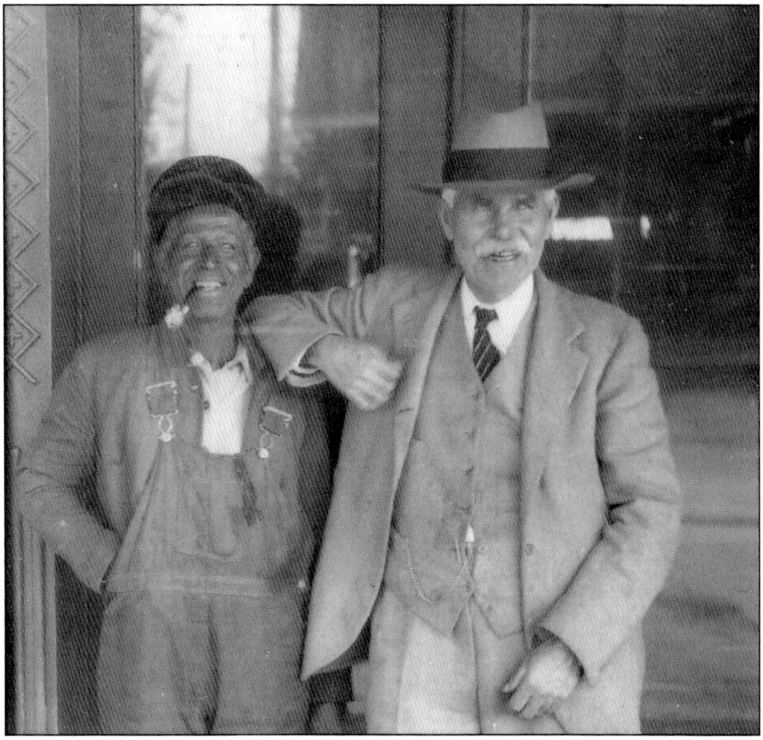

Frankie Paden and J. H. Johnston, 1930. Paden (left) loaded and hauled bales of cotton and rope from Woodstock to the mill in Canton. (Courtesy of Preservation Woodstock, Inc.)

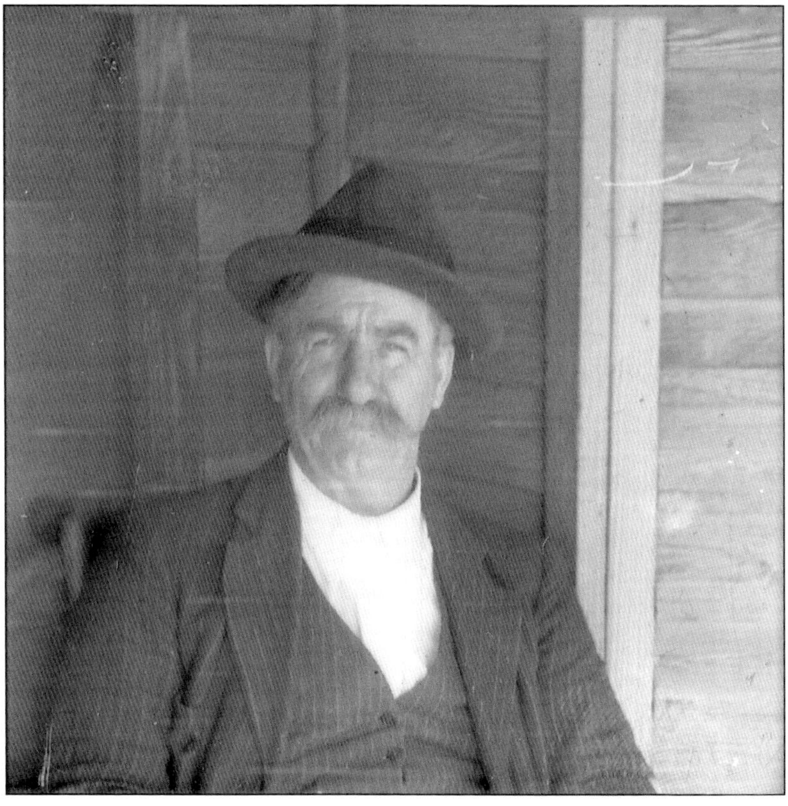

Barber John Barnett, 1930. Barnett operated a barbershop during the 1920s and 1930s. Barnett charged 25¢ for a haircut, and hot baths were available at his shop. (Courtesy of Preservation Woodstock, Inc.)

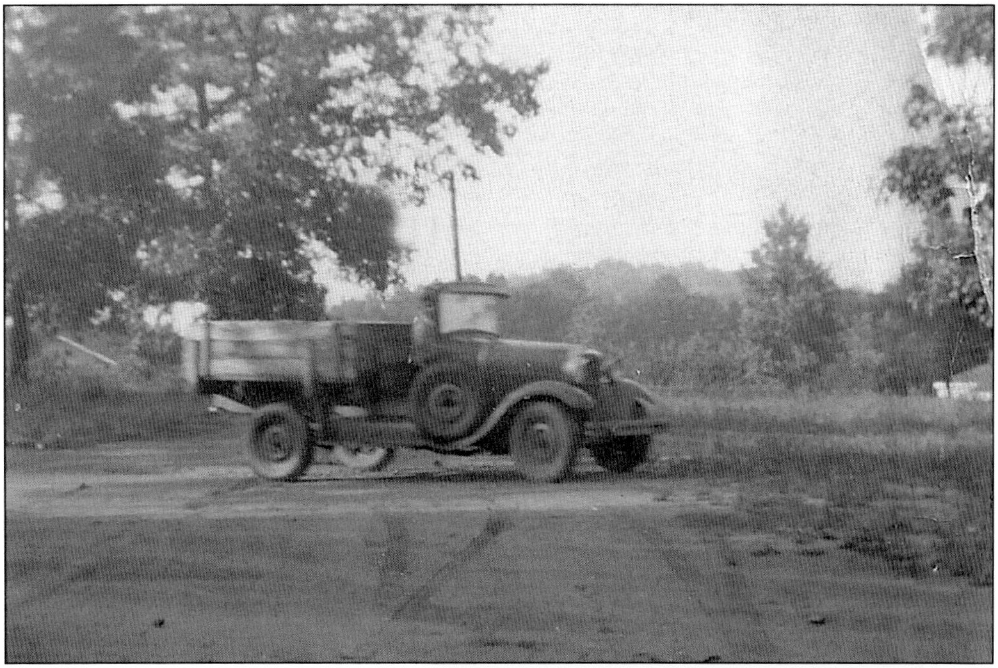

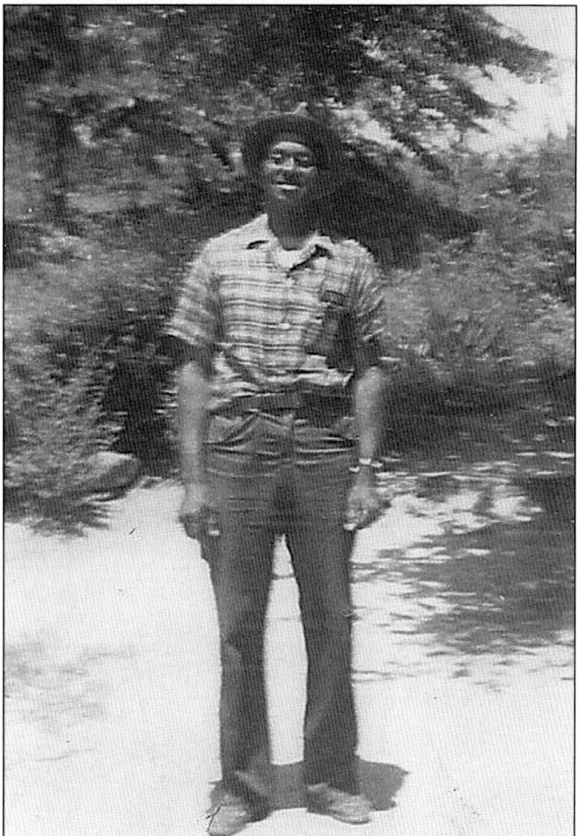

Charlie Webb, 1930s. Webb served many Woodstock residents for 42 years, picking up trash for residents with his 1928 Model A Ford that he converted into the town's garbage truck. He later purchased a 1958 Chevrolet truck to replace the Model A. Webb charged 75¢ to $1 a month to collect residential garbage. Webb lived all his life on Arnold Mill Road. He lived to be 91 years old. (Both courtesy of Charlie Webb Jr.)

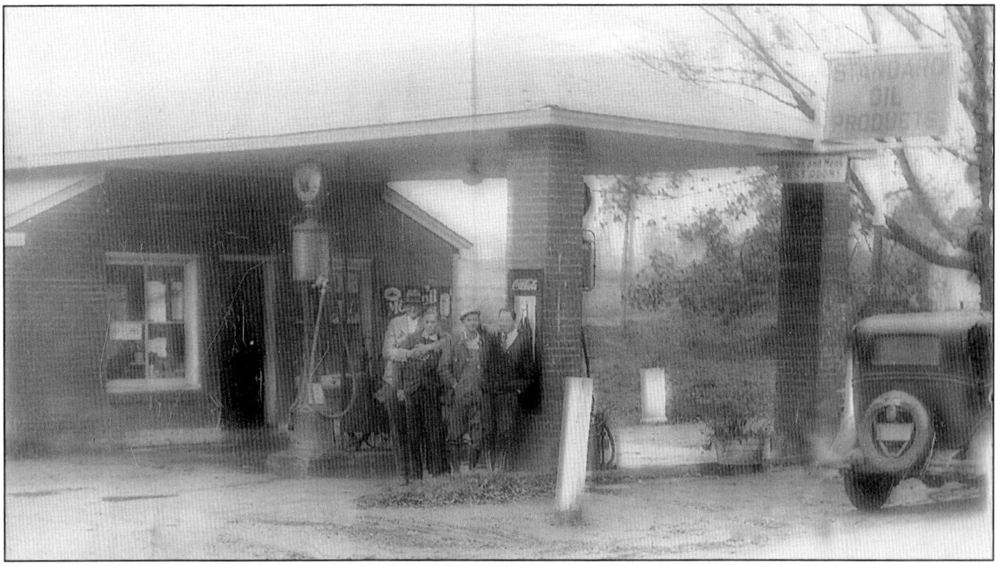

Greenhouse Service Station, 1935. Gilbert Reeves built this grocery and filling station, located on Highway 5 south of town near Reeves Florist, in 1935. Andrew Rice Fowler originally owned 1,000 acres on which Reeves built the Greenhouse Service Station. Reeves married Fowler's daughter, Ruth. Reeves developed other businesses south of town to serve the rural, agricultural area. Reeves leased the station to Sam Priest. In 1939, Priest became partners with Carl Dunn, who eventually acquired the business. Due to its significant historic construction, it is on the Historic American Buildings Survey (Library of Congress). It was demolished in 1992. (Courtesy of Preservation Woodstock, Inc.)

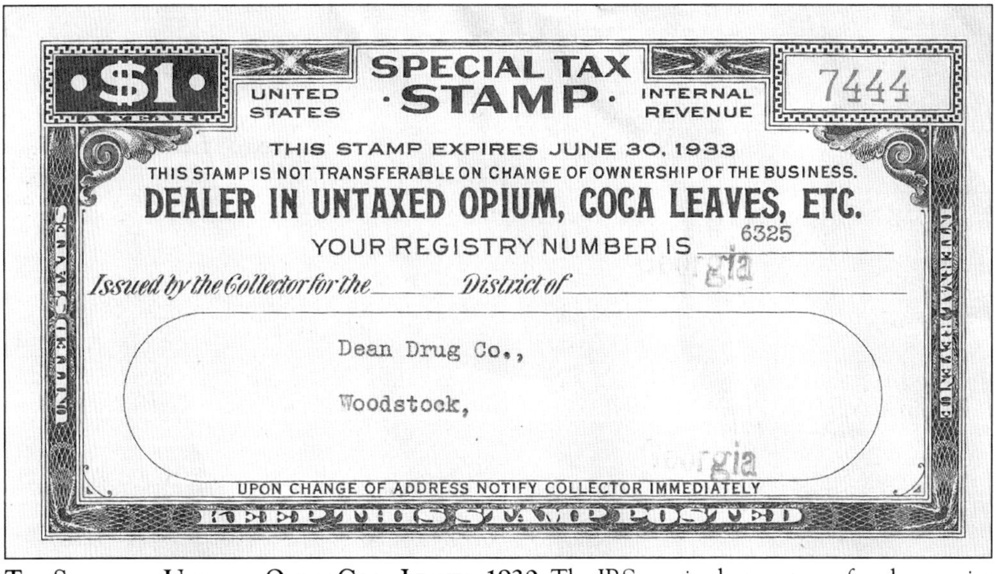

$1 A YEAR

UNITED STATES · SPECIAL TAX STAMP · INTERNAL REVENUE

7444

THIS STAMP EXPIRES JUNE 30, 1933

THIS STAMP IS NOT TRANSFERABLE ON CHANGE OF OWNERSHIP OF THE BUSINESS.

DEALER IN UNTAXED OPIUM, COCA LEAVES, ETC.

YOUR REGISTRY NUMBER IS 6325

Issued by the Collector for the ______ *District of* ...gia

Dean Drug Co.,

Woodstock,

...gia

UPON CHANGE OF ADDRESS NOTIFY COLLECTOR IMMEDIATELY

KEEP THIS STAMP POSTED

UNITED STATES — INTERNAL REVENUE

Tax Stamp for Untaxed Opium Coca Leaves, 1930. The IRS required a tax stamp for pharmacies to sell items containing opium and coca leaves. Dean Drug Store sold drug items such as patent medicines and remedy powders. Throughout the 19th century, opium was available as a drug in patent medicines. The drug's use became fairly widespread during the Civil War. A tariff was imposed on opium importation. Before 1914, the use and manufacture of morphine and cocaine was also permitted under federal law. (Courtesy of Preservation Woodstock, Inc.)

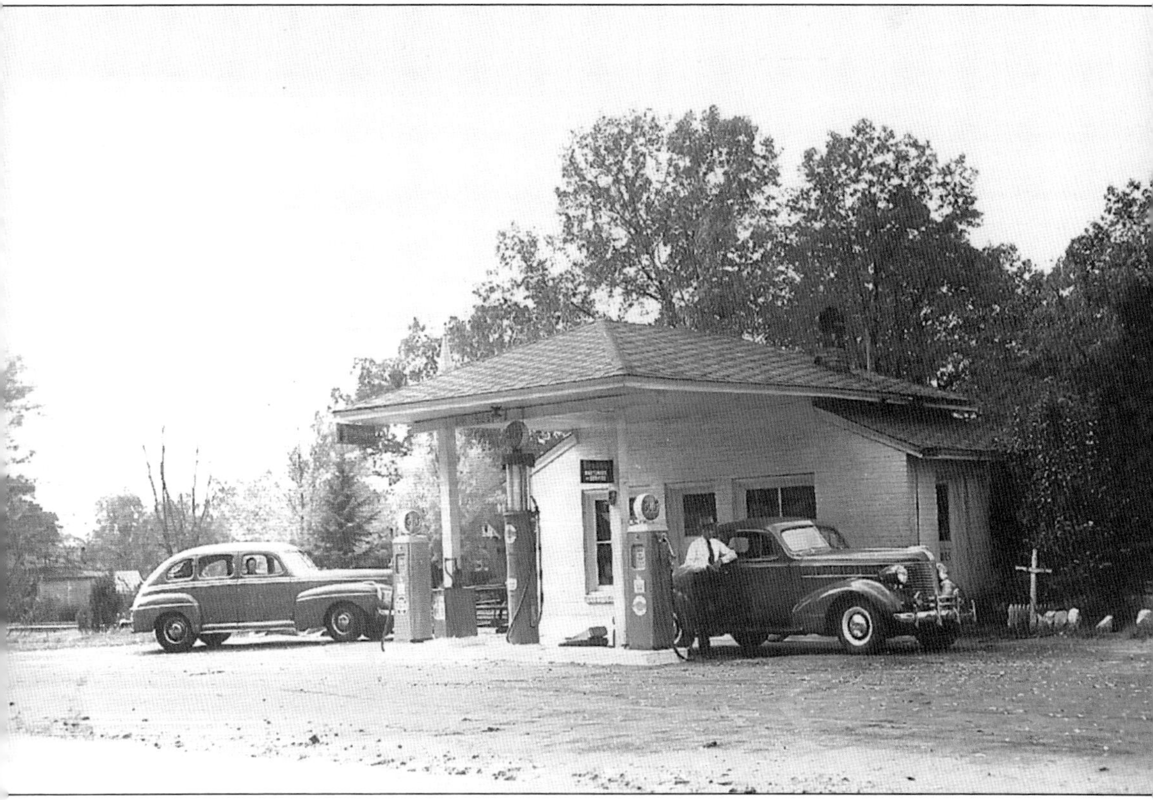

HANK PRIEST SERVICE STATION, 1943. Hank Priest owned and operated the service station during the 1940s and later. Priest later operated an auto parts store with his wife, Lee Etta Payne, on Main Street. (Courtesy of Stanley Johnston.)

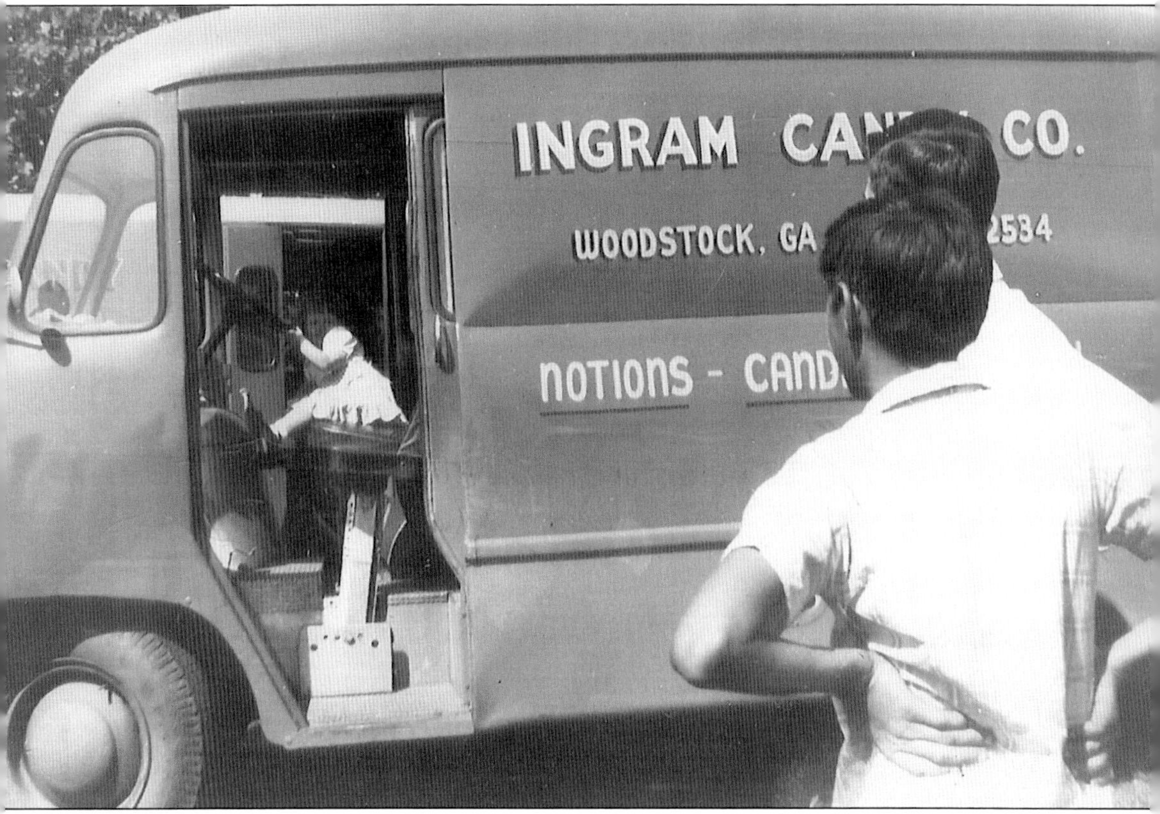

INGRAM CANDY COMPANY, MID-1940S. V. T. Ingram Sr. operated a "rolling store" and wholesale delivery to local Woodstock businesses. Ingram later ran a candy store next to the theater. Rolling stores were popular before and after World War II in small towns. Although residents still made shopping trips to town businesses, rolling stores were traveling convenience stores that offered merchandise such as farm produce, notions, cold drinks, candy, and even live chickens. The rolling stores were often delivery trucks, pickup trucks, or altered school buses. Pictured are Hunter Ingram (left) and Tip Ingram Jr. (right). The girl in the truck is their sister Mary Lois Ingram. (Courtesy of James Parker.)

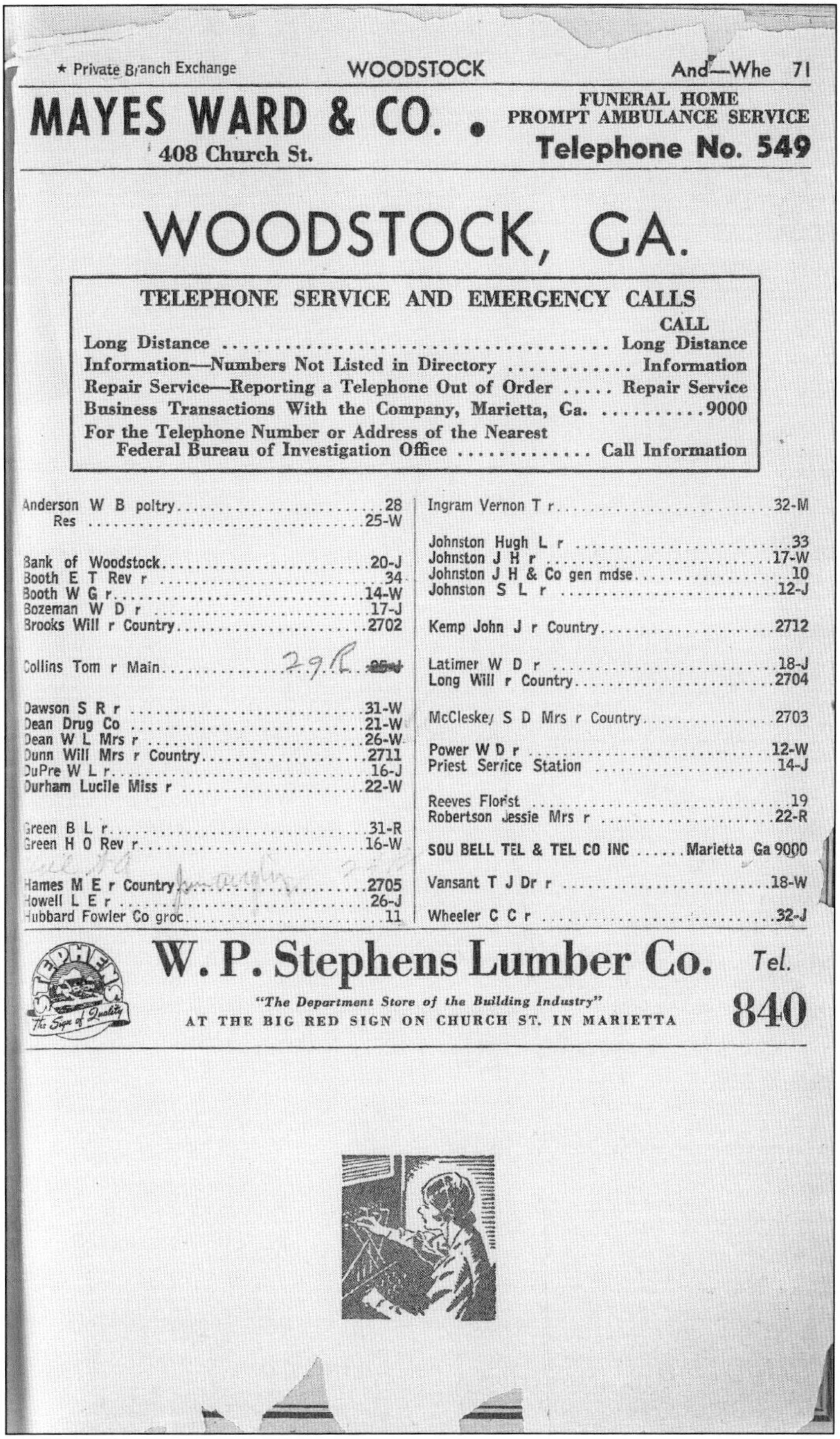

★ Private Branch Exchange — WOODSTOCK — And—Whe 71

MAYES WARD & CO. • FUNERAL HOME PROMPT AMBULANCE SERVICE
408 Church St. — Telephone No. 549

WOODSTOCK, GA.

TELEPHONE SERVICE AND EMERGENCY CALLS

	CALL
Long Distance	Long Distance
Information—Numbers Not Listed in Directory	Information
Repair Service—Reporting a Telephone Out of Order	Repair Service
Business Transactions With the Company, Marietta, Ga.	9000
For the Telephone Number or Address of the Nearest Federal Bureau of Investigation Office	Call Information

Anderson W B poltry ... 28
Res ... 25-W

Bank of Woodstock ... 20-J
Booth E T Rev r ... 34
Booth W G r ... 14-W
Bozeman W D r ... 17-J
Brooks Will r Country ... 2702

Collins Tom r Main ... 29 R [illegible]

Dawson S R r ... 31-W
Dean Drug Co ... 21-W
Dean W L Mrs r ... 26-W
Dunn Will Mrs r Country ... 2711
DuPre W L r ... 16-J
Durham Lucile Miss r ... 22-W

Green B L r ... 31-R
Green H O Rev r ... 16-W

Hames M E r Country ... 2705
Howell L E r ... 26-J
Hubbard Fowler Co groc ... 11

Ingram Vernon T r ... 32-M

Johnston Hugh L r ... 33
Johnston J H r ... 17-W
Johnston J H & Co gen mdse ... 10
Johnston S L r ... 12-J

Kemp John J r Country ... 2712

Latimer W D r ... 18-J
Long Will r Country ... 2704

McCleskey S D Mrs r Country ... 2703

Power W D r ... 12-W
Priest Service Station ... 14-J

Reeves Florist ... 19
Robertson Jessie Mrs r ... 22-R

SOU BELL TEL & TEL CO INC ... Marietta Ga 9000

Vansant T J Dr r ... 18-W

Wheeler C C r ... 32-J

WOODSTOCK TELEPHONE DIRECTORY, 1946. The phone directory of only a few pages included 10 communities outside of Atlanta. The Woodstock business and residential page consisted of 35 entries. (Courtesy of Alice Dean Felton.)

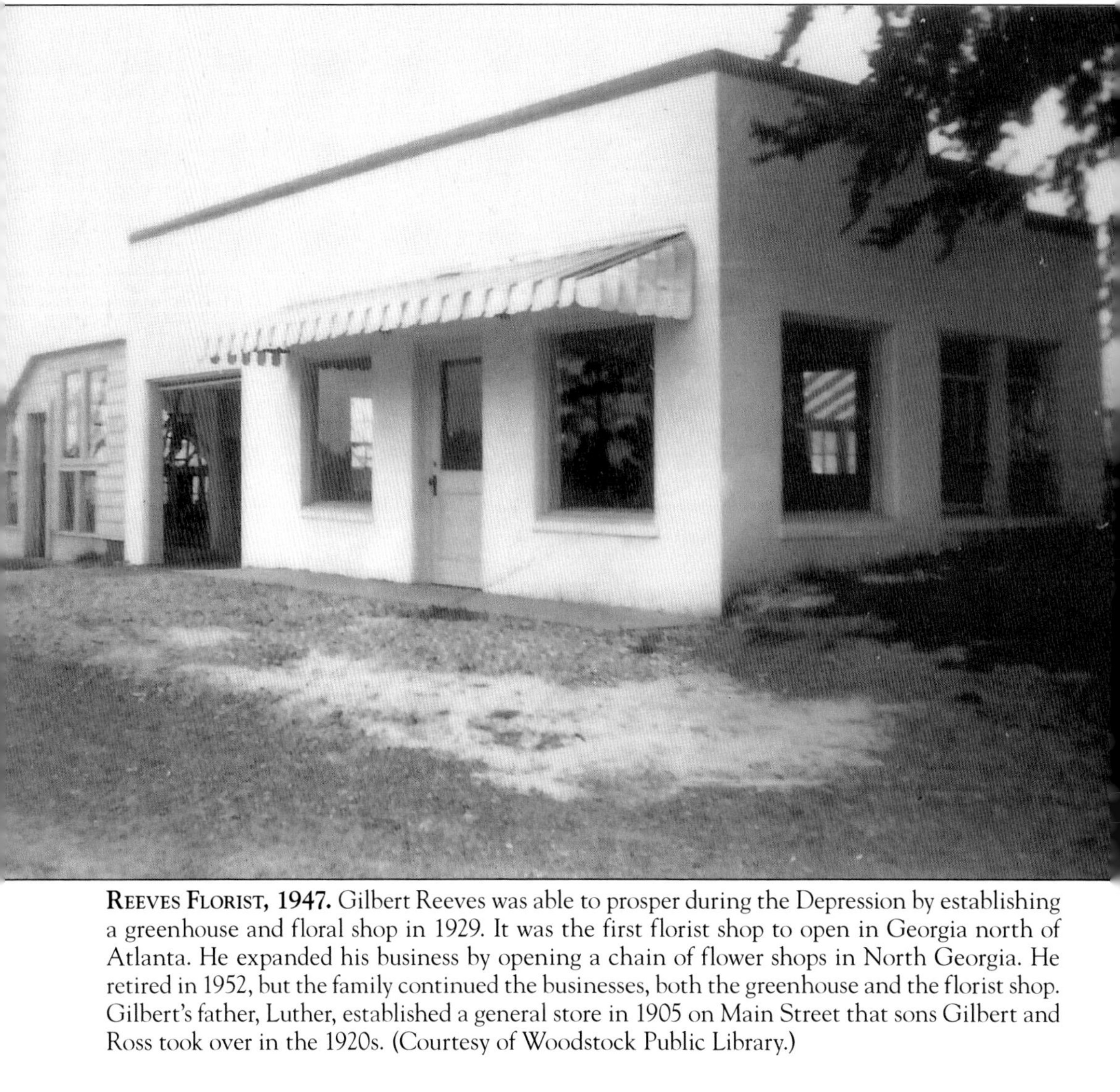

Reeves Florist, 1947. Gilbert Reeves was able to prosper during the Depression by establishing a greenhouse and floral shop in 1929. It was the first florist shop to open in Georgia north of Atlanta. He expanded his business by opening a chain of flower shops in North Georgia. He retired in 1952, but the family continued the businesses, both the greenhouse and the florist shop. Gilbert's father, Luther, established a general store in 1905 on Main Street that sons Gilbert and Ross took over in the 1920s. (Courtesy of Woodstock Public Library.)

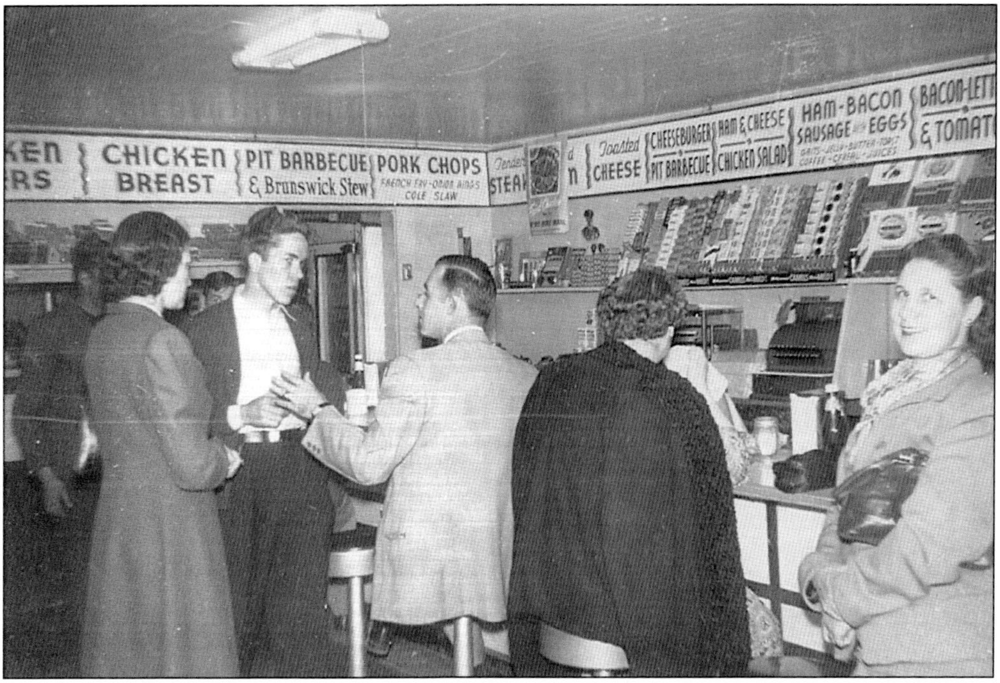

Dixie Inn, 1948. Pictured are, from left to right, Sara Frances and Speer Ramsay, Hugh and Sara Lou Johnston, and Pearl Nelson Parker. The Dixie Inn became a well-known restaurant located at the corner of Highways 92 and 5. People as far away as Marietta and Atlanta came to eat at the curbside service restaurant. Ed Mulkey opened the restaurant in 1947. Dixie Inn was best known for barbecue pork, fried chicken, and catfish. Customers could put a nickel in the jukebox and listen to the music through speakers outside the restaurant. The restaurant changed hands in 1963 and was renamed Shepherd Inn. Bill Tasker, the new owner, kept the restaurant going until March 1964, when it was destroyed by fire. The restaurant was rebuilt and was known as the Old Dixie Inn. (Courtesy of James Parker and Mary Ann Eubanks.)

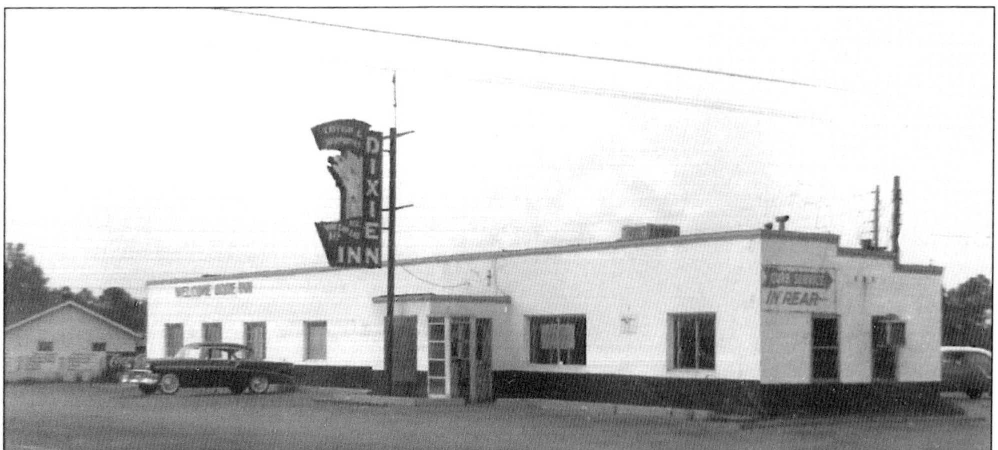

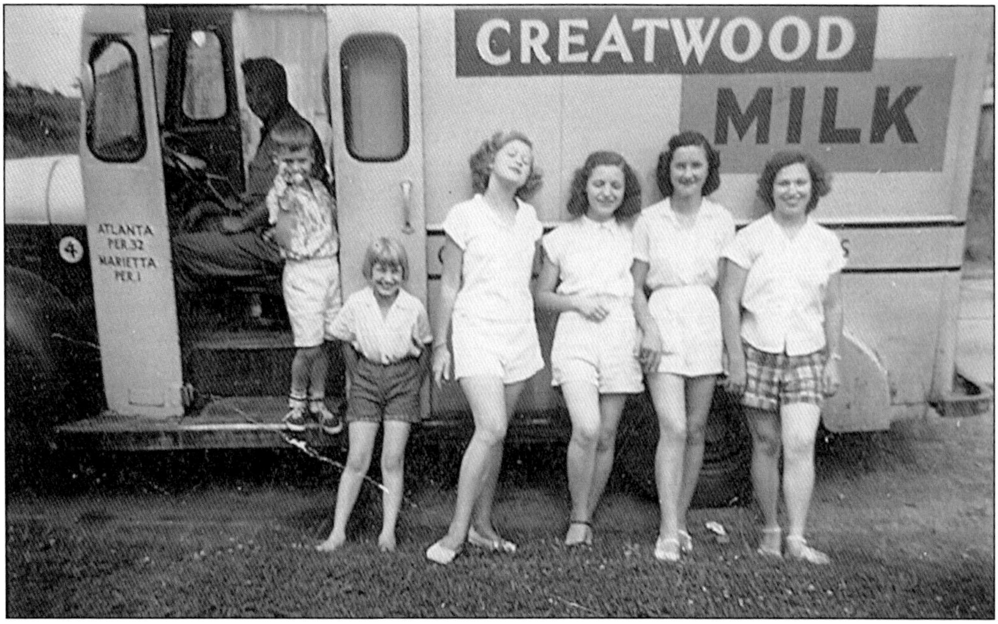

CREATWOOD DAIRY TRUCK, SOUTH MAIN STREET, 1949. Pictured are, from left to right, an unidentified driver, James Parker on truck step, Twila Parker, Mary Ann Parker, Faye Crow, Mildred Booth, and Jeanette Parker. (Courtesy of James Parker.)

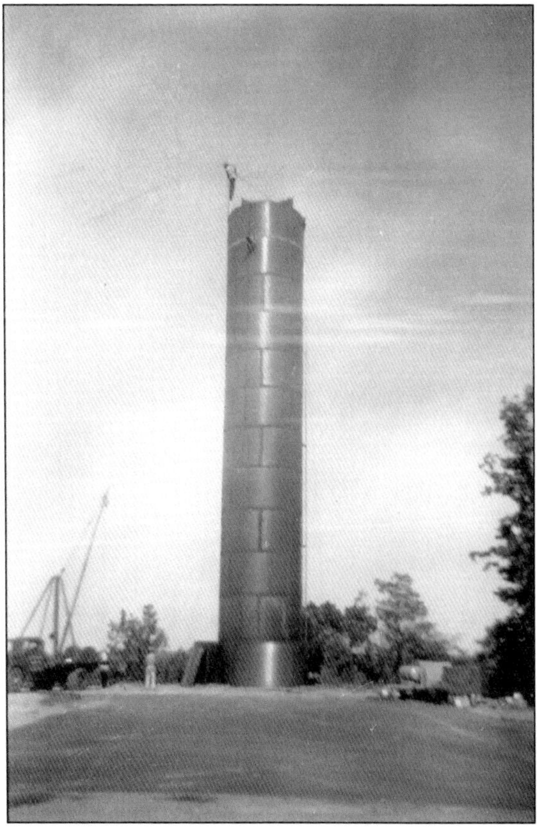

WOODSTOCK WATER TOWER, 1949. Located behind Woodstock School, the water tower supplied water pressure to residents. The tower was the first water system after individual wells were used. Before Woodstock provided a city water system, they placed the water tank at the highest point in town, thereby creating the water pressure to supply water to the houses below. The water tower was dismantled, a section at a time, and removed when it was no longer needed. The city installed the first water system in 1952. (Courtesy of James Parker.)

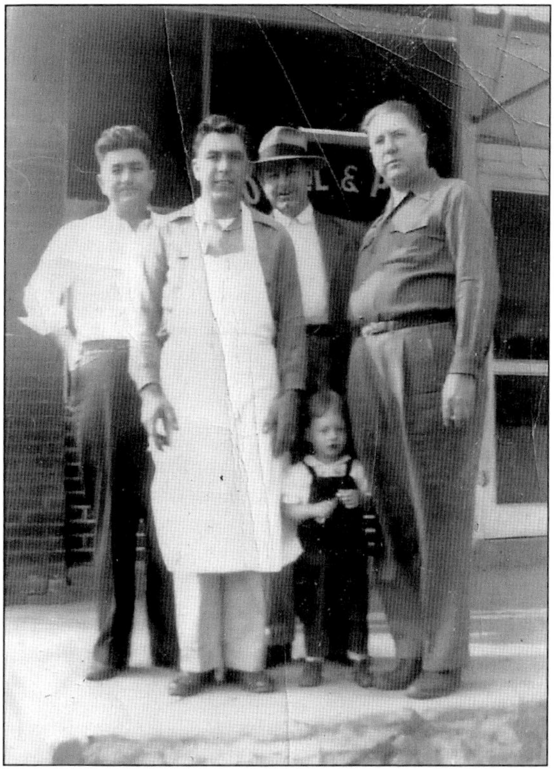

Howell-Poor Grocery, 1949–1956. Luther Howell and James Poor (Howell's son-in-law) operated the grocery store together. Before 1935, Luther Howell, his brothers, and father owned and operated a cotton gin, sawmill, and gristmill north of Woodstock. Pictured from left to right are Hoyt Howell, Herbert Howell, Luther Howell, and Pierce Howell and his daughter. (Courtesy of Jeanne Cosey.)

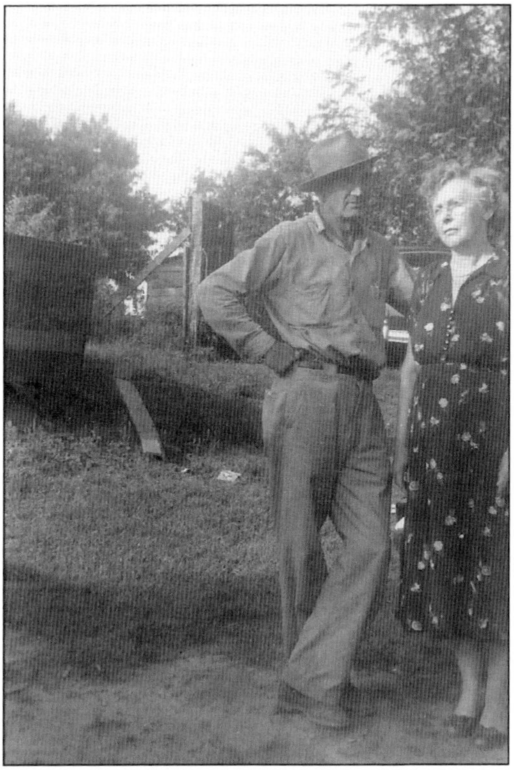

Floyd Nim McArthur, Late 1940s. McArthur worked for W. B. Anderson Feed and Poultry Company in the late 1940s. McArthur transferred the chickens to factories and other states by truck. McArthur moved to Woodstock in the early 1930s from Pickens County. McArthur is pictured with his wife, Tinie Grizzel McArthur. (Courtesy of Jeanette Parker McArthur.)

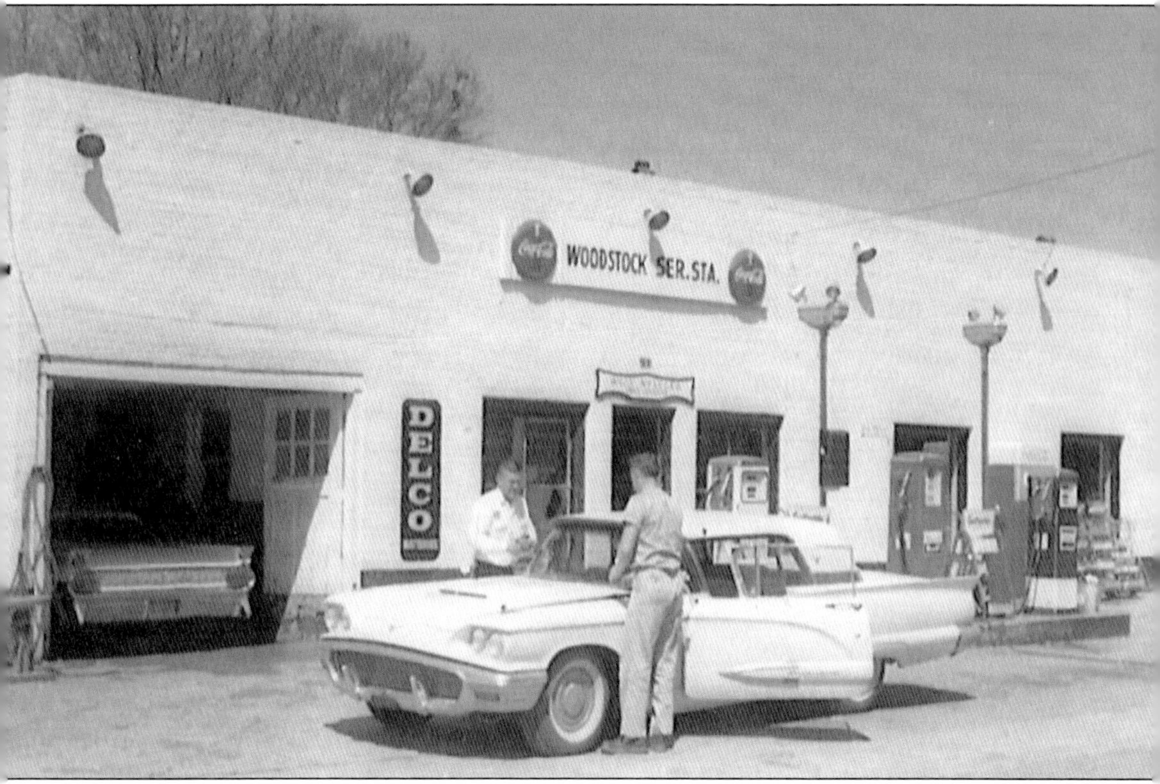

Woodstock Service Station, 1950s. Billy Wheeler operated the service station in the late 1950s. The station was situated near Woodstock Elementary at the intersection where Rope Mill Road and Main Street converge. (Courtesy of Stanley Johnston.)

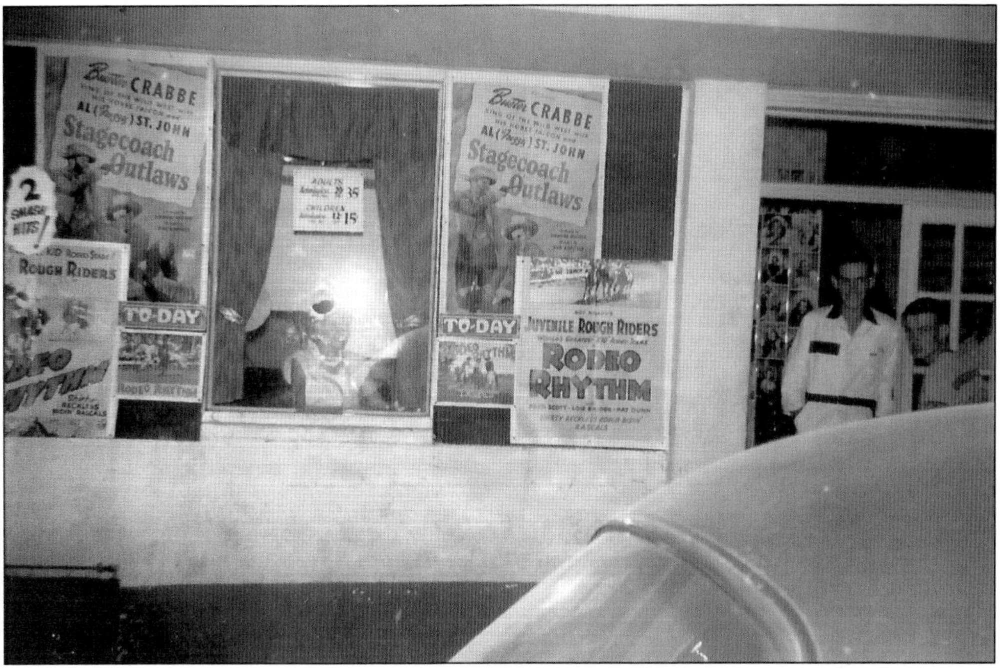

Woodstock Theatre, Closing Night, August 12, 1950. On May 13, 1947, J. M. Holliday and J. P. Duckett obtained a license by the city to open a motion picture house in Woodstock. The theater was not allowed to show movies on Sundays or during church hours. The theater reopened for a brief time but burned to the ground on Saturday night, November 25, 1950. (Courtesy of Preservation Woodstock, Inc.)

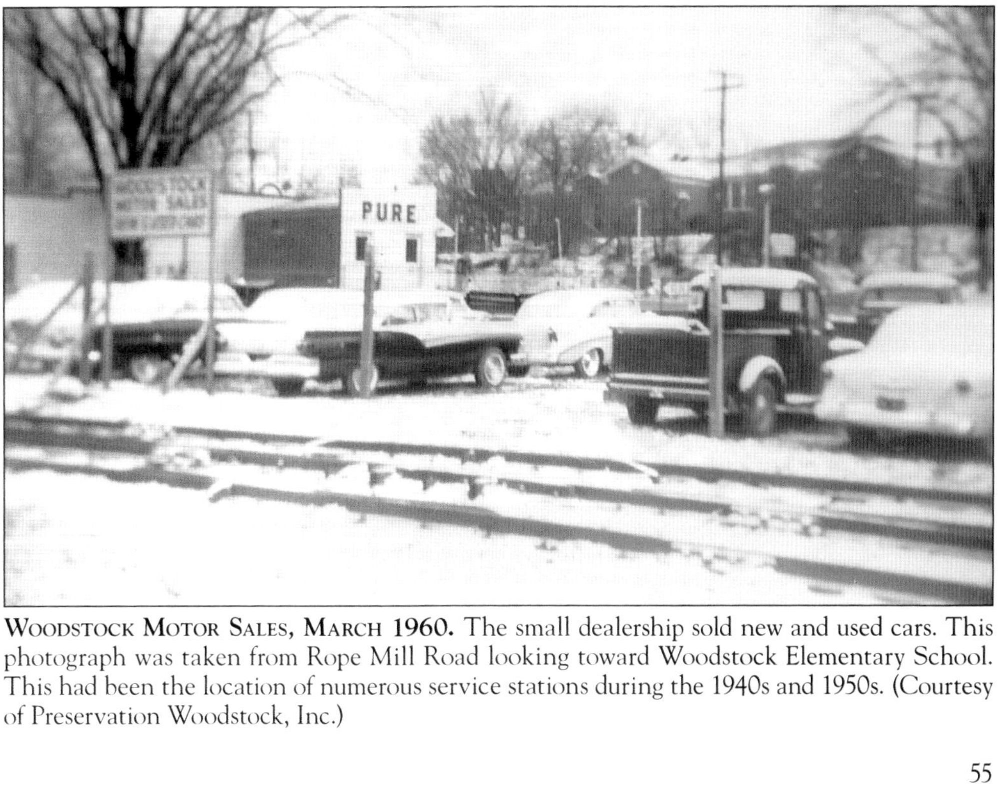

Woodstock Motor Sales, March 1960. The small dealership sold new and used cars. This photograph was taken from Rope Mill Road looking toward Woodstock Elementary School. This had been the location of numerous service stations during the 1940s and 1950s. (Courtesy of Preservation Woodstock, Inc.)

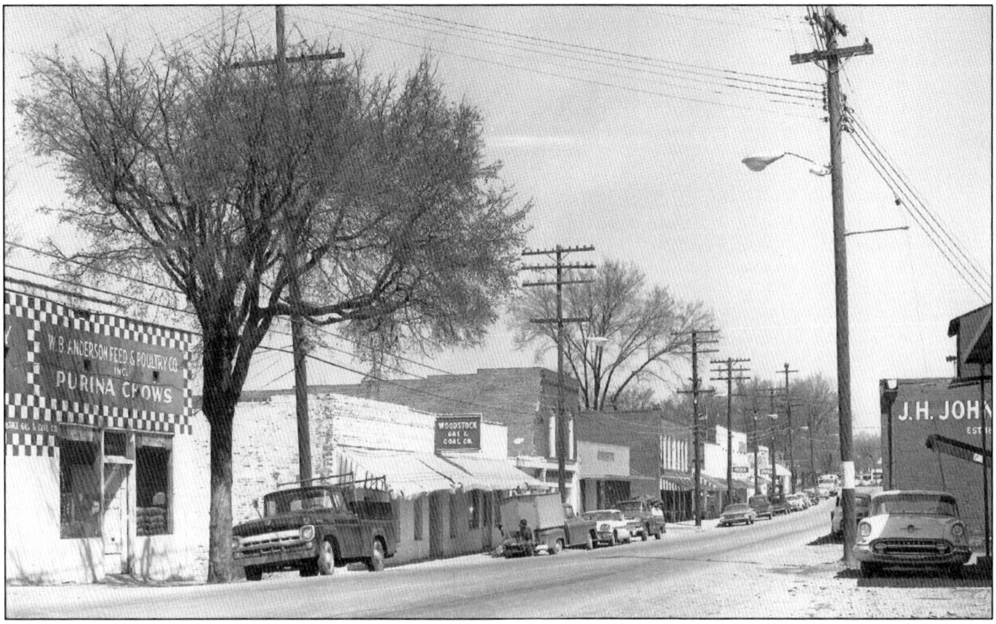

Downtown Woodstock, 1960. W. B. Anderson owned and operated W. B. Anderson Feed and Poultry Company and Woodstock Gas and Coal Company. He sold coal brought by rail to Woodstock. Anderson later sold feed at his business. In the 1960s, Anderson established Woodstock Premium Propane Gas Company at the same location. (Courtesy of Preservation Woodstock, Inc.)

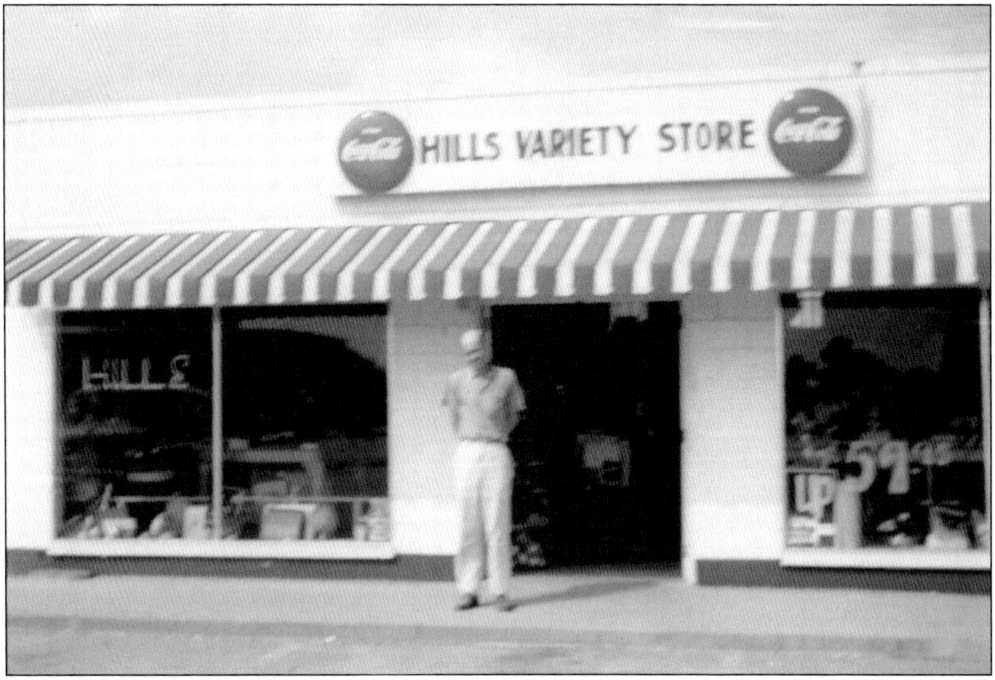

Hills Variety Store, 1962. Chester Hill is pictured outside the variety store that operated next door to Dean Drug Store. Hill also had worked for the Johnston Company and later worked for Economy Food, the grocery store operated by Howell and Poor. (Courtesy of Russ Sims.)

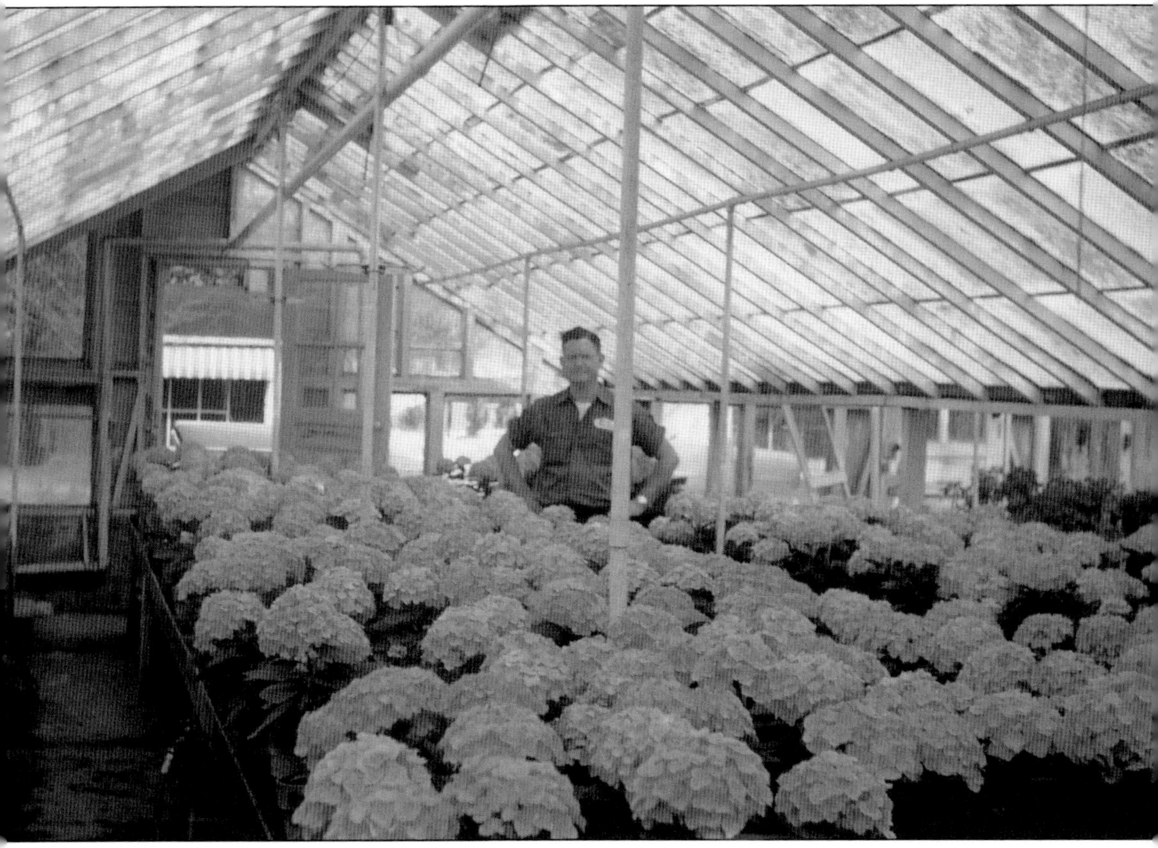

Reeves Greenhouses, 1962. John Reeves operated the greenhouses in 1962. Gilbert Reeves, his father, established the greenhouses as part of his floral business in 1929. John Reeves was one of the first fire chiefs for the South Cherokee Fire Department. The business is continued by family members. (Courtesy of Russ Sims.)

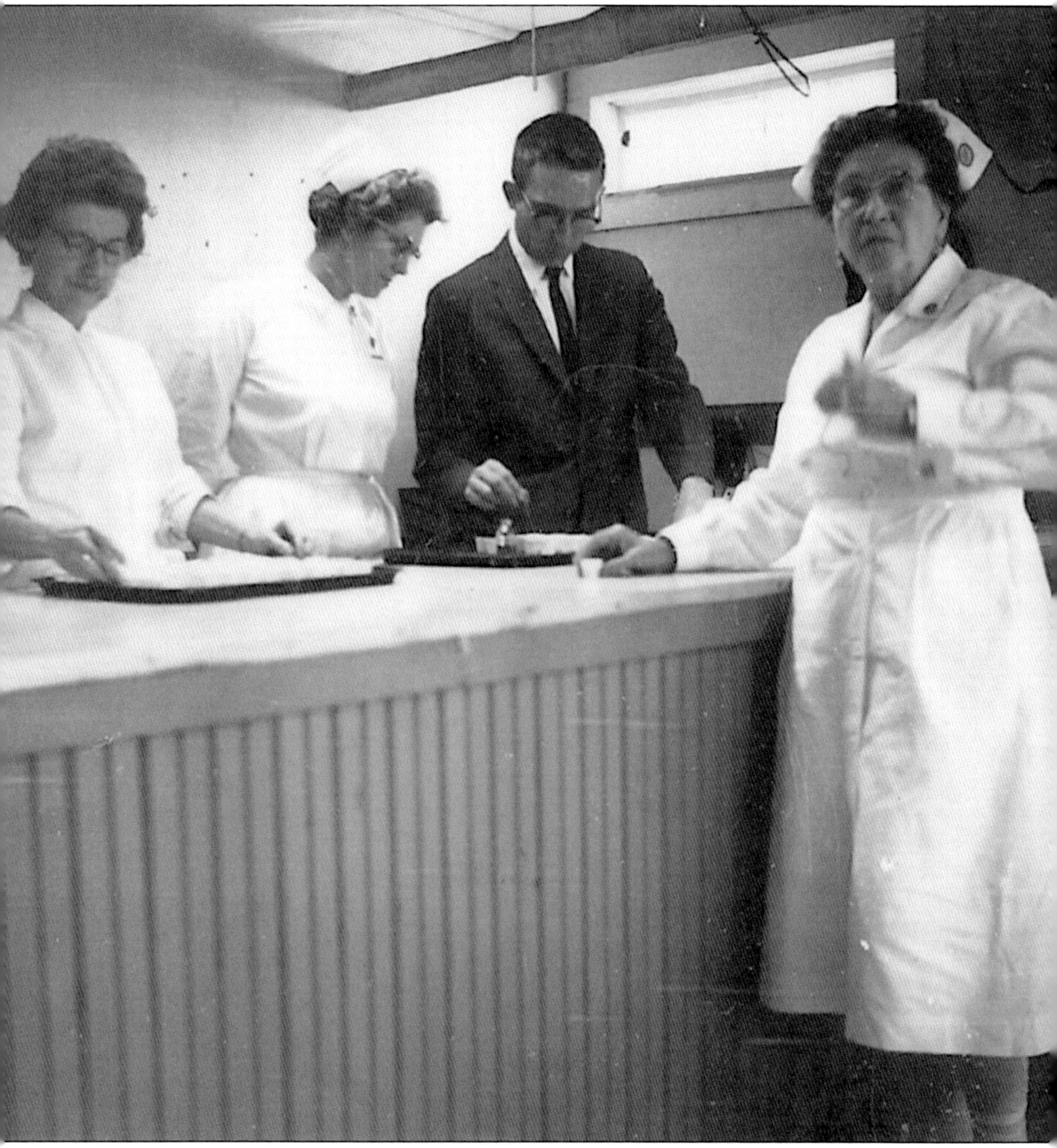

WOODSTOCK MEDICAL CLINIC, 1964. From left to right, Evelyn Chambers, Edna Whitmire, Dr. A. Evan Boddy, and an unidentified nurse update medical records at Woodstock Medical Clinic. Boddy came to Woodstock as a physician in 1962 after studying medicine at Emory University School of Medicine. He opened the medical clinic that year and a nursing home in 1979. The brick one-story clinic located between the Dean home and the McAfee home had four examining rooms, two waiting rooms, an X-ray room, and a nurse station. A nonprofit corporation was established with seven trustees that financed the clinic from interest-bearing certificates bought by residents. He and other community leaders were instrumental in opening Woodstock's first hospital in 1969. Chambers became the city clerk and later the first female mayor. (Courtesy of Woodstock Public Library.)

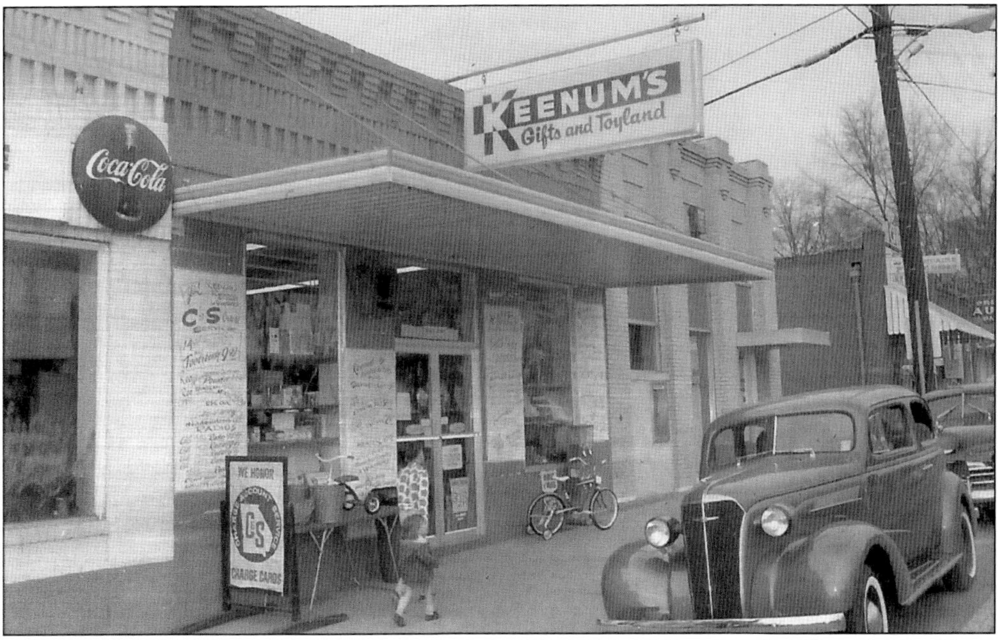

Keenum's Toyland, 1964. Don Keenum opened Keenum's Toyland in the Chandler Building. The business was an all-purpose drugstore but sold particularly toys. Keenum held contests for children such as model car contests, and children earned points for every toy purchased in the store that counted toward another toy. (Courtesy of Don Keenum.)

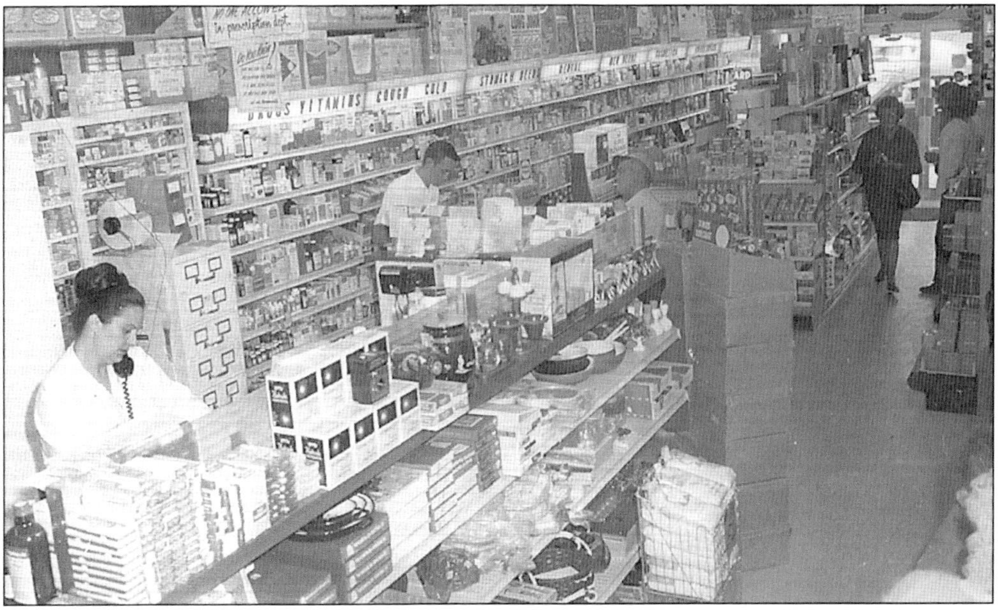

June Keenum, First Woman Pharmacist, 1966. June Keenum was the only female pharmacist when she graduated from Southern College of Pharmacy in Atlanta, now College of Pharmacy and Health Sciences of Mercer University, in 1952. She became the only female pharmacist at Kennestone Hospital in Marietta in 1954. She and her husband, Don, also a pharmacist, opened Keenum's Pharmacy in 1961. Buddy Hulsey worked for the Keenums before and after he graduated from pharmacy school. (Courtesy of Don Keenum.)

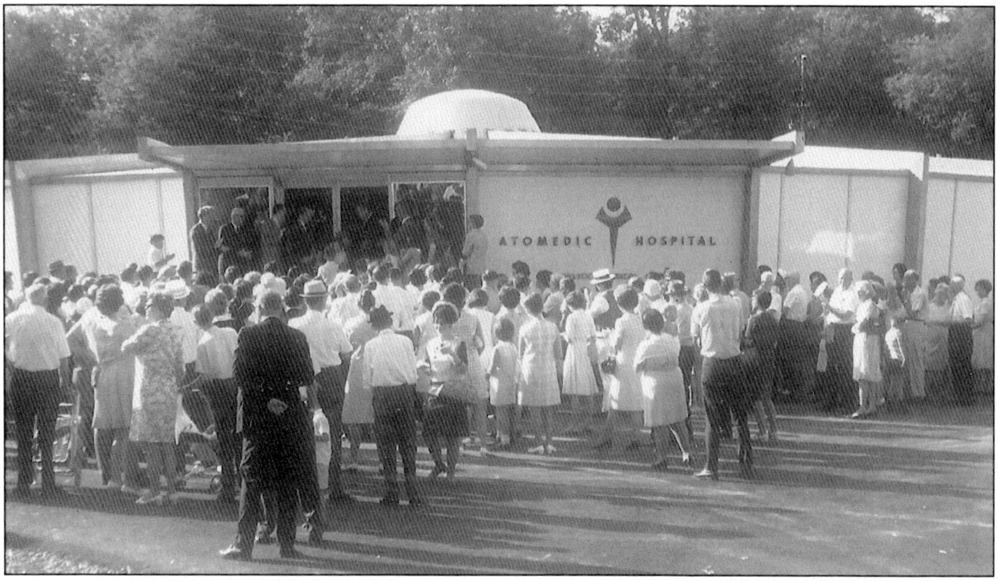

DEDICATION OF CHEROKEE ATOMEDIC HOSPITAL, 1969. The space-age 22-bed hospital was moved piece by piece in 1967 from Montgomery, Alabama, to become the first hospital in Woodstock. The concept building was displayed at the World's Fair in New York in 1965–1966. A revolutionary concept of the time, the hospital was equipped with closed-circuit televisions to monitor patients, a computer that dispensed medications, linens, and medical supplies. The hospital operated under a contract by the Atomedic Research Center of Florida. Drs. J. Thomas Cooper, A. Evan Boddy, and Robert Townsend were the first physicians to work at the new hospital. (Courtesy of Sara Frances Dial Ramsay.)

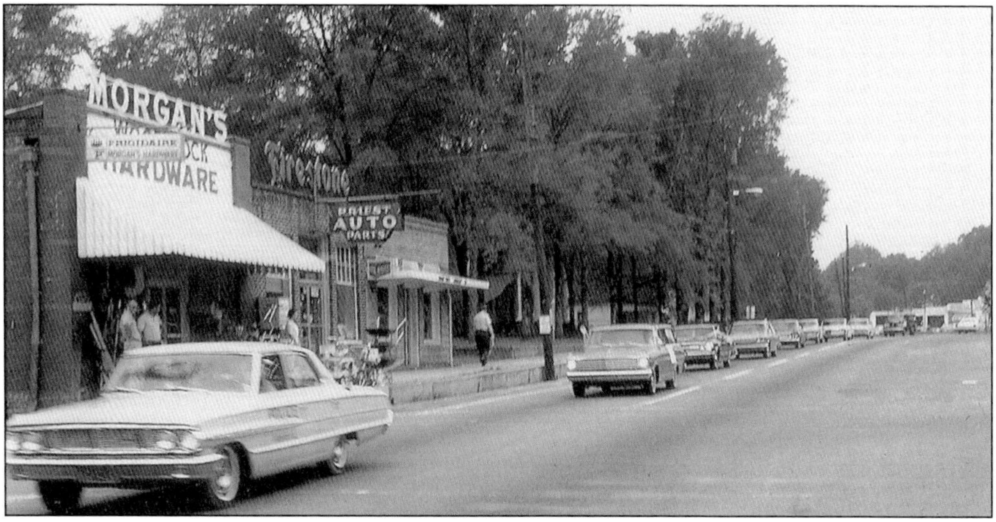

MORGAN HARDWARE AND PRIEST AUTO PARTS, LATE 1960S. O. E. Morgan opened Morgan's Hardware Store in 1961. He and his brother A. R. opened a hardware store in 1939 in Canton. The Canton store closed in the late 1960s. Hansel ("Hank") Priest operated a service station in 1939, at Rope Mill Road and Main Street. In 1947, he expanded the business by adding a garage and an auto dealership. In 1955, Priest dropped the auto sales and continued operating the station. Then in 1959, he opened and operated Priest Auto Parts on Main Street until his retirement in 1973. (Courtesy of Carolyn Fox Hitt.)

Five

Founding Families

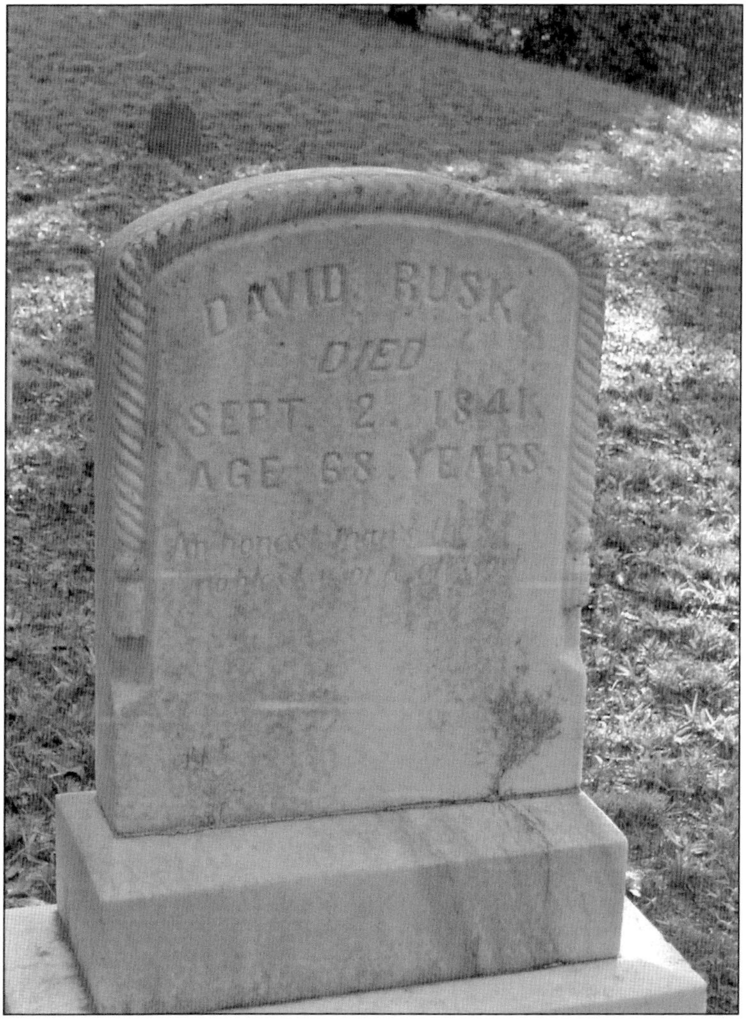

David Rusk, Early Settler. David Rusk was born in Northern Ireland around 1790. He and his wife, Jane Gourley, immigrated to Charleston, then to a farm just outside of Woodstock around 1831. He decided to settle in the Woodstock area to take advantage of the land lottery enactment. His great-grandson, Dean Rusk, became secretary of state during the Kennedy and Johnson administrations. (Courtesy of Felicia Whitmore.)

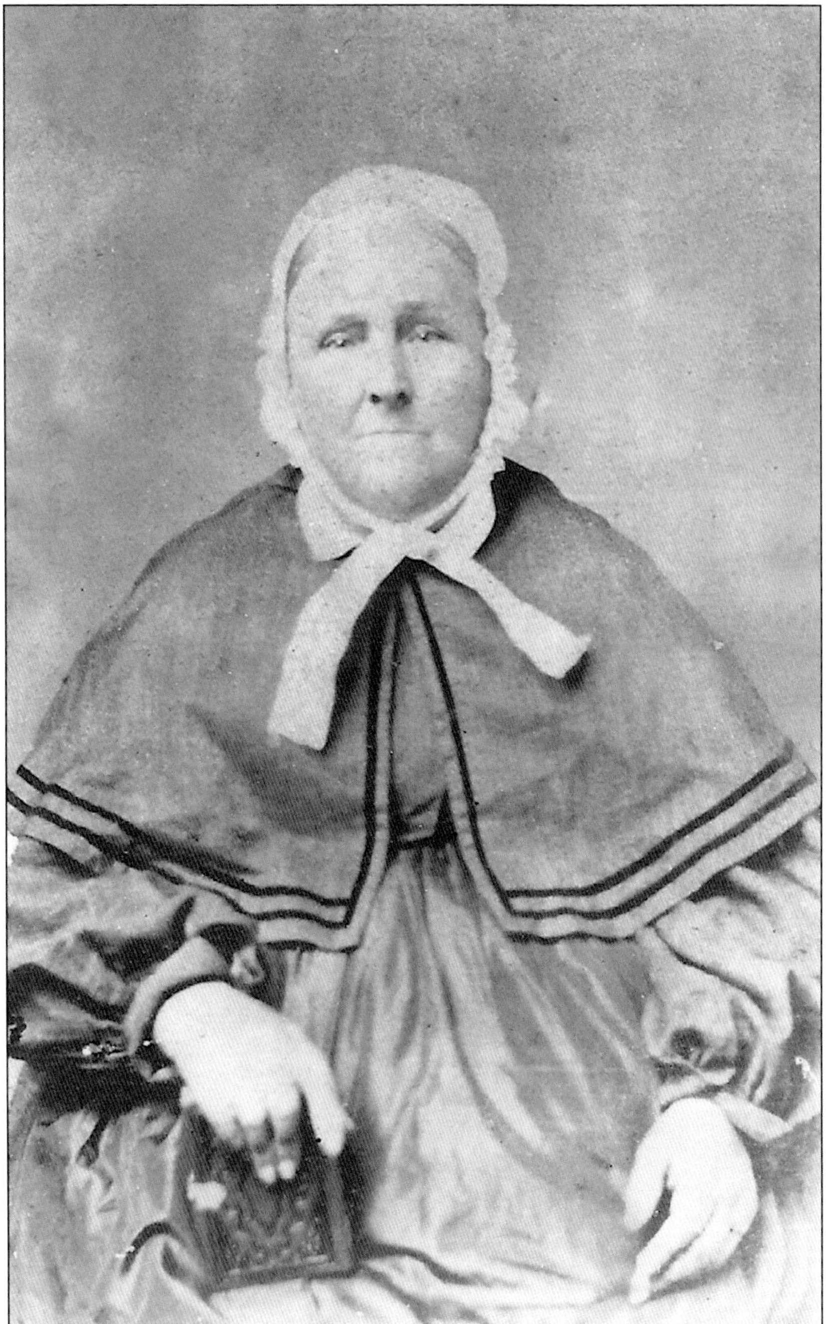

Aralinta Choice Dial, Early Settler. Aralinta Dial, born in 1802, was among the first white settlers in the Woodstock area. She married Joseph Stallsworth Dial, who was born in 1793 in South Carolina. Stallsworth Dial purchased many lots left from settlers who had acquired them through the land lottery. Dial accumulated extensive acreage from Woodstock to Sweats Mountain. He built a large home on his working farm, and he and Aralinta raised five children: William Choice, Cyrus, Tully John, Hastings Joseph, and Mary Elizabeth. William Choice Dial became a captain in the Confederate army. (Courtesy of Harold Johnston.)

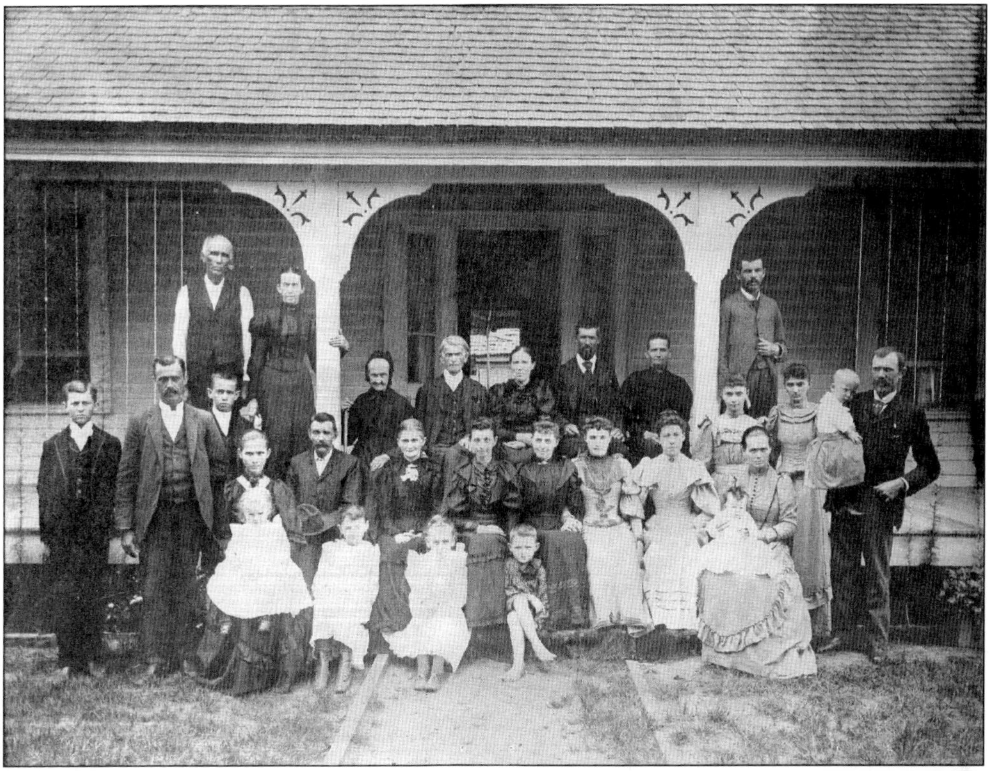

Saye Family Reunion, 1898, Celebrating Elizabeth Saye's 90th Birthday. Brothers George and Charles Barnes moved to Woodstock in 1839. Their sister Elizabeth and her husband, William Saye, settled on 80 acres in 1843 near Little River and what is now Arnold Mill Road. They cleared the land and built grist and sawmills. (Courtesy of Felicia Whitmore.)

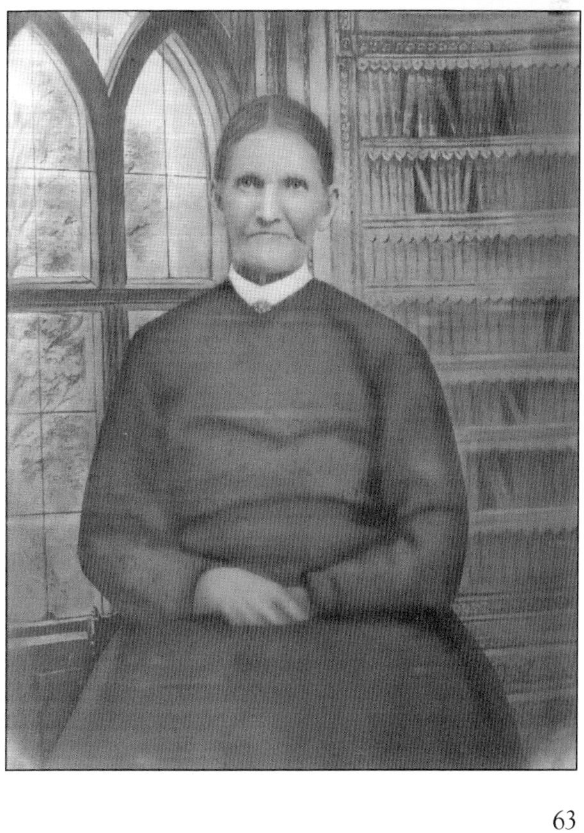

Elizabeth Sledge Johnston, Early Settler. Sledge Johnston is pictured in this painted portrait from 1875. Her hard features indicate the difficult life she had on the frontier and farms of North Georgia. She was born in Warren County, North Carolina, in 1814 where her parents were raised, and she died in Woodstock in 1892. Her son, J. H. Johnston, established one of the first businesses in Woodstock and created the Bank of Woodstock in 1905. (Courtesy of Harold Johnston.)

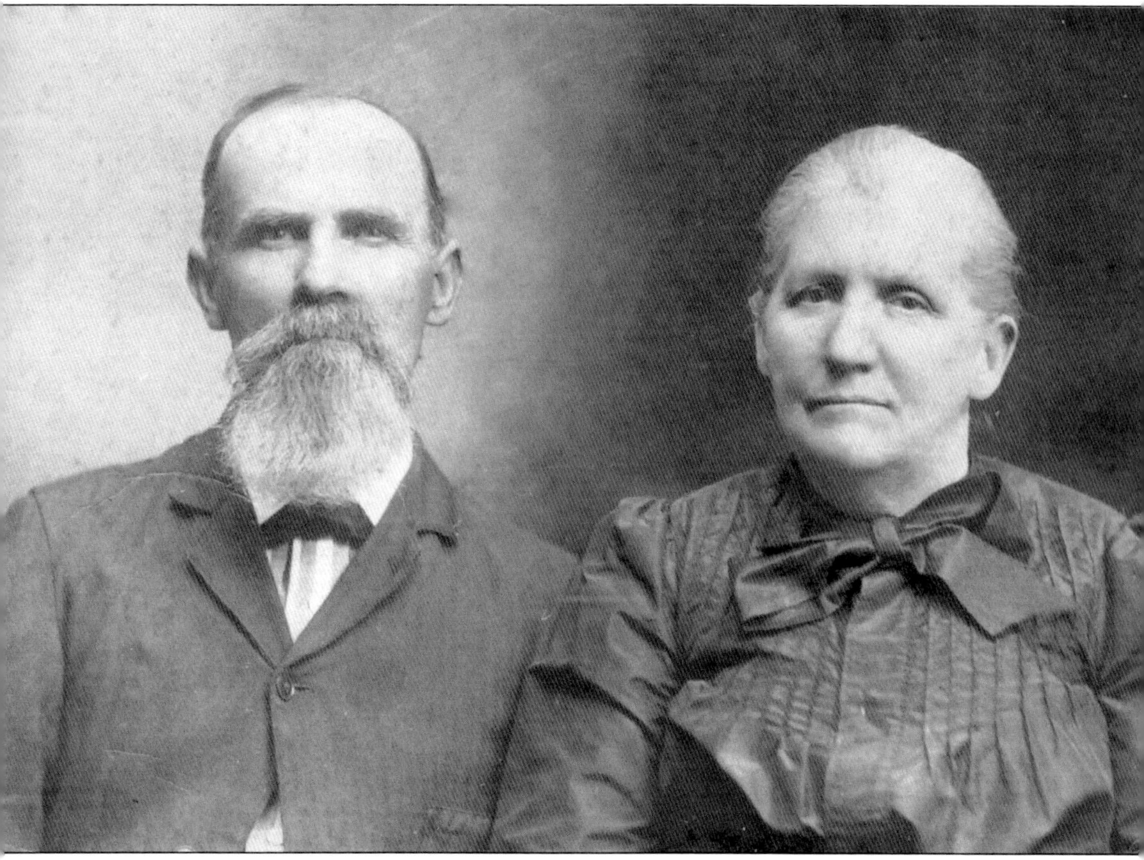

WILEY PARKS DOBBS AND SELENA ANN DUPREE DOBBS, C. 1911. Wylie Parks Dobbs (1844–1913) was the 11th of 12 children of Burrell Dobbs (born in 1800) and his wife, Margaret. Burrell and his brother Baalam brought their families to Cherokee County and settled near Woodstock. Later they moved to Lickskillet and farmed on Hickory Flat Road. Both were farmers and fortunate drawers in the Cherokee Land Lottery of 1827. Their land was located east of Woodstock. Selena Ann Dupree (1845–1929) was the daughter of William and Myra Dupree, early Woodstock settlers. Wylie and Selena married in 1866 and raised eight children. Dobbs served in the Civil War with the Phillips' Legion. When he returned from the war, he worked as a farmer and merchant. (Courtesy of Marilyn Dobbs Morrell.)

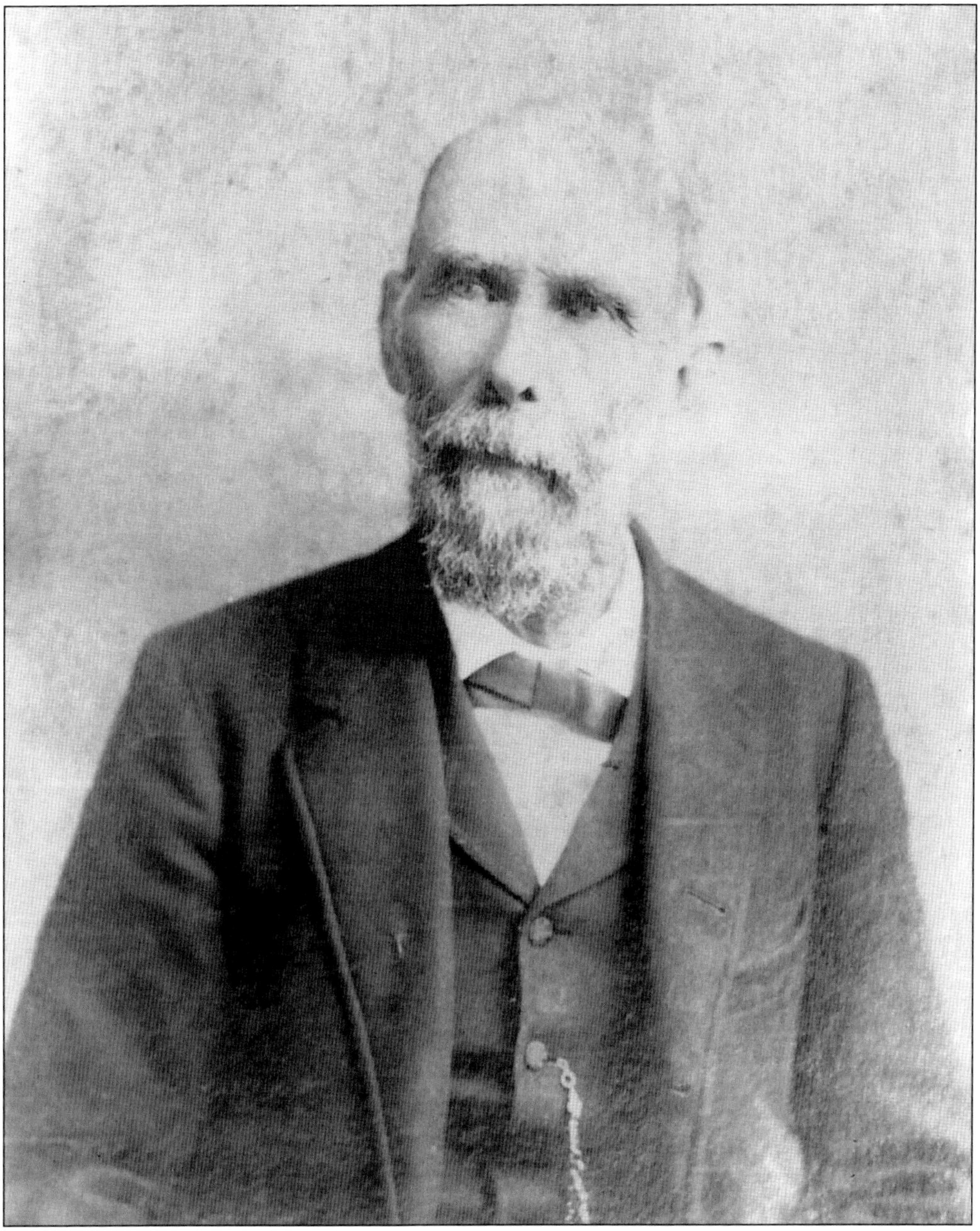

William Hiram Dean, Physician and Pastor. Dean (1824–1912) graduated from the Medical College of Georgia in Augusta and practiced medicine for one year at Oak Hill in Newton County before settling in Woodstock. He built a log house in 1851 in town. Dean served in the Confederacy as a surgeon. Dean rode horseback to patients' homes with a saddlebag containing medications strapped to his horse. Dean served as pastor periodically for Enon Baptist Church from 1862 until 1884. The Dean family grew cotton and alfalfa on their farm. (Courtesy of Alice Dean Felton.)

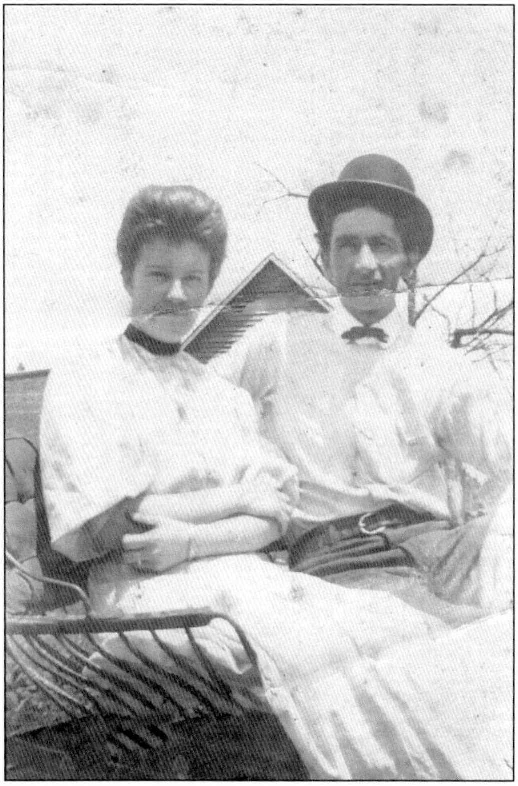

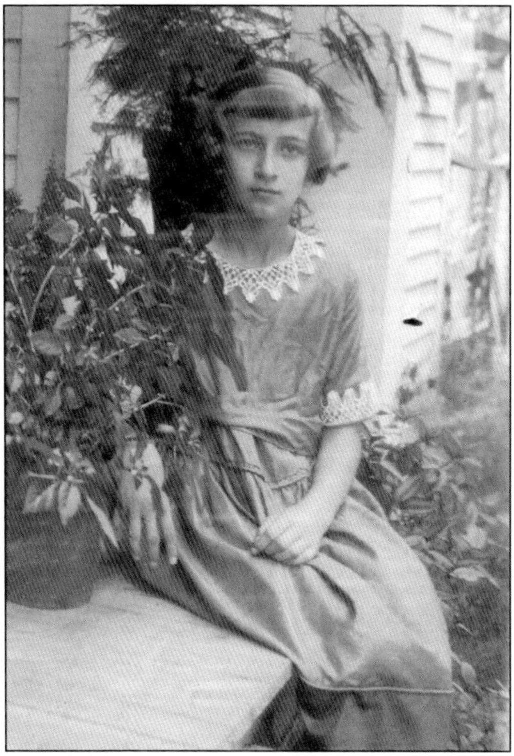

LAURA MAYE DOBBS AND CLAUDE CHANDLER, 1908. Laura Maye died 21 days after giving birth to their daughter, Maye, in 1910. Maye was raised by her grandmother, Amanda Chandler Edwards, who lived on Elm Street. Claude Chandler later married Maude Gober. Chandler and Wylie Dobbs Sr. opened a general store on Main Street in 1905. The store balcony held caskets that Chandler and Dobbs sold. Chandler also taught at Little River Academy and became the town's undertaker. Chandler lived to be 101. Maye Chandler attended Georgia State College for Women in Milledgeville, graduating with a teacher's (education) degree in 1929. She married the son of her father's store business partner, Wylie Dobbs Jr., after he graduated from Georgia Tech in 1931. They raised two children, Marilyn and Amanda. She taught at Mountain View School and at Blackwell School, where she started a music program. Maye Chandler started playing piano at age six and continued to perfect her talent all her life. She played for community events and at Woodstock Methodist Church. She was a regular pianist on Sundays at Reinhardt College into her 80s. (Both courtesy of Marilyn Dobbs Morrell.)

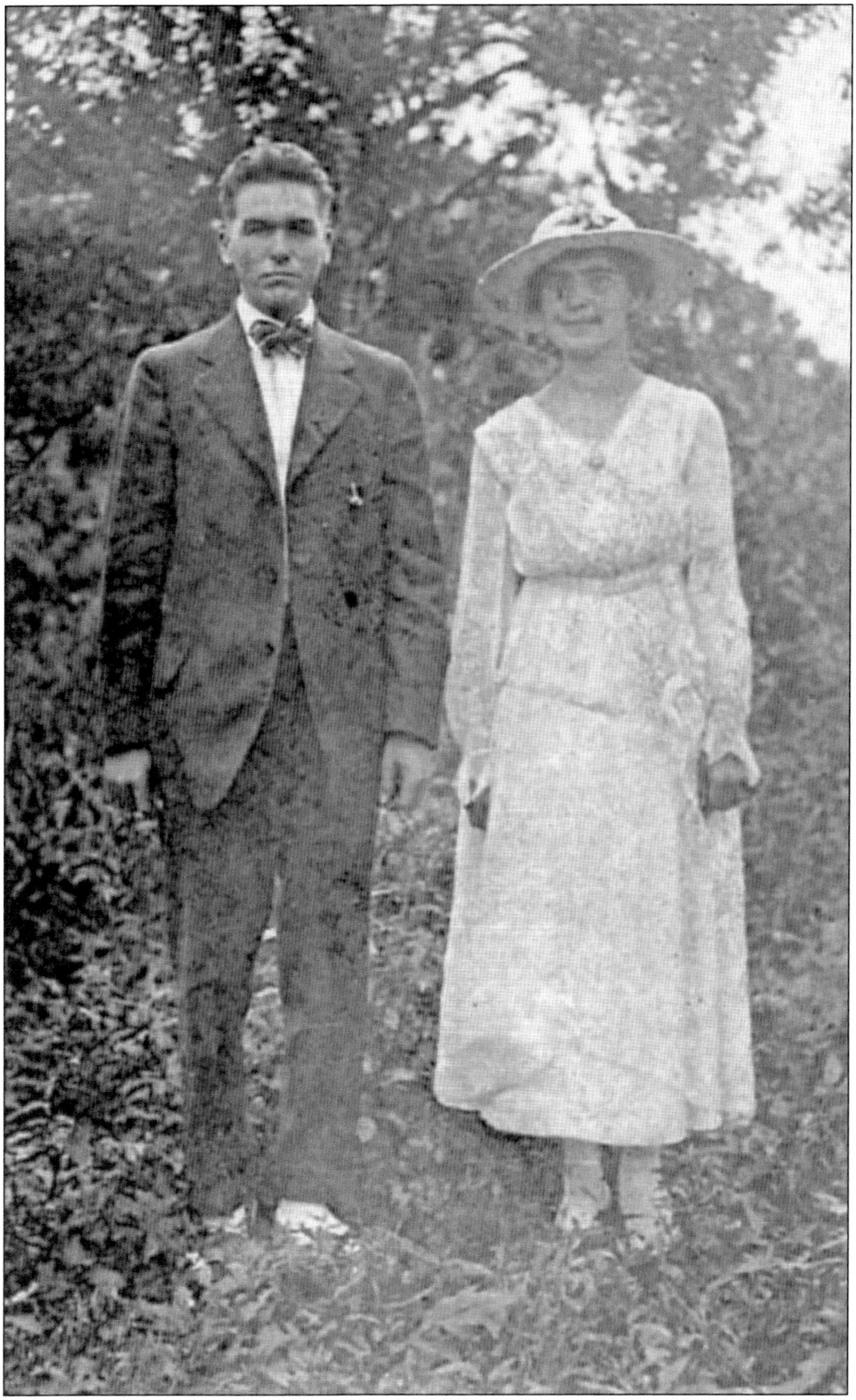

EDGAR AND CORA HASTY POOR, C. 1915. Edgar Poor's parents settled around Bells Ferry Road, but Edgar became a farmer and carpenter in Woodstock, where he raised a family. The Poors lived west of Woodstock Methodist Church. Their son, Arthur Lee, later worked for the Bank of Woodstock. (Courtesy of Elaine Hubbard.)

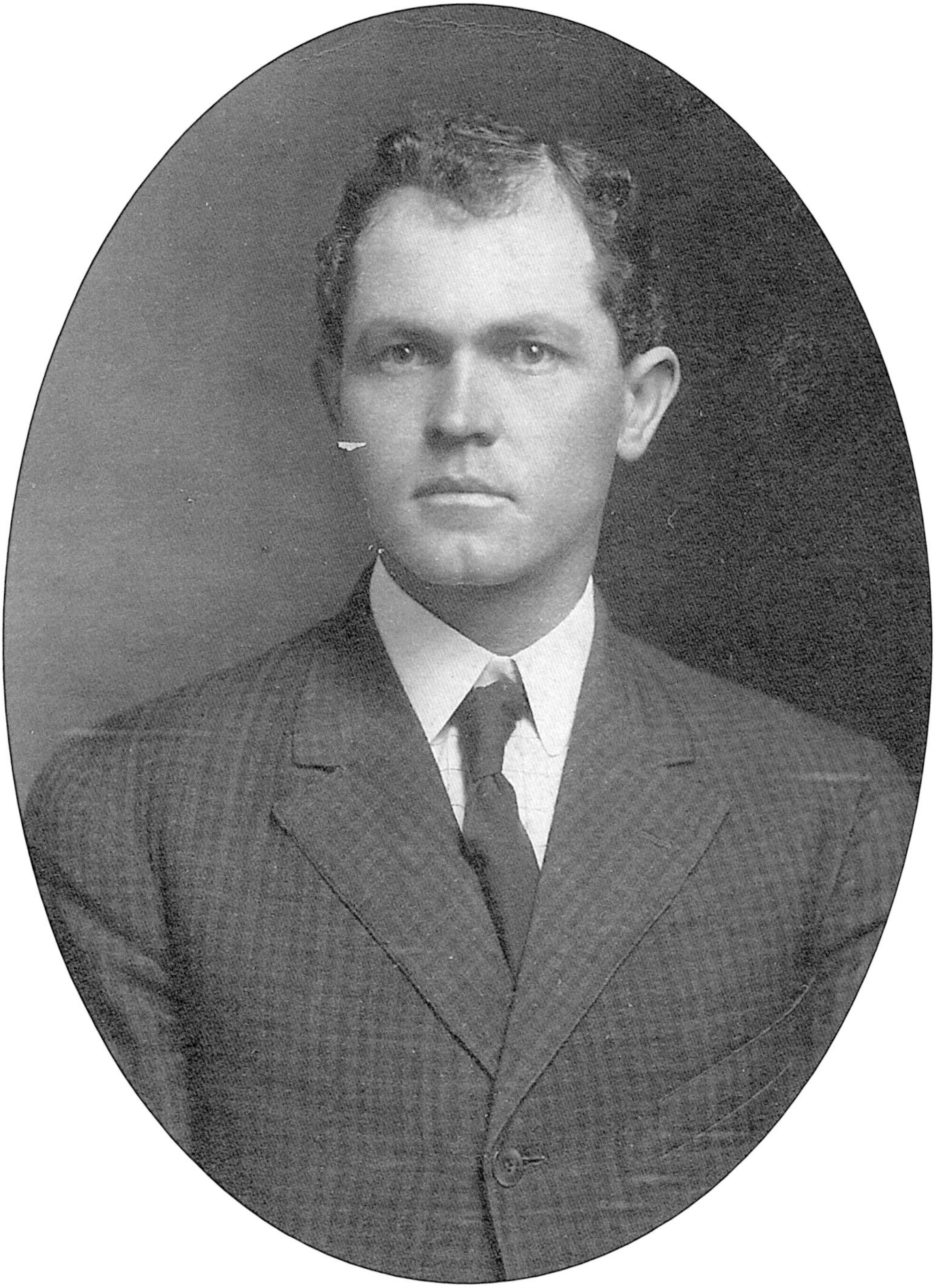

EMMETT DIAL, POSTMASTER, 1917. Dial's father was William Stallworth (1851–1928), and his mother was Esther Rusk. Dial was a rural mail carrier when postal service was known as Rural Free Delivery (RFD). He became postmaster in 1917 and served until 1933. He married Mary Claude Simpson in 1914. Simpson was a granddaughter of Cherokee pioneer Dr. John Torrentine, one of the first physicians in the Hickory Flat area. Dial was the grandson of Col. James Edward Rusk. (Courtesy of Sara Frances Dial Ramsay.)

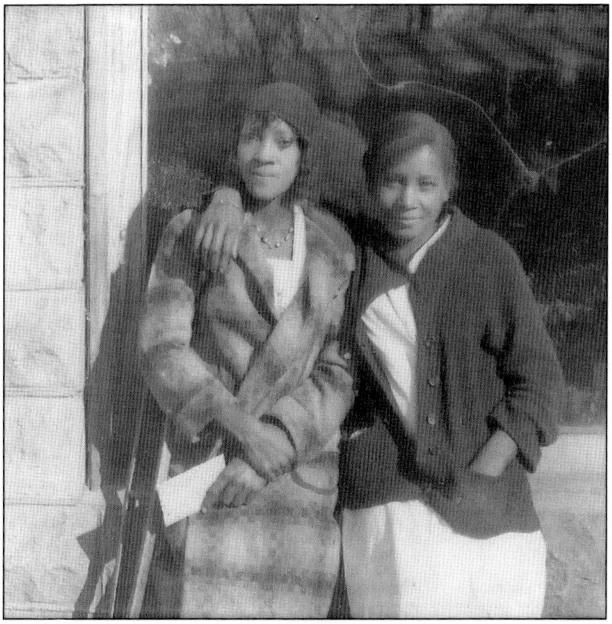

Minnie and Jeanette Maroney, c. 1930. The mother of the Maroney sisters, Laura, was an early Woodstock settler. The Maroney family lived on Arnold Mill Road. (Courtesy of Preservation Woodstock, Inc.)

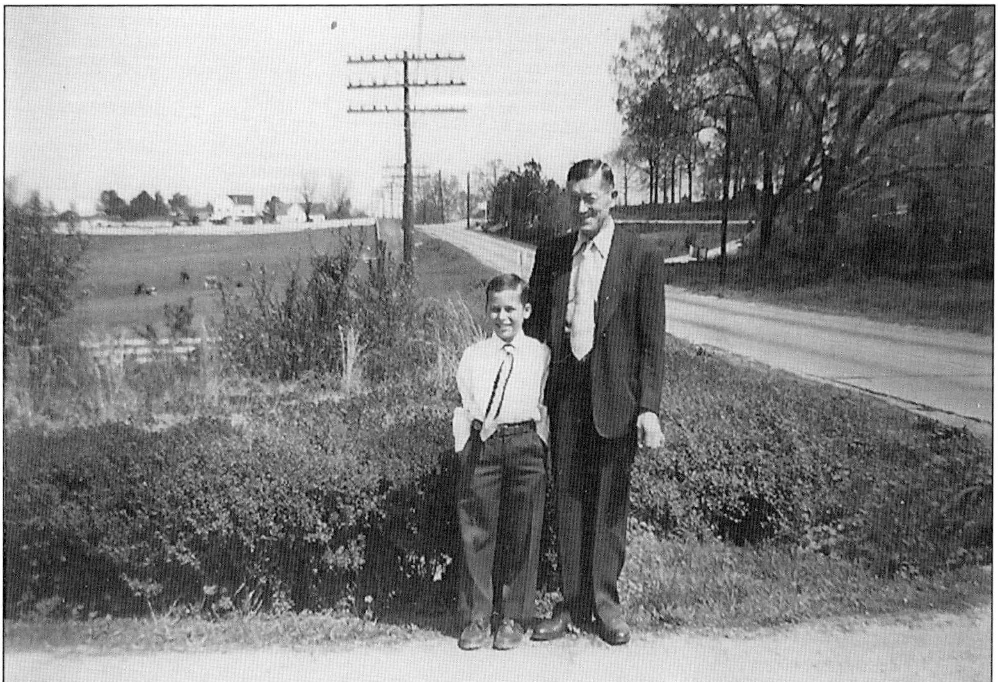

James Calvin Parker and Son James, 1950. Parker and his son are pictured on Highway 5 across from one of the cotton gins in Woodstock. The view is looking north. Born in 1903, Parker worked as a painter, mechanic, and carpenter. He also worked at Lockheed in Marietta. Parker became mayor of Woodstock in 1968 and active in the city council. He also served as a judge for the city. He remained active in the Lions Club and Freemasonry and established the first Eastern Star organization in Woodstock with his wife, Pearl. (Courtesy of Mary Ann Parker Eubanks and Jeanette Parker McArthur.)

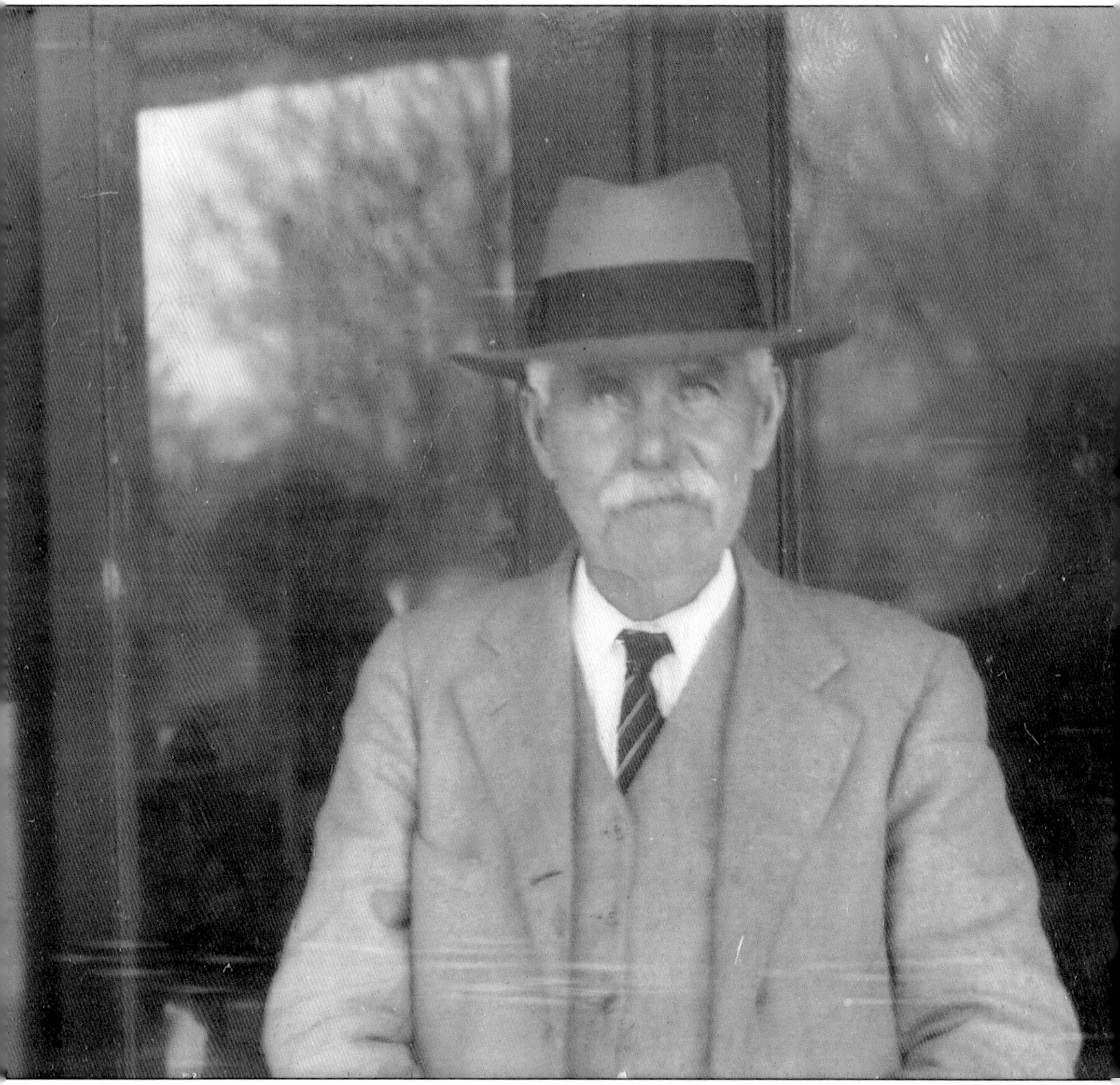

J. H. Johnston, 1930. Johnston was born in 1855 and received only six months of education. J. H. Johnston's father, Dr. Medicine Johnston, lost everything during the Civil War. He and his father cut cordwood to make a living. His father died when he was 14, leaving him to support his mother and his nine-year-old sister. When he was 15, he saved enough money to buy corn and a cow and rented a little farm from T. J. Baldwin. By 1870, he bought property near Moon's Station not far from Kennesaw, cleared it, and cultivated it as a farm. He also worked at the Cox gold mine for $1 a day. Just a few years later, he had paid off the land and purchased 125 acres. He was only 21. He bought a 60-acre farm on Rope Mill Road in 1887 and established J. H. Johnston Mercantile Company in 1888. He served as a state senator in 1890–1891. He established the Bank of Woodstock in 1905 and was the only bank within 10 miles of Woodstock until 1974. (Courtesy of Preservation Woodstock, Inc.)

Six

ORIGINAL HOMES

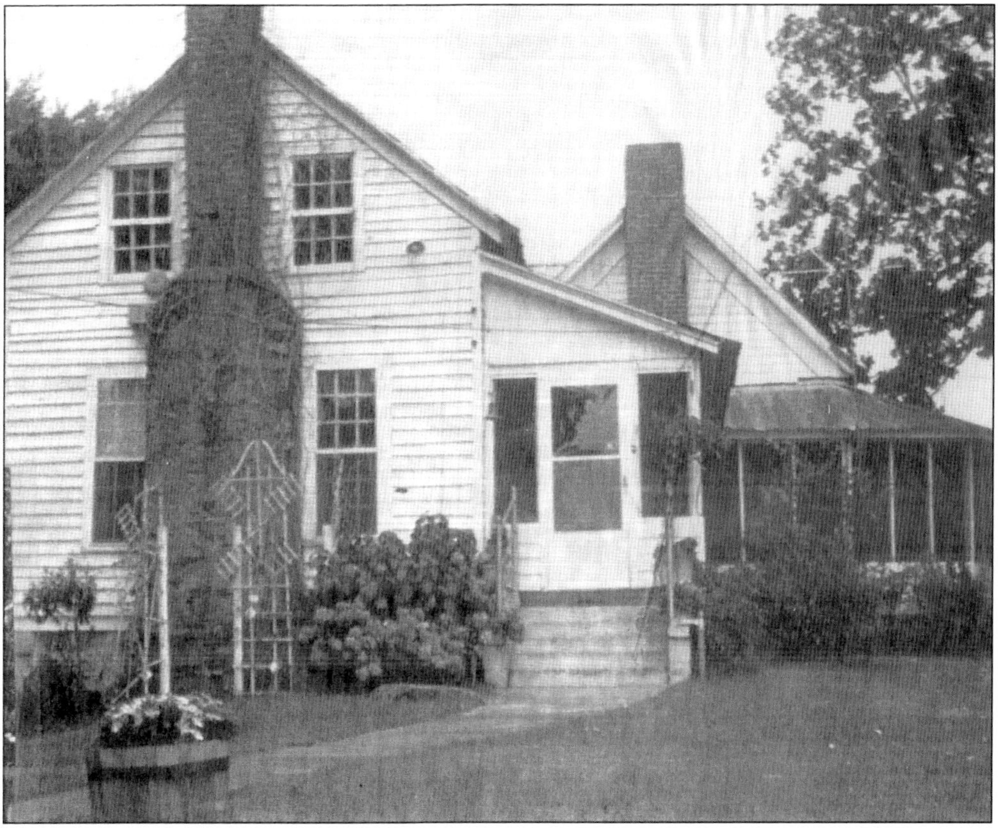

BROOKS FARM HOME, MID-1800S. Five generations of the Brooks family lived on the farmstead on Highway 5 and 92 just south of Woodstock, from 1875 until 1998. The Brooks family acquired the land from Levi Durham. Martha Elizabeth McCleskey inherited 200 acres from her father when she married James Radford Brooks in 1875. Their son James G. Brooks and Elizabeth Routh Brooks lived there until their deaths in 1931 and 1976, respectively. The Brooks family grew cotton and vegetables and raised livestock. When James Brooks died in 1931, Elizabeth and her children continued running the farm. Daughter Martha Routh, age 12, cooked for the family while her mother worked as a nurse. When Elizabeth's son Radford married in 1941, he and his wife, Ara, took over the farm. Elizabeth later ran a boardinghouse in Marietta for travelers and young working women. (Courtesy of Patricia Daves Freeman.)

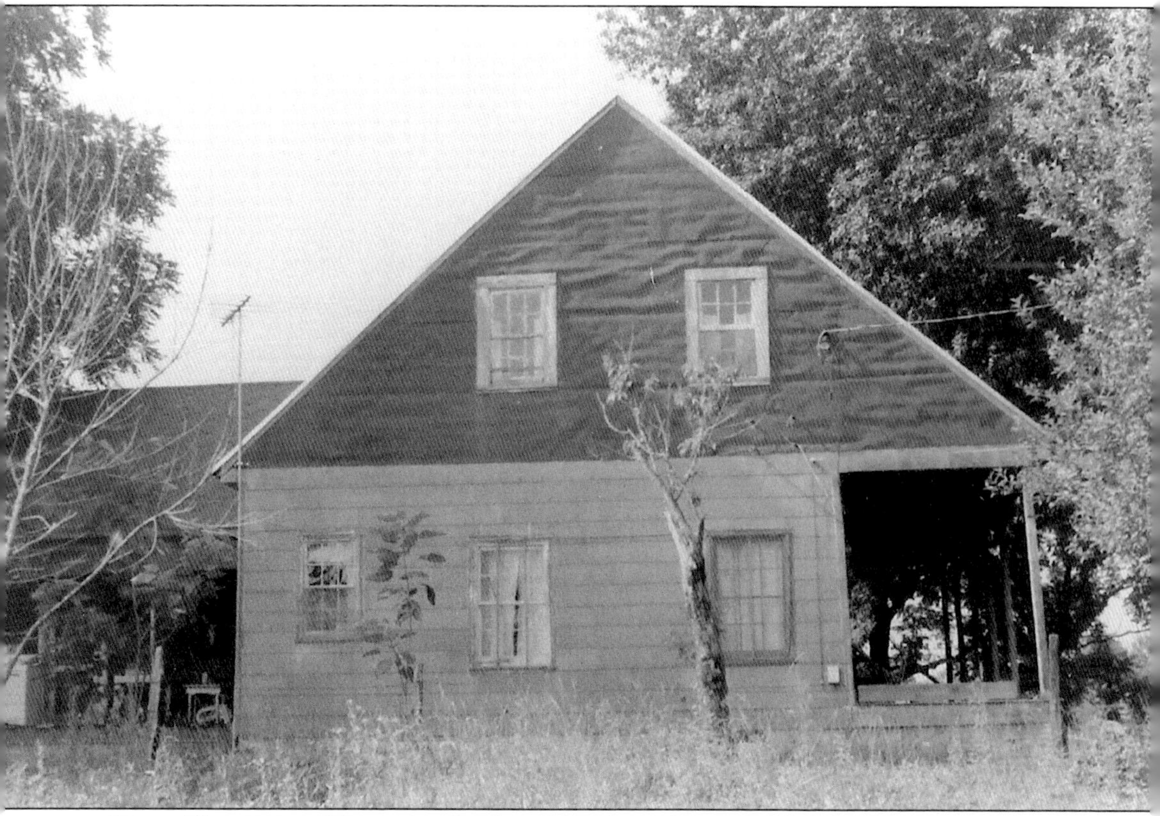

HANEY HOMESTEAD, MID-1850S. Brothers J. Singleton (1829–1892) and Jacob Haney (1820–1883) came to Woodstock by oxcart in 1852 from Spartanburg, South Carolina, after marrying sisters. They purchased adjoining properties north of town on Highway 5 near what is now Enon Cemetery. The Haney brothers farmed their property. Jacob Haney died when his son David was five years old. Nancy Spear Haney raised the children and managed the farm. Most of her servants were her husband's freed slaves. She and the family stayed on the homestead until 1910, when they moved into a large home in town. Jacob Haney served in the Georgia Militia in the Civil War and was captured at Vicksburg. (Courtesy of Virginia Switzer Wald.)

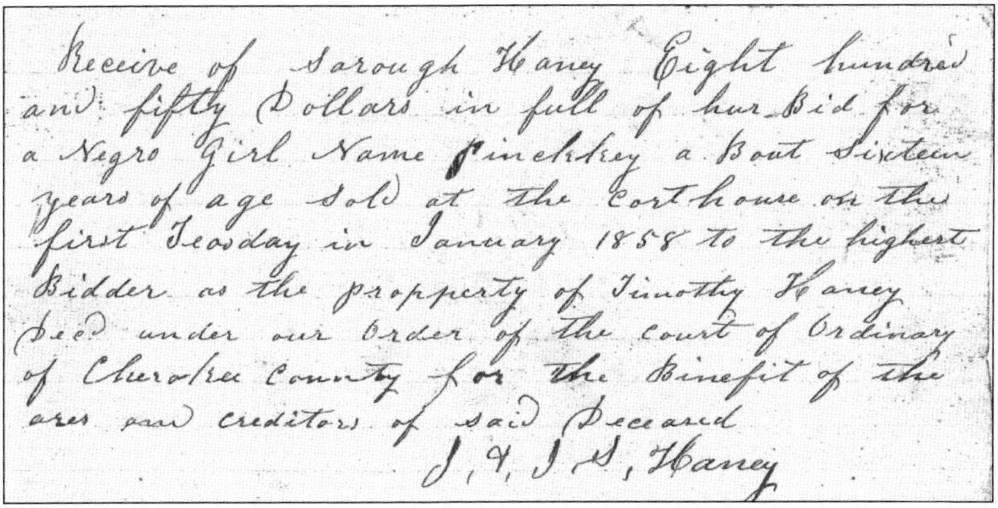

Receive of Sarough Haney Eight hundred and fifty Dollars in full of her Bid for a Negro Girl Name Pinchkrey a Bout Sixteen years of age Sold at the Cort house on the first Teasday in January 1858 to the highest Bidder as the propperty of Timothy Haney Dec'd under our Order of the court of Ordinary of Cherokee County for the Binefit of the ares and creditors of said Deceased

J. & J. S. Haney

BILL OF SALE FOR SLAVE GIRL, 1858. At the time, $850 would buy about 20 acres of land; buying slave labor at that price did not seem like good business. The document reads, "Receive of Sarough Haney Eight hundred and fifty dollars in full of her bid for a Negro Girl Name Pinchbrey a Bout Sixteen years of age sold at the Cort House on the first Tuesday in January 1858 to the highest Bidder as the property of Timothy Haney dead under our order of the court of Ordinary of Cherokee County for the benefit of the ares and creditors of said Deceased. Signed, J. & J. S. Haney." (Courtesy of Virginia Switzer Wald.)

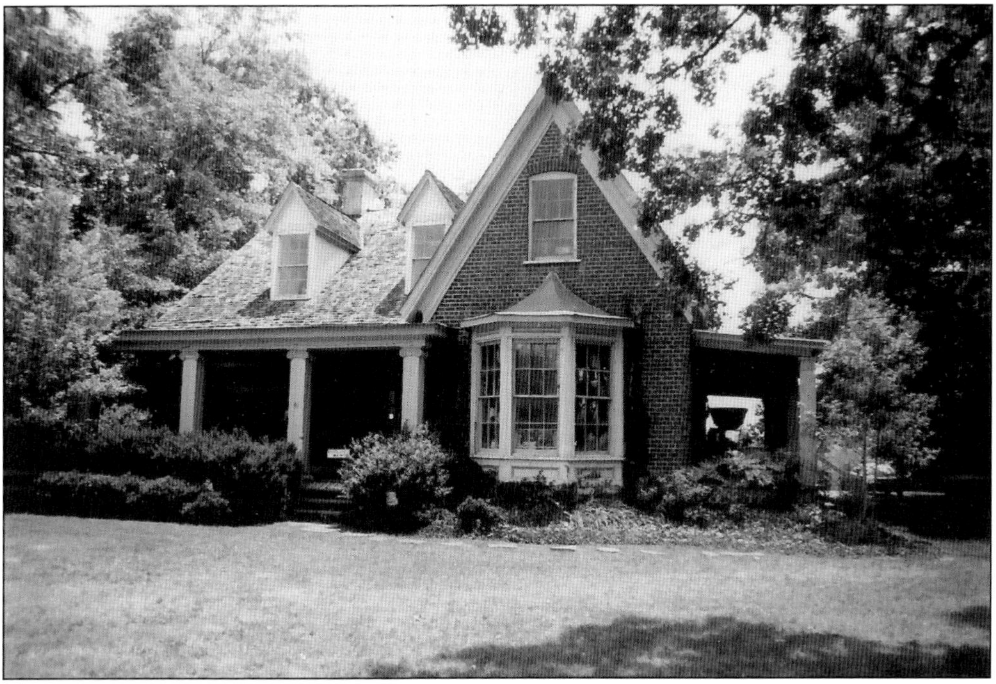

DEAN HOME, 1875. The Dean home was purportedly constructed from bricks made on the premises around 1875 by Dr. G. A. Merritt. Dr. Will Dean and his wife, Lou, married in 1883 and lived there throughout their lives. Widowed in 1906, Lou remained in the home until her death in 1945. The home remained in the Dean family for over 100 years. (Courtesy of Alice Dean Felton.)

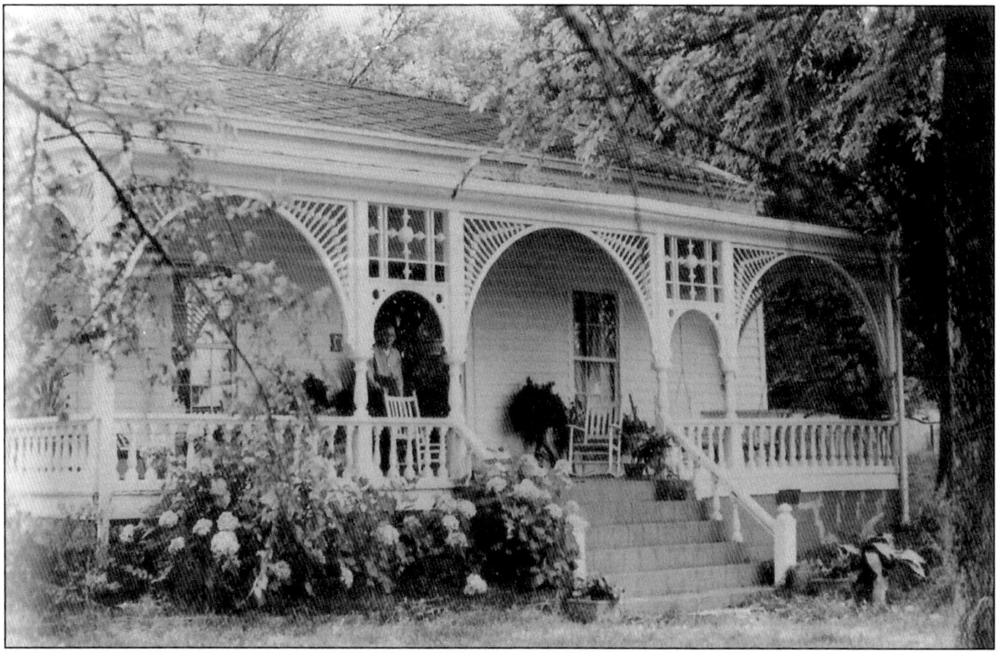

Fowler/Hendrix Home, c. 1869. George Thomas Fowler (1848–1923) inherited land south of the depot. Fowler hired men to work his farm, and families lived in tenant houses on his property. He owned a grocery store in town until 1921. He married Eliza Wood in 1869. (Courtesy of William Johnston.)

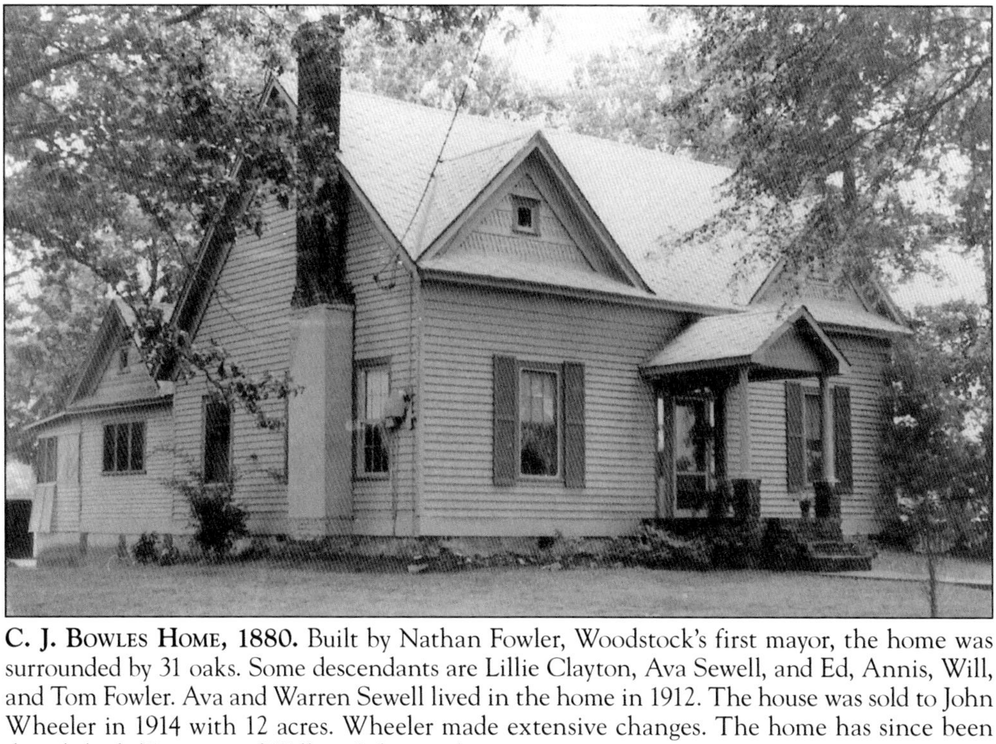

C. J. Bowles Home, 1880. Built by Nathan Fowler, Woodstock's first mayor, the home was surrounded by 31 oaks. Some descendants are Lillie Clayton, Ava Sewell, and Ed, Annis, Will, and Tom Fowler. Ava and Warren Sewell lived in the home in 1912. The house was sold to John Wheeler in 1914 with 12 acres. Wheeler made extensive changes. The home has since been demolished. (Courtesy of William Johnston.)

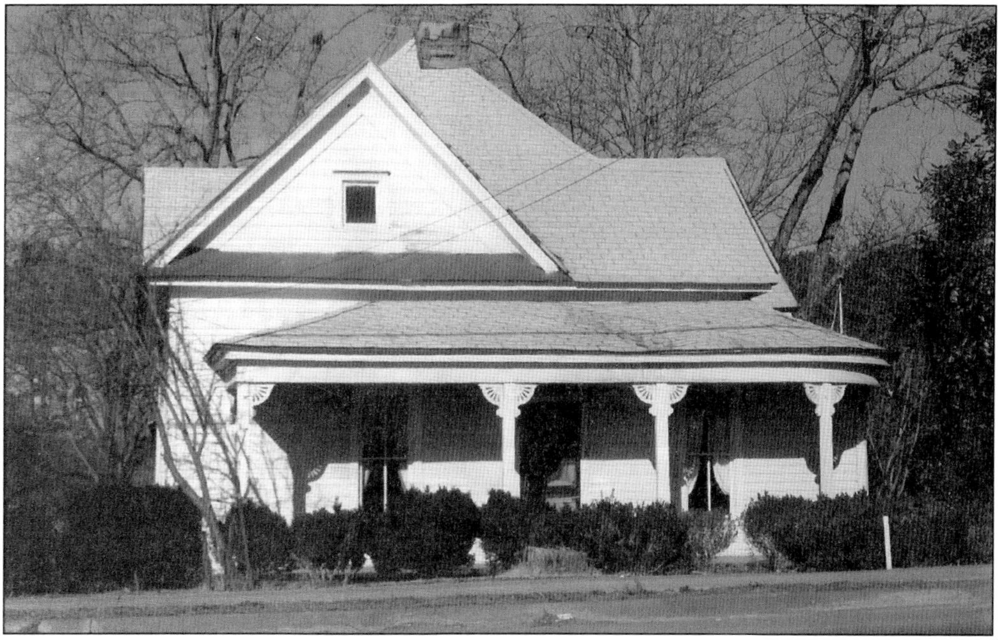

Neese/Gober/Johnston Home, 1890. The white framed house with one peak and a porch with small lattice on the pillars is located on South Main Street. The home is currently owned by William Johnston. John W. Gober, a preacher for Woodstock United Methodist Church, lived in the home during the 1920s. (Courtesy of William Johnston.)

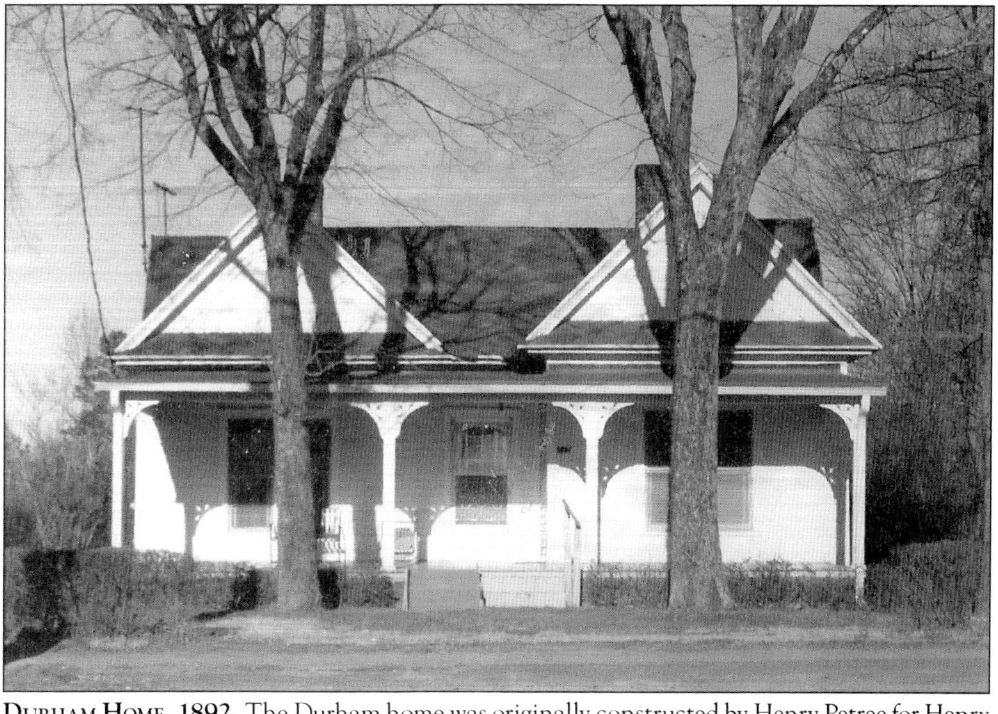

Durham Home, 1892. The Durham home was originally constructed by Henry Petree for Henry Kemp in 1892. Lucille and Jay Durham bought the house in 1963. The home has been occupied by local businesses since Lucille Durham's death in 1992. (Courtesy of William Johnston.)

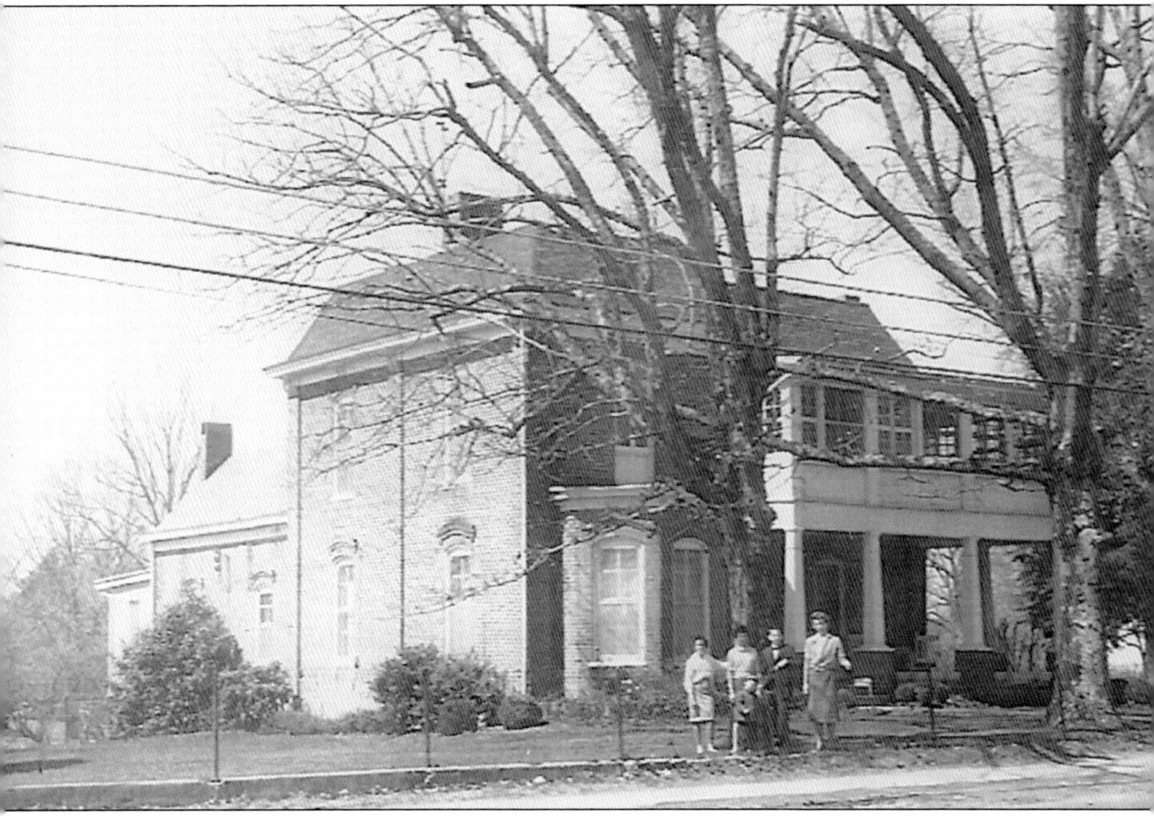

W. H. PERKINSON HOME, 1880. The French Colonial home was constructed from bricks made in Woodstock. Perkinson installed a coal-burning furnace and a running water system in the home. Five sons and one daughter lived there. William Howard Perkinson was a physician and a plantation owner. According to the Georgia Census of 1850, Perkinson owned 10 slaves ranging from age 12 to age 50. They probably worked on the plantation for Perkinson. Perkinson was one of several local farmers who formed the Woodstock Agricultural Society in the 1880s. The farmers frequently met to discuss and record their experiments with crops, soil tests, and improvements. In 1885, the members wrote an agriculture column that appeared in the *Cherokee Advance*. Perkinson also served as postmaster in 1880. Smith Johnston Jr. purchased the home in 1949. The home was torn down and became the location of the Bank of Woodstock. Pictured is the Johnston family in 1962. (Courtesy of Preservation Woodstock, Inc.)

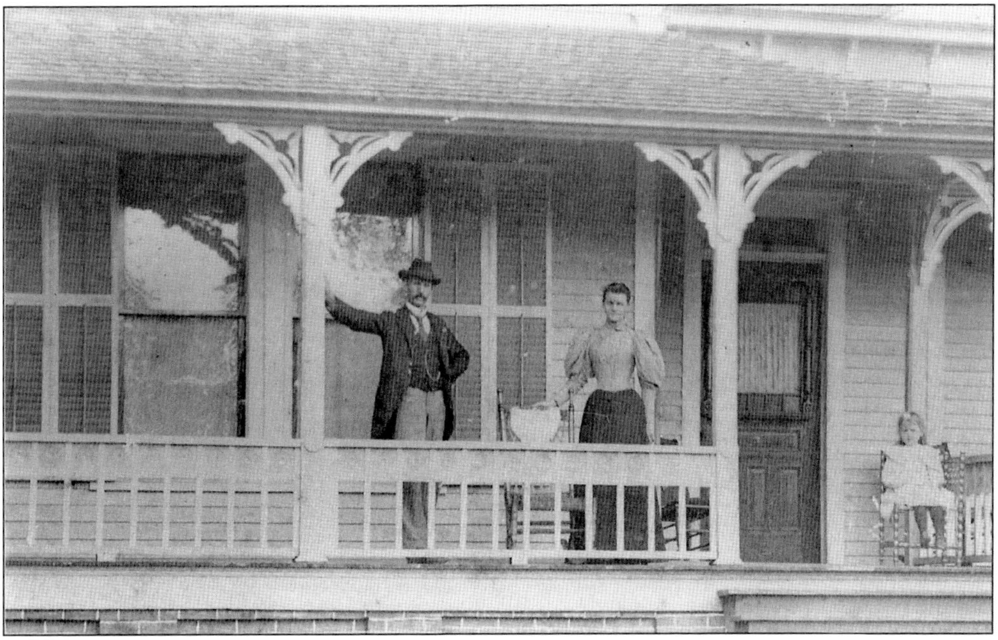

LATHEM HOME, 1894. Jim and Lizzie Lathem are pictured with Florine Dial (seated). Later Dr. Van Sant owned the home until it burned in the late 1950s. The home was located at the corner of East Main and Arnold Mill Road. Florine Dial was the daughter of William C. Dial Jr. and Dollie Gresham Dial, who died at age 21 when Florine was only two years old and her sister Dollie was six weeks old. Florine lived with her Aunt Lizzie and Uncle Jim, and Dollie was raised by her grandmother Dollie Sueanna Gresham. The Lathems operated a boardinghouse in their home. Florine Dial married Smith Johnston in 1917. (Courtesy of William Johnston.)

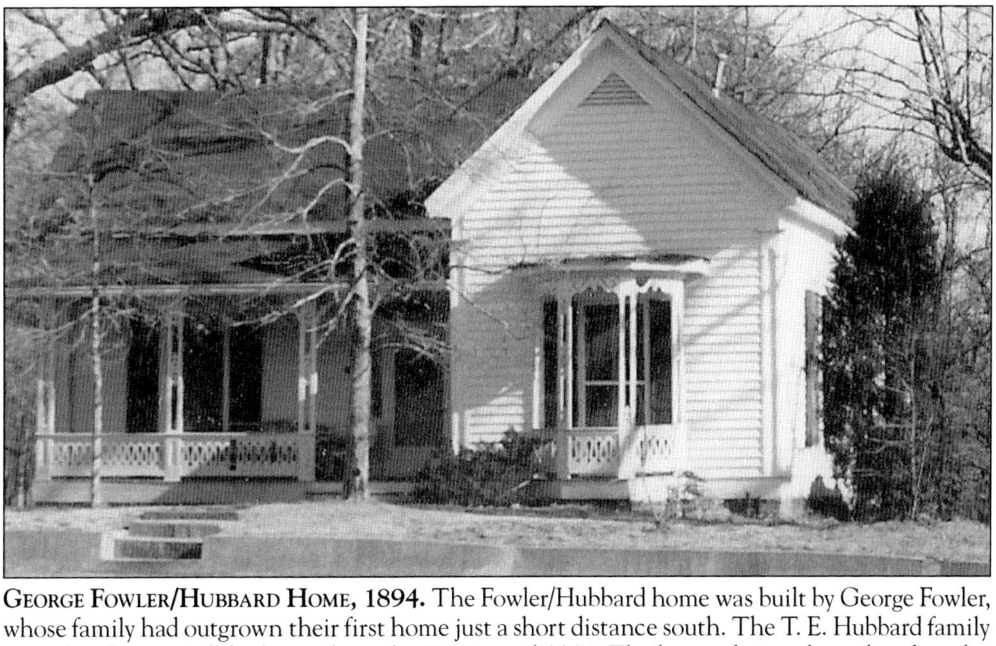

GEORGE FOWLER/HUBBARD HOME, 1894. The Fowler/Hubbard home was built by George Fowler, whose family had outgrown their first home just a short distance south. The T. E. Hubbard family owned and occupied the home from the 1940s until 2004. The home, facing the railroad tracks, is still standing. (Courtesy of William Johnston.)

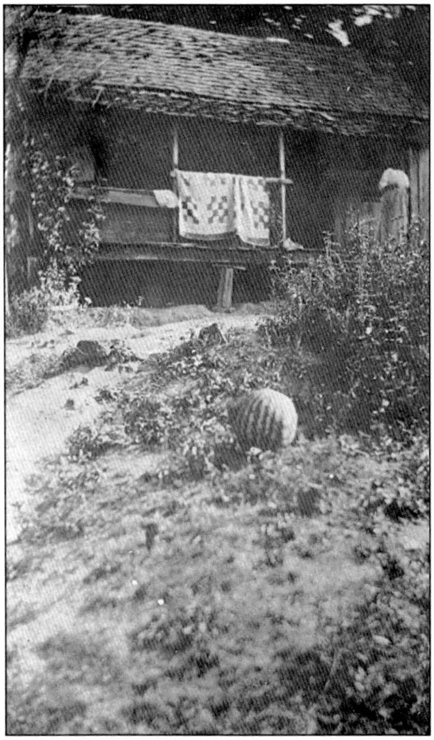

Maroney Home, c. 1900. The Maroney family resided on Arnold Mill Road, next door to Magnolia Thomas. Laura Maroney hauled water from the branch, a stream near the corner of Main Street and Arnold Mill Road, to wash clothes during the late 1800s. She was paid $1 for a batch of washed clothes. She carried the basket of clothes on her head and walked to houses to deliver the newly washed clothes. (Courtesy of City of Woodstock.)

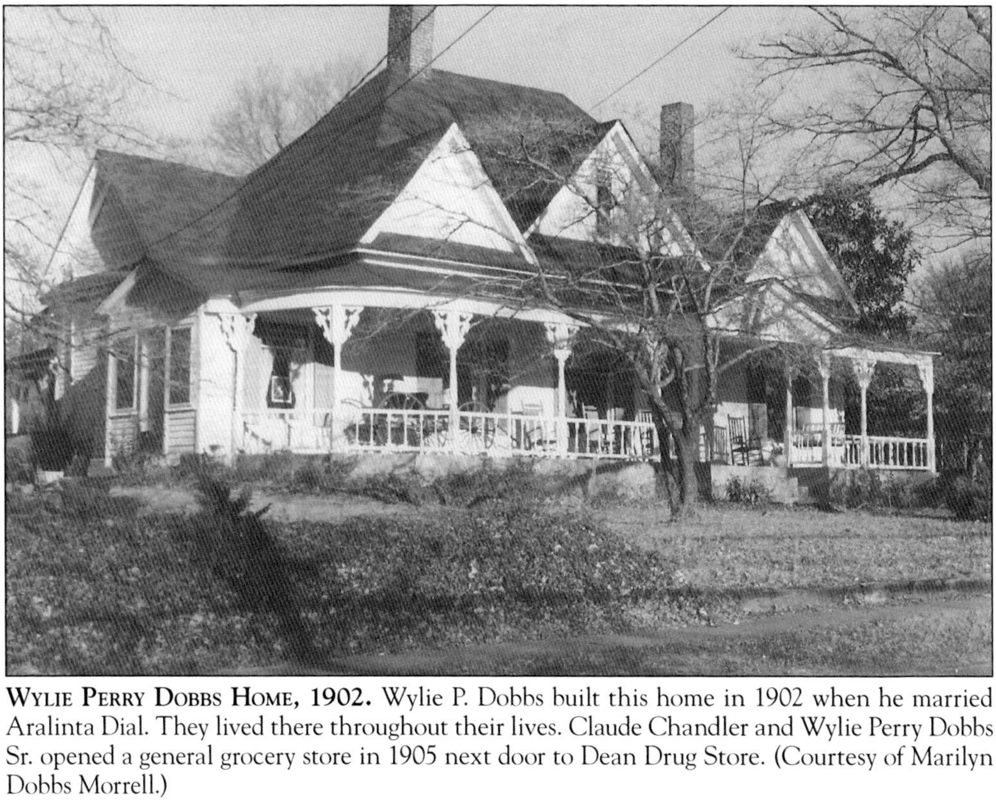

Wylie Perry Dobbs Home, 1902. Wylie P. Dobbs built this home in 1902 when he married Aralinta Dial. They lived there throughout their lives. Claude Chandler and Wylie Perry Dobbs Sr. opened a general grocery store in 1905 next door to Dean Drug Store. (Courtesy of Marilyn Dobbs Morrell.)

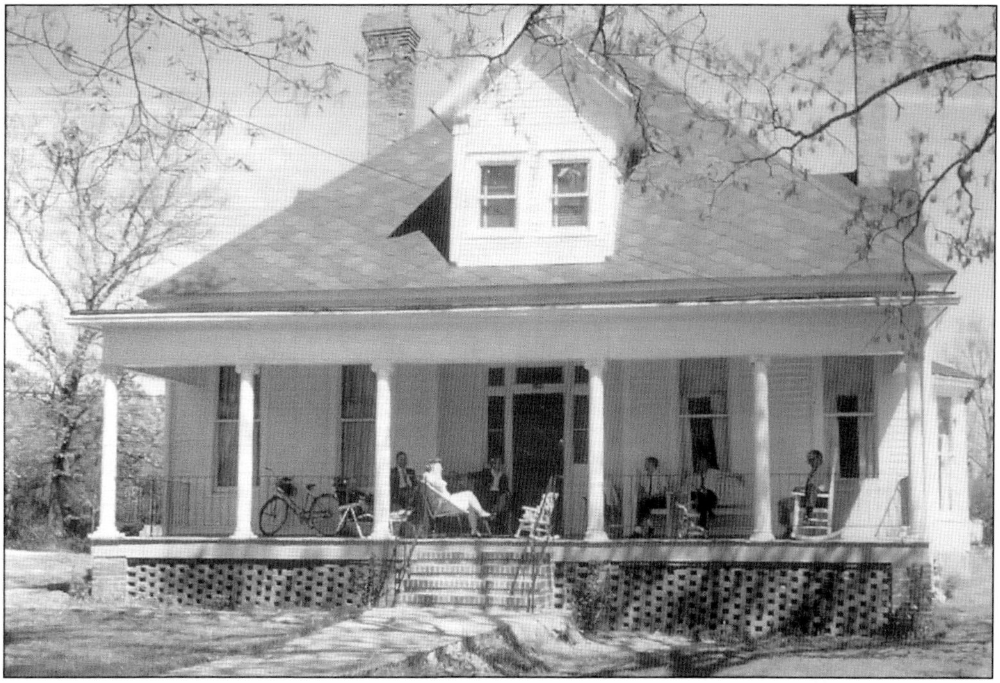

McAfee Home, c. 1905. Hubert Sr. and Eva Dean McAfee moved into the new home when they married. Eva was the daughter of Dr. Will Dean. Eva and her mother, Lou, who had been widowed for 40 years, died on the same day, July 26, 1945. The home later burned. The property is the site of the city park. (Courtesy of Millicent Barnes Fox.)

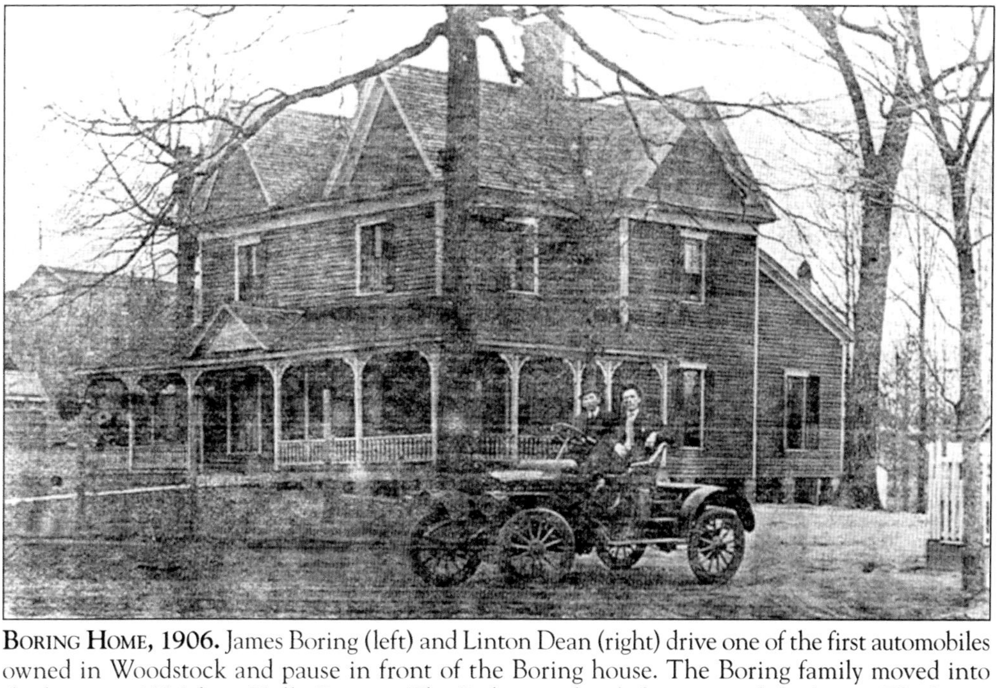

Boring Home, 1906. James Boring (left) and Linton Dean (right) drive one of the first automobiles owned in Woodstock and pause in front of the Boring house. The Boring family moved into the home in 1906 from Holly Springs. The Perkinson family later owned the home. The home burned on Christmas Day in 1925. (Courtesy of Alice Dean Felton.)

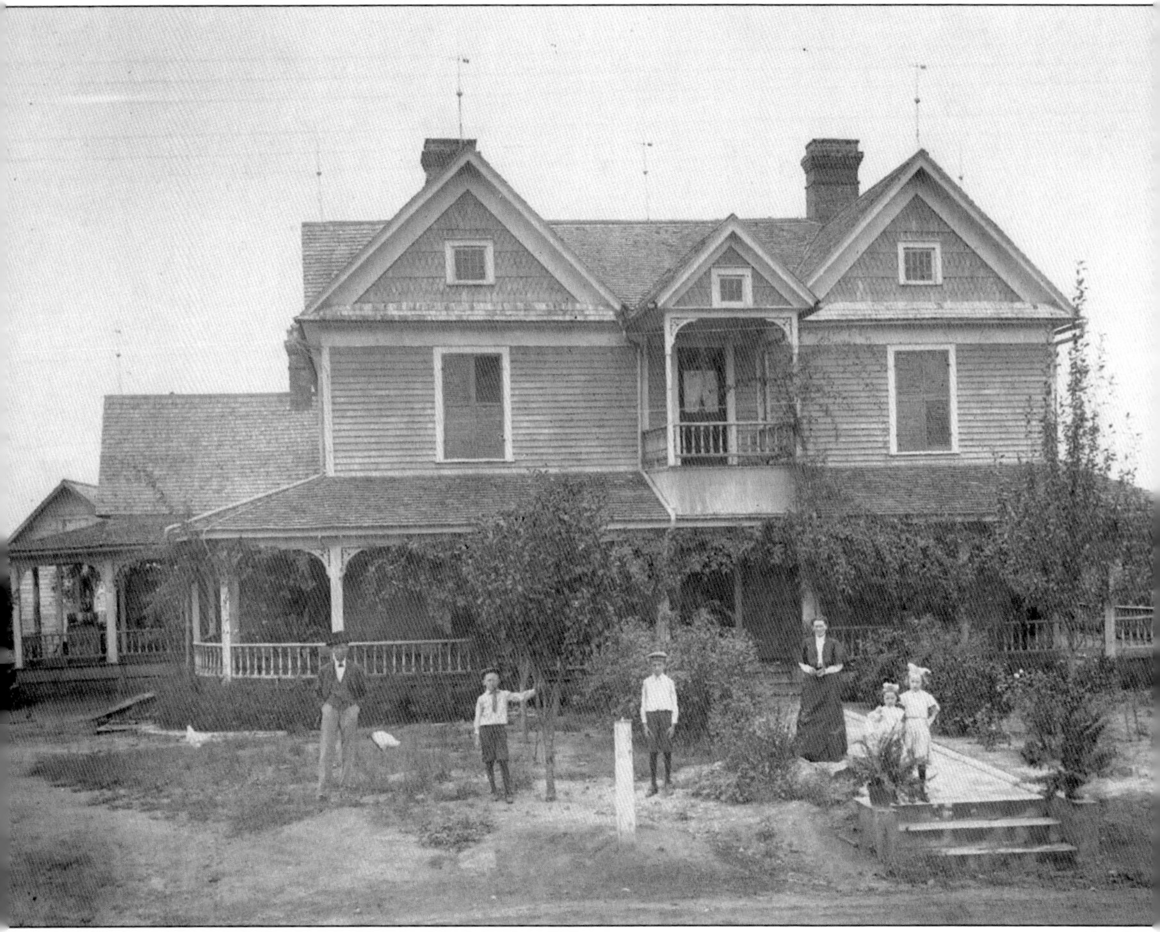

FOWLER HOUSE, C. 1906. Andrew Rice Fowler built a home on property near the corner of Highways 92 and 5. Fowler hired tenant farmers to work the cotton fields on the land. Fowler came to Woodstock from Cobb County. When he was 16 years old, his brothers and his father were away fighting in the Civil War, leaving Andrew Rice to care for his mother and sisters. His father returned weak and sick from the hardships of the war. He died not long after returning to his family. Later Fowler's daughter Ruth and her husband, Gilbert, lived in the home. Pictured are, from left to right, Andrew Rice Fowler, Andrew Herbert Fowler, Thomas Clyde Fowler, Molly Bentley Fowler, Ruth Irene Fowler, and Myrtie Fowler. (Courtesy of Russ Sims.)

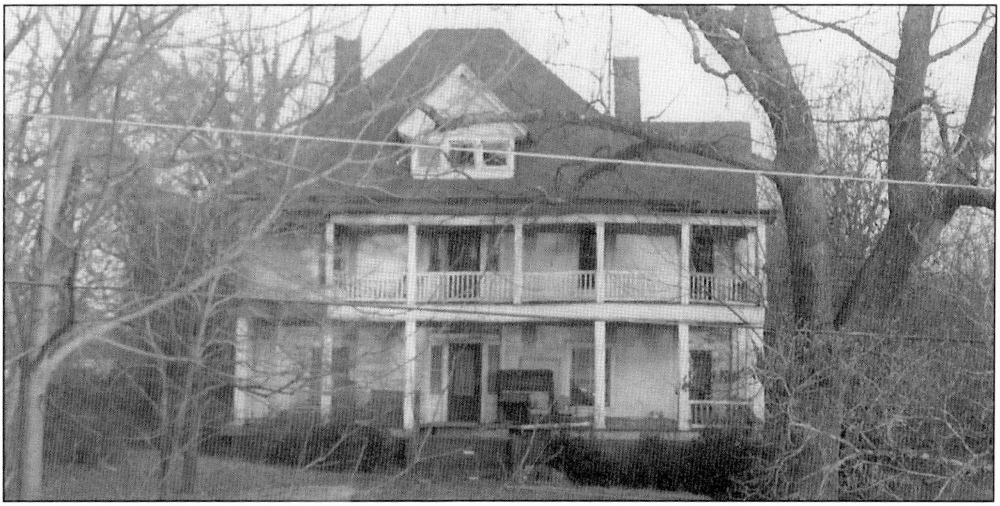

Iris Dobbs Home, 1908. Cicero Chappel (1847–1912) and Sarah Dupree Dobbs (1848–1931) raised their daughter Iris and their other children in the large, two-story framed home with two-tiered front wraparound porches. Cicero Dobbs was a successful Woodstock farmer in the mid- to late 1800s. Iris lived in the home on Wheeler Street until her death in 1966. The home came into disrepair and was demolished in 1992. (Courtesy of William Johnston.)

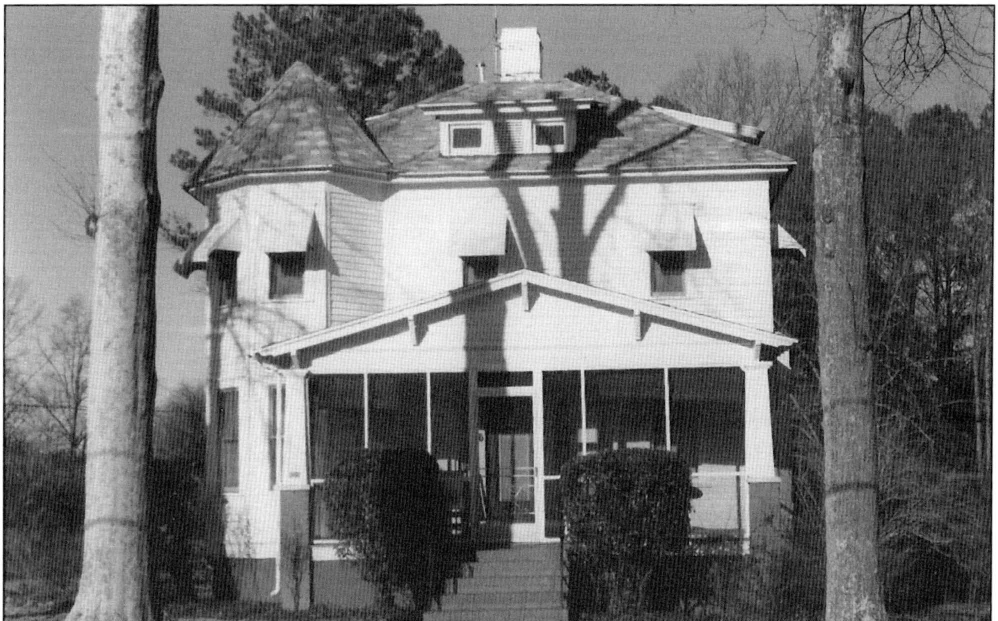

Bozeman Home, c. 1910. The turn-of-the-century home has an asymmetrical front with a bay window at the side, four fireplaces, and pine wood floors. W. D. Bozeman (1873–1944), the original homeowner, and Dave Haney (1878–1930) ran Haney-Bozeman General Mercantile Company and Cotton Brokers on the corner of Main and Church Streets. Their business thrived until the boll weevil and the Depression ruined most cotton businesses. The Bozemans raised four daughters in the home on Rope Mill Road, and the last surviving daughter, Sarah, lived in the home until her death in the late 1990s. All the sisters were teachers except Mildred, who married James Newton Barnes, one-time mayor of Woodstock. (Courtesy of William Johnston.)

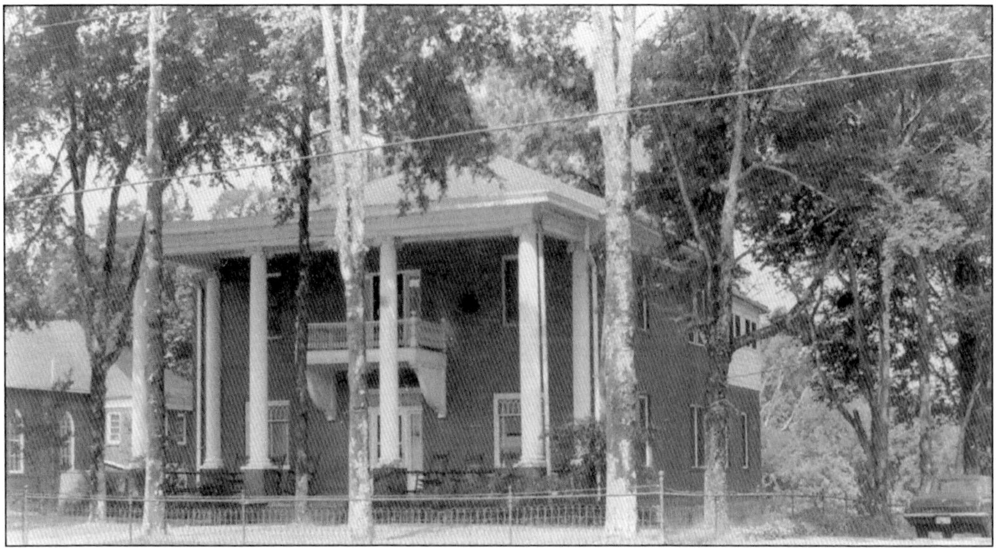

J. H. Johnston Home, 1913. Rebuilt following a fire that destroyed the wood two-story frame home, the large home on the small lot, adorned with six white Ionic columns on the front porch, contained brass spittoons in the living room. This home was the only white-column house in Woodstock. Woodstock Baptist Church next door also burned, but both were rebuilt with matching brick. Joe Johnston, son of J. H., lived in the 14-room home until his death in 1978. The home is now a business. (Courtesy of William Johnston.)

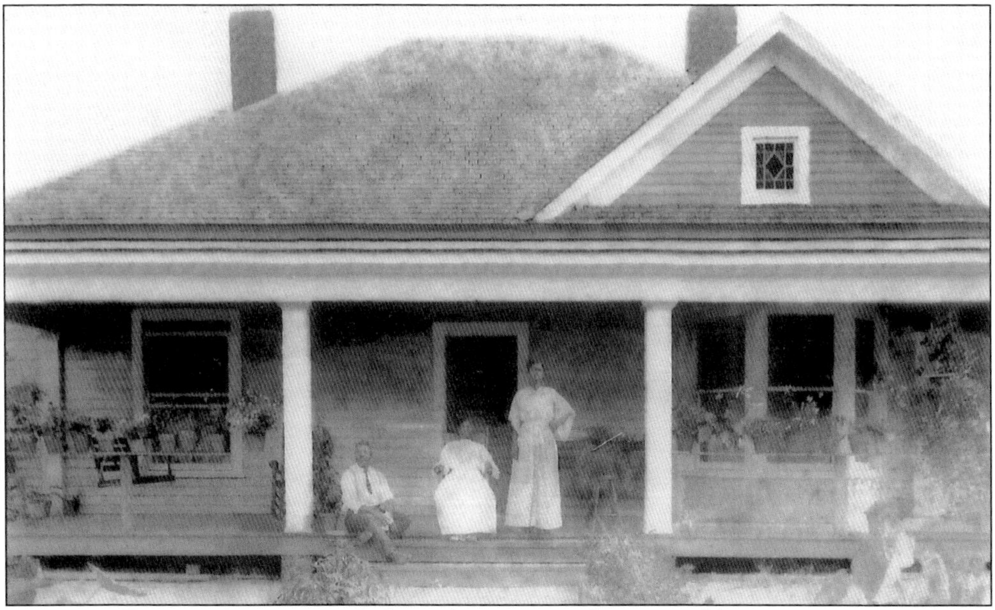

Magnolia Thomas Home, 1915. Robert Thomas, one of six sons of farming parents, purchased 1.5 acres for $300 on Arnold Mill Road in 1911. Later he built a home for his mother, Caroline, and his sister Magnolia. Magnolia Thomas taught at Canton, TooNigh, Bethel, Orange, and Hickory Flat schools and attended Spelman Seminary, graduating in 1918. She also attended Tuskegee Institute in Alabama during the summer terms. Thomas witnessed the transition from segregation to integration in the schools in her lifetime. The home burned in 2008 and is being rebuilt. (Courtesy of Preservation Woodstock, Inc.)

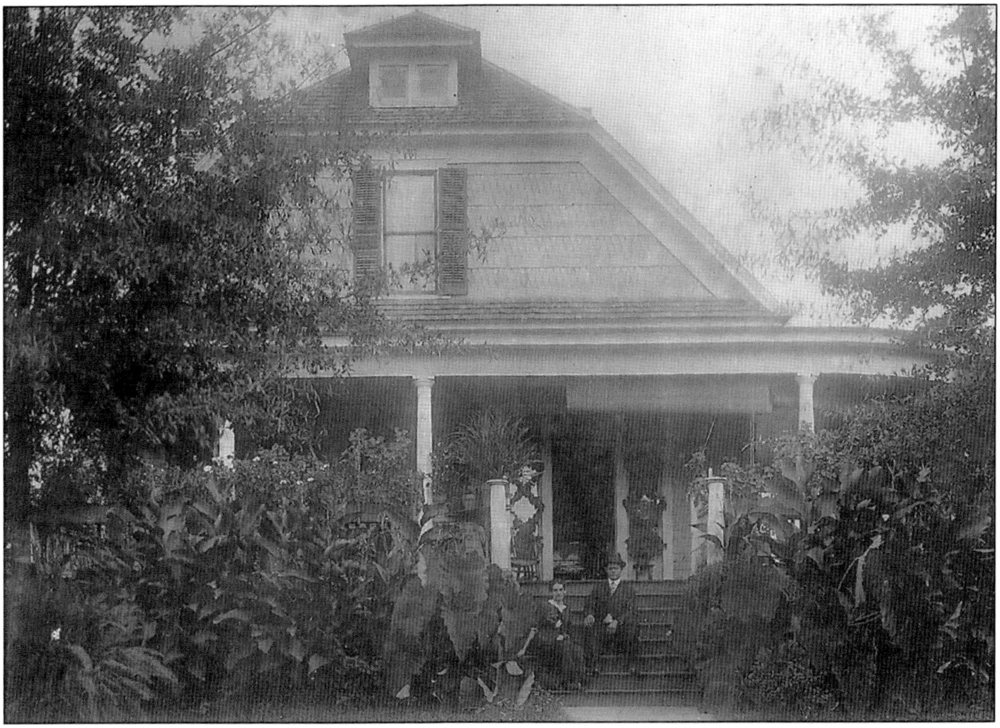

EMMETT D. DIAL HOME, 1916. Emmett Dial was a rural mail carrier when postal service was known as Rural Free Delivery (RFD). He became postmaster in 1917 and served until 1933. He married Mary Claude in 1914. Their daughter Sara Frances Dial Ramsay still occupies the home. (Courtesy of Sara Frances Dial Ramsay.)

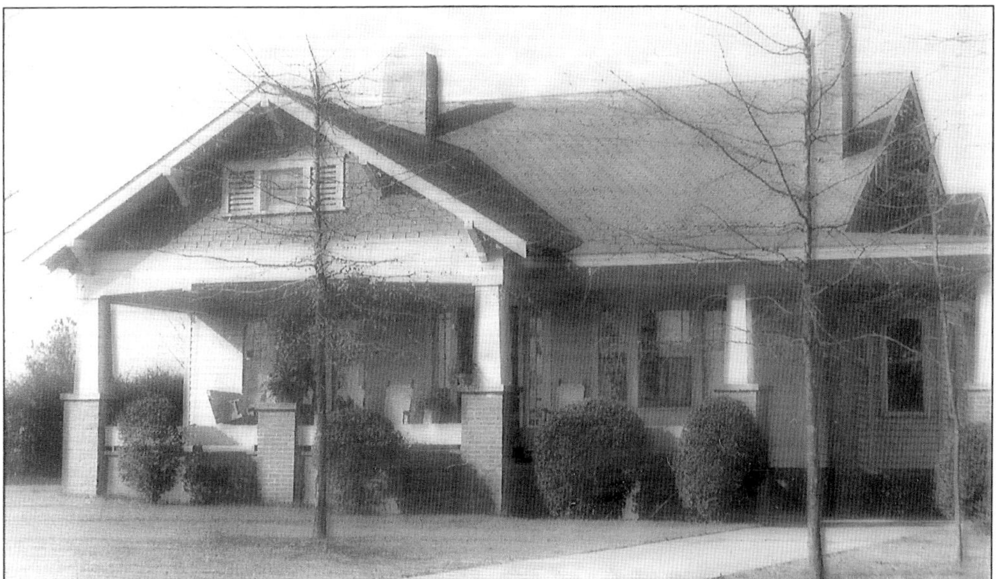

CHANDLER/LINTON DEAN HOME. Claude Chandler sold the house to Linton Dean in 1931. Linton's daughter Elizabeth; her husband, Bill Drinkard; and their sons occupied the home with Linton after death of his wife, Alice. (Courtesy of Alice Dean Felton.)

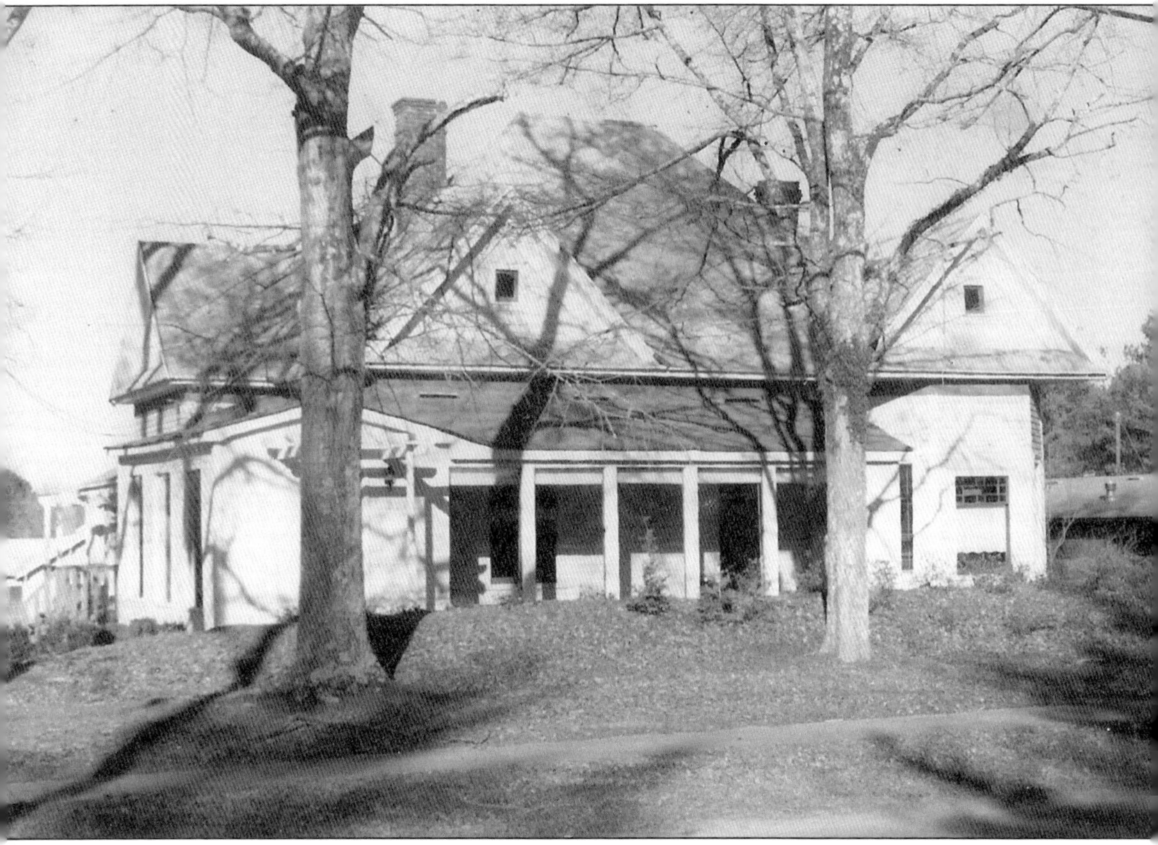

DAWSON HOME, 1909. Sam and Georgia Dawson raised their two children, James and Sally, in this home. Dawson had a general dry goods store in Woodstock until he retired. The house was originally surrounded by porches, and a walkway led from the street to the home. Dawson built a chicken house, tennis racquetball courts, and an area for croquet. Dawson also built a log-cabin playhouse for his daughter, Sally. Sally and her husband, George Parr, operated Dawson-Parr Department Store in Woodstock. Sally Parr became a teacher at Woodstock Elementary School. (Courtesy of William Johnston.)

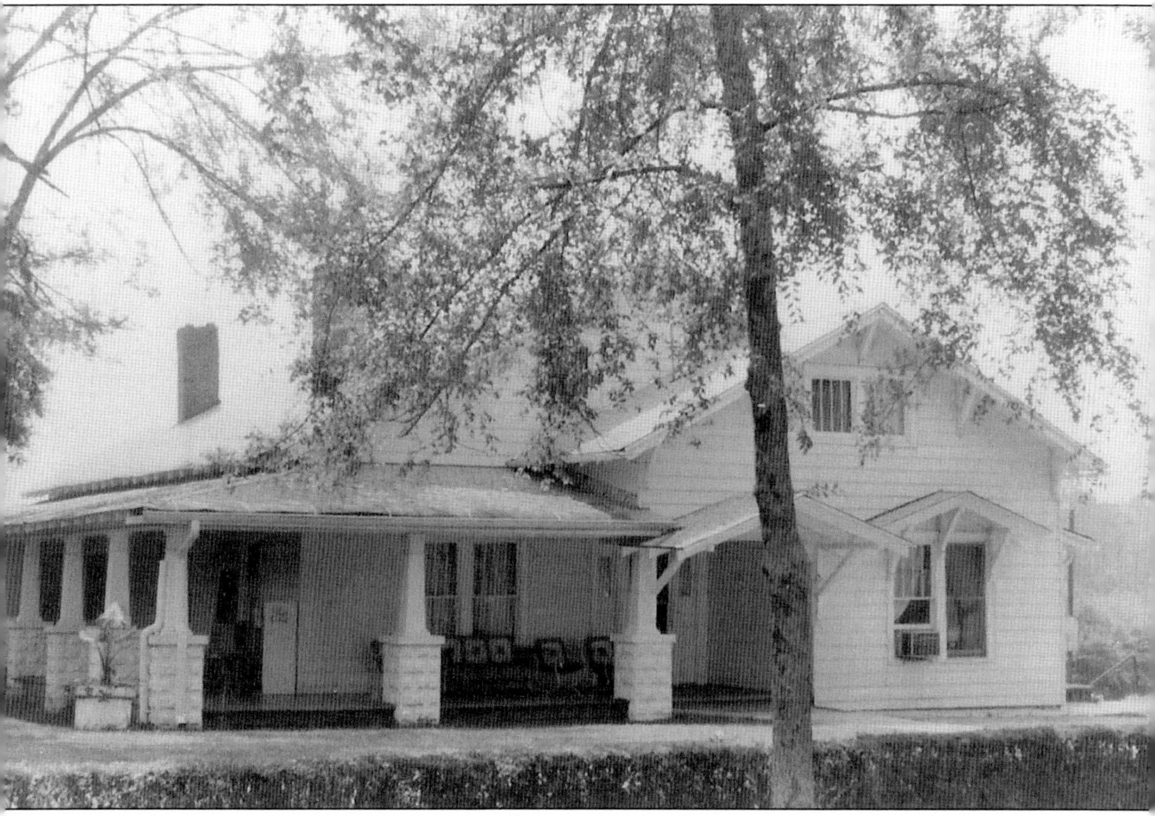

LATIMER/CARPENTER HOME, 1919. Originally occupied by the Pierce Latimer family, the house became the home place of the Carpenter family and birthplace of renowned Southern League pitcher Lew Carpenter. Carpenter first starred at Georgia Tech as a pitcher and was known for a 22-2 season with the Atlanta Crackers in the 1940s. He also worked at the Bell Bomber Plant while on the baseball team. The home became Woodstock Funeral Home. (Courtesy of Preservation Woodstock, Inc.)

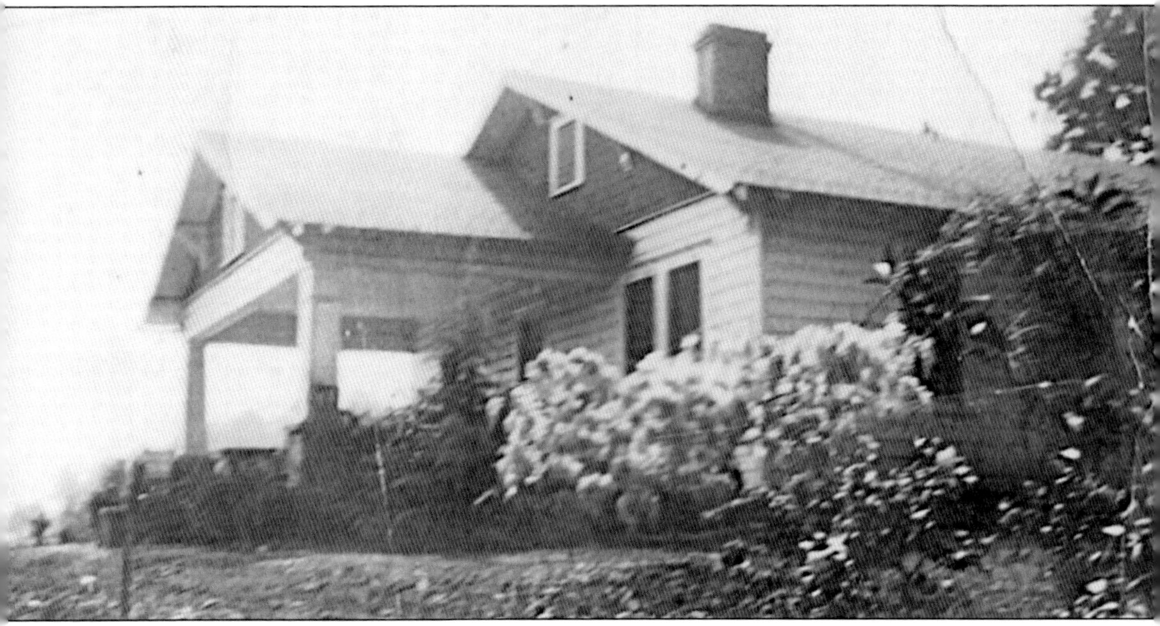

Clyde Fowler Home, 1896. John Miller McAfee, white ancestor of Atlanta's mayor Maynard Jackson, owned a large tract of land at the corner of Highways 5 and 92. Georgia's Reconstruction governor Rufus Bullock purchased the land from Melinda McAfee in 1868. He built a large, three-story barn to house Thoroughbred horses. His political career soured when he was accused of corruption. He sold the land to his friend George Moore, resigned as governor, and returned to New York. N. A. Fowler purchased the land in 1883, and it remained in the Fowler family for 100 years. Clyde Fowler later inherited the land when the barn was crumbling and the home was collapsing. The remains of the barn and the home later became a landmark. Fowler built a home on the hill at the southwest corner of Highways 5 and 92. (Courtesy of Tom Fowler.)

Seven

CHURCHES

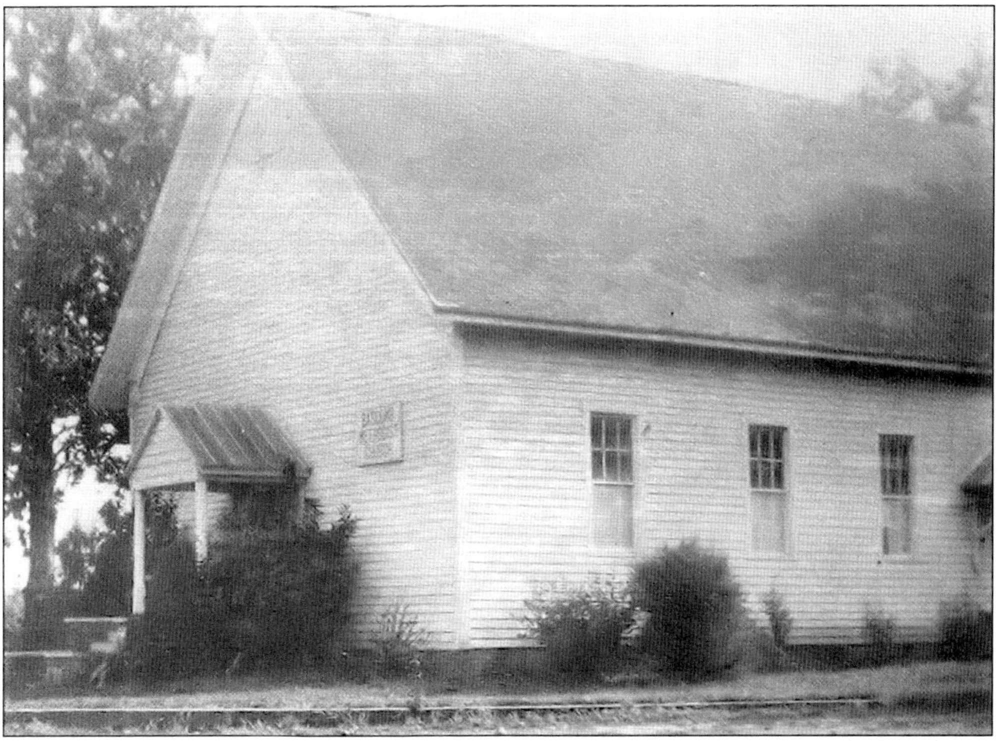

BASCOMB UNITED METHODIST CHURCH, ESTABLISHED 1830. Bascomb United Methodist Church was organized in a log cabin in 1830. It also served as a school until 1945. The church was used as a campsite of the 123rd Illinois Regiment during the Civil War. Union soldiers daily raided the local farmers for food and livestock. A second log cabin was built where the current church cemetery is located. It is unknown how long that structure existed. Church membership outgrew the log cabin in the 1880s, and a new wood building was constructed. W. R. Page deeded the land to the church for the new building in 1883. In 1933, the congregation remodeled the building, added four Sunday school rooms, and built a balcony. (Courtesy of Preservation Woodstock, Inc.)

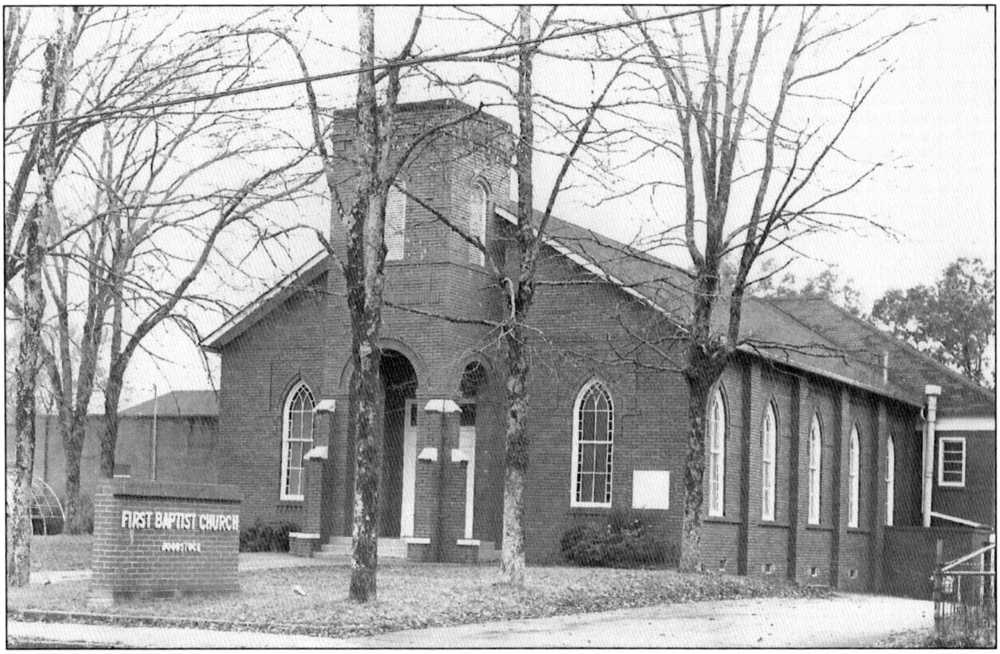

ENON/FIRST BAPTIST CHURCH, ESTABLISHED 1837. The church, originally named Enon Baptist, was established in 1837 with 12 members. The original church was located near Rubes Creek and Little River. The cemetery exists on the original location of the church. The congregation moved to town in 1879, and the chapel was built in 1913 after a fire destroyed the church and the Johnston home next door. Both were rebuilt with matching brick. The congregation moved again in the 1990s. (Courtesy of Carolyn Fox Hitt.)

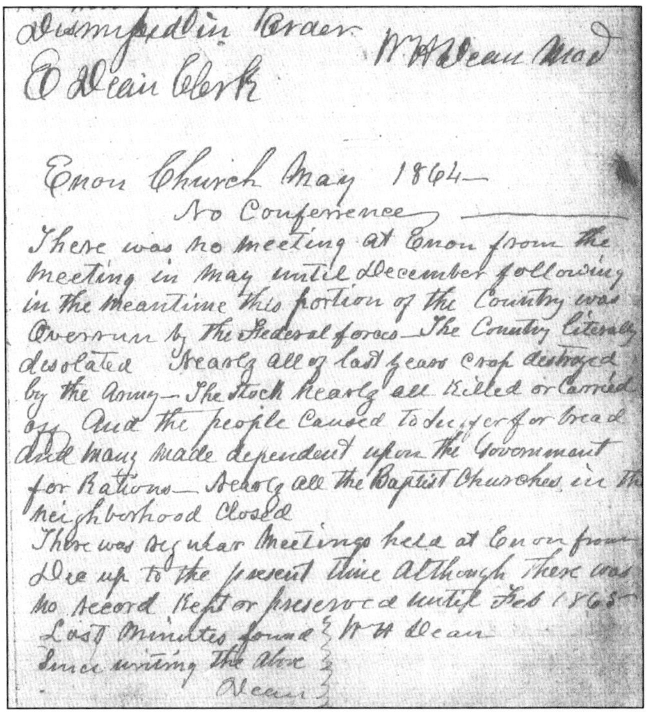
Dismissed in Order W H Dean Mod
E Dean Clerk

Enon Church May 1864
No Conference
There was no meeting at Enon from the
meeting in May until December following
in the meantime this portion of the Country was
Overrun by the Federal forces The Country literally
desolated Nearly all of last years crop destroyed
by the Army The stock nearly all killed or carried
off And the people caused to suffer for bread
and many made dependent upon the Government
for Rations Nearly all the Baptist Churches in the
neighborhood Closed
There was regular Meetings held at Enon from
Dec up to the present time although there was
no record kept or preserved until Feb 1865
Last Minutes found } W H Dean
Since writing the above }
Dean }

ENON BAPTIST CHURCH MINUTES, 1864. The church minutes dated May 1864 describe the devastation of the Civil War. Crops were destroyed and livestock killed or carried away by the Union soldiers. Churches were closed because of the war. (Courtesy of Woodstock Public Library.)

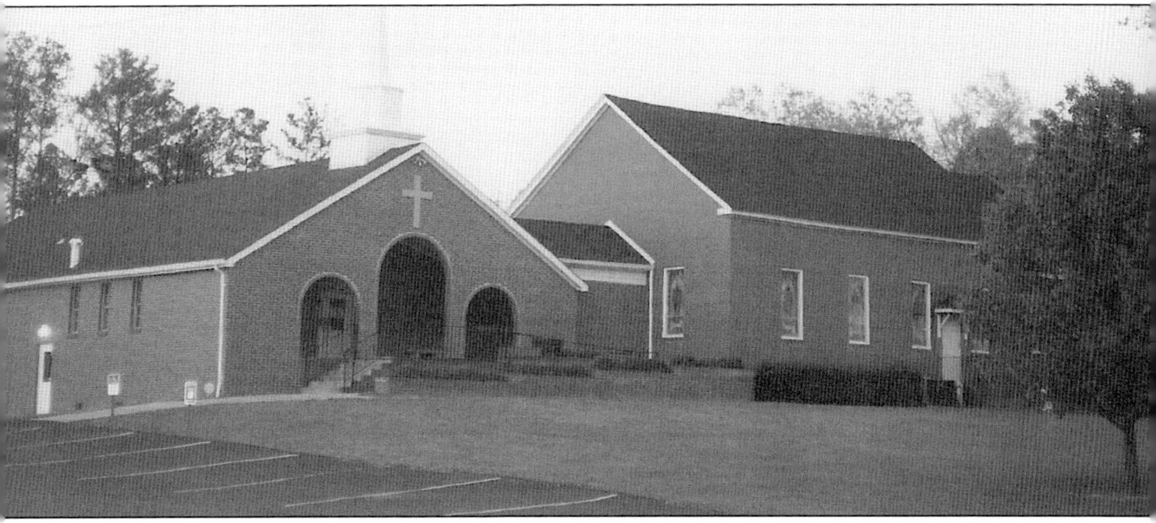

LITTLE RIVER METHODIST CHURCH, ESTABLISHED 1830. Little River Methodist Church, located east of Woodstock on Highway 92 near Sweats Mountain, was organized in 1830. The original structure built on Trickum Road was constructed of cut logs on the bank of Little River near Evan's Bridge, 1 mile from the current site. The original building also served as Little River Academy. In 1854, a framed pine sanctuary was constructed. A weather-beaten gravestone from 1858 in the cemetery pays tribute to one of the first pastors, Joseph W. Pharr. An old antelope horn was used to call camp meetings to order until they were discontinued in 1912. Early parishioners traveled by horse and wagon to services once a month. As was customary, African Americans were buried in a separate section of the cemetery. (Courtesy of Preservation Woodstock, Inc.)

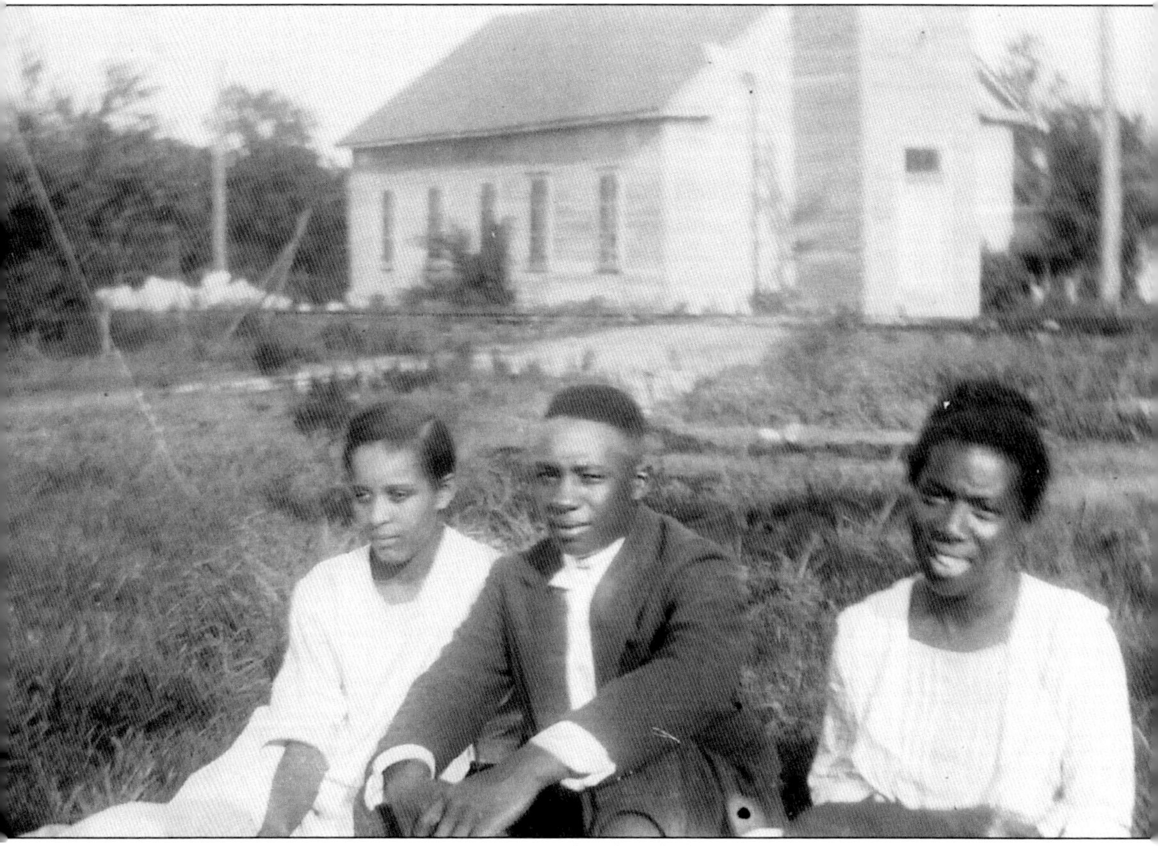

Bethel AME Church, Established 1867. The church, located on Trickum Road, also served as a school, and a cemetery was established. The church burned in 1950, and the congregation combined with the AME church on Arnold Mill Road. (Courtesy of Preservation Woodstock, Inc.)

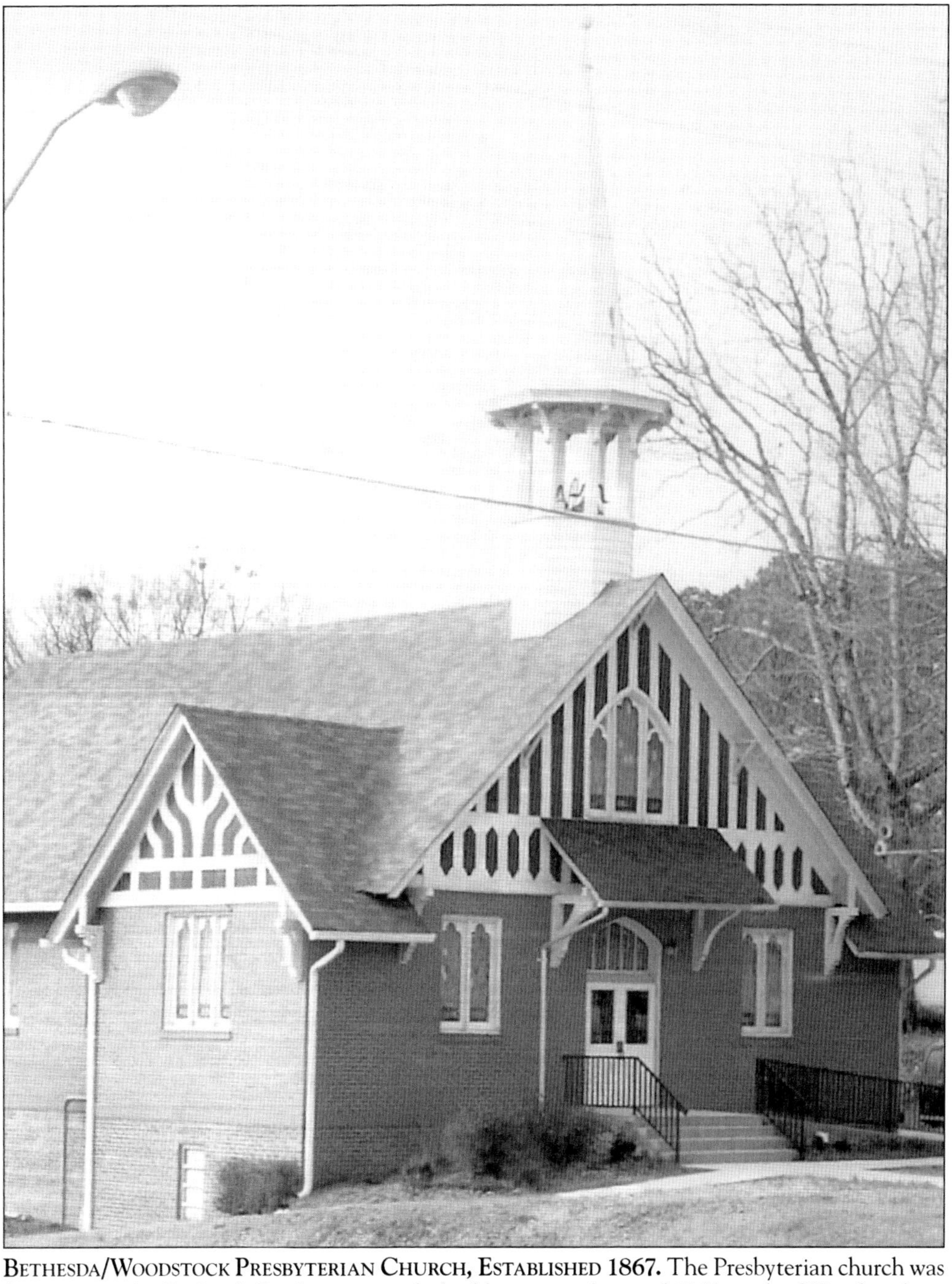

BETHESDA/WOODSTOCK PRESBYTERIAN CHURCH, ESTABLISHED 1867. The Presbyterian church was first organized as Bethesda Presbyterian and a building erected around 1867 north of Woodstock on Sixes Road with R. W. Milner as pastor. In 1916, the church burned, leaving a small congregation without a building. For seven years, members met in tents, homes, and at the nearby Lebanon Baptist Church for services. They named their displaced church Bethesda II. The congregation constructed a brick building from insurance money in 1923 on North Main Street and Rope Mill Road and renamed the church Woodstock Presbyterian Church. The first pastor in the new church was Gray McClintock. (Courtesy of Preservation Woodstock, Inc.)

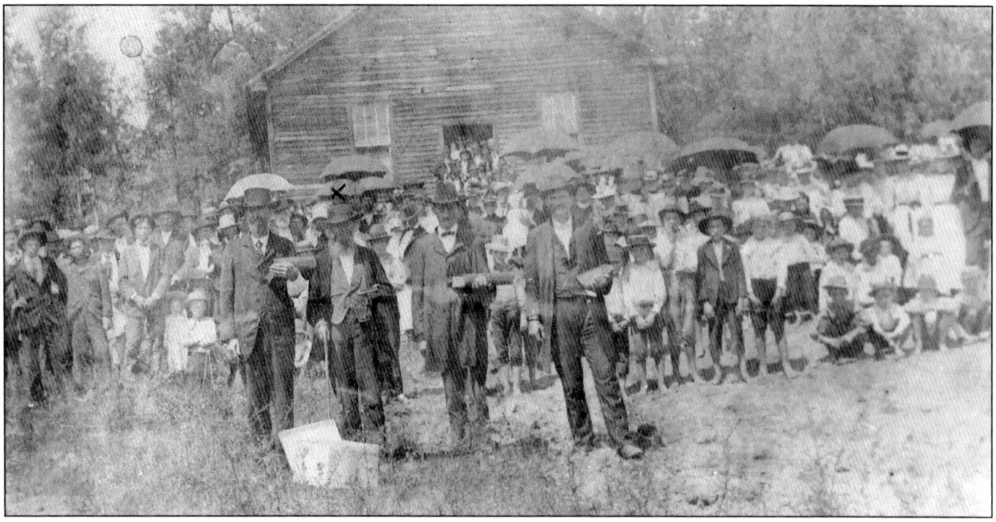

Mill Creek Baptist Church, Established 1879. Twenty-two charter members established and constructed Mill Creek Baptist Church in 1879 on East Cherokee Drive. By 1925, the church grew to 185 members, outgrowing their church building. Members constructed a new building on the same property that same year. The congregation organized a school in the original church building until 1918, when they decided to construct a new structure. The school existed until 1942 when it consolidated with Woodstock Elementary. The school building was demolished in 1947 to create a church cemetery. (Both courtesy of Mary Ann Parker Eubanks and Jeanette Parker McArthur.)

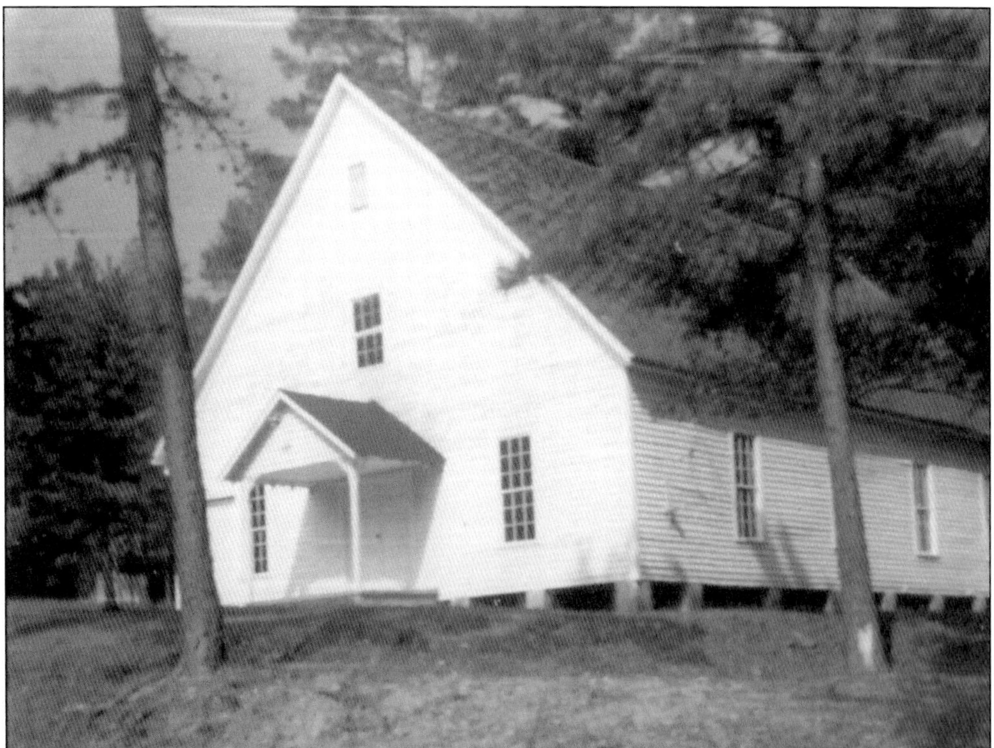

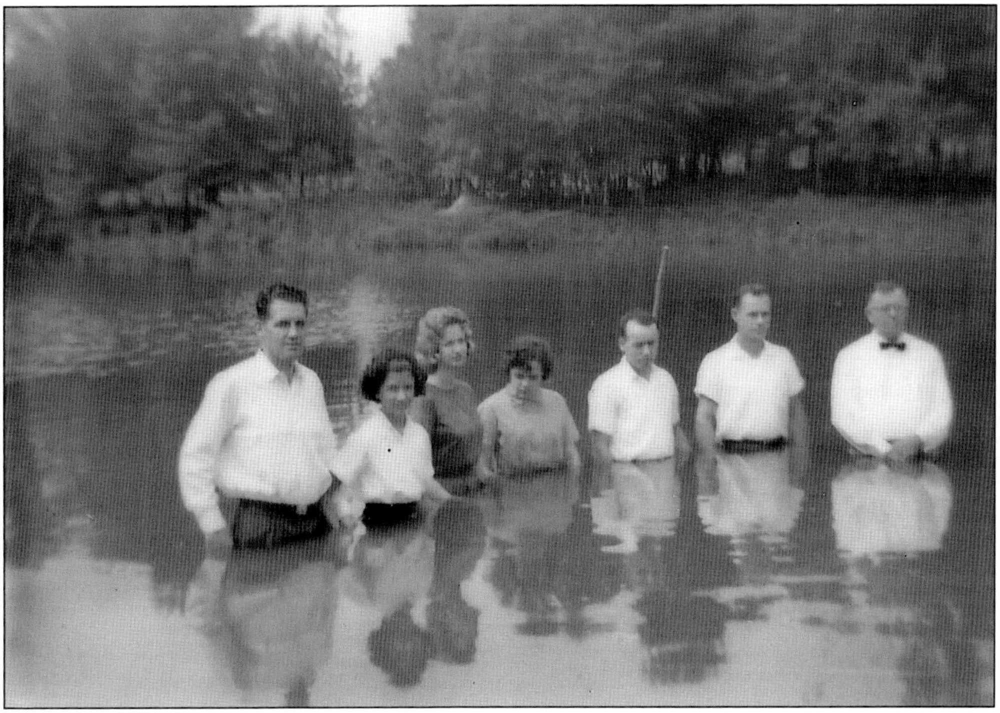

Summer Revival, Mill Creek Baptist Church, 1964. Pictured from left to right are Paul Eubanks, Nancy Eubanks, Wilene Abernathy, Carol Eubanks, Claud McArthur, Donald Eubanks (pastor), and Hansel Hagood. (Courtesy of Mary Ann Parker Eubanks and Jeanette Parker McArthur.)

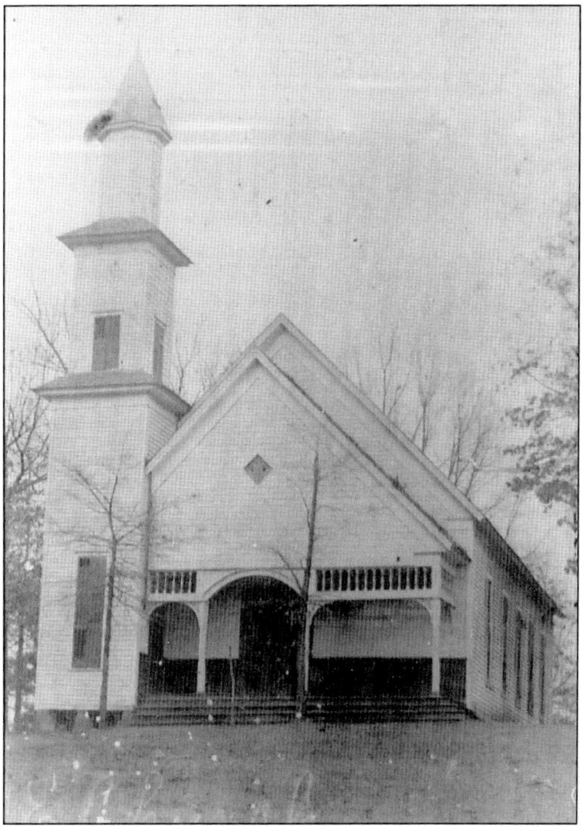

Woodstock United Methodist Church, Built 1889. Before the church was built, the congregation worshipped at Enon Baptist Church. The church made its first structure improvement in 1924. The first couple to be married in the church was Will and Berta Dean in 1915. (Courtesy of Harold Johnston.)

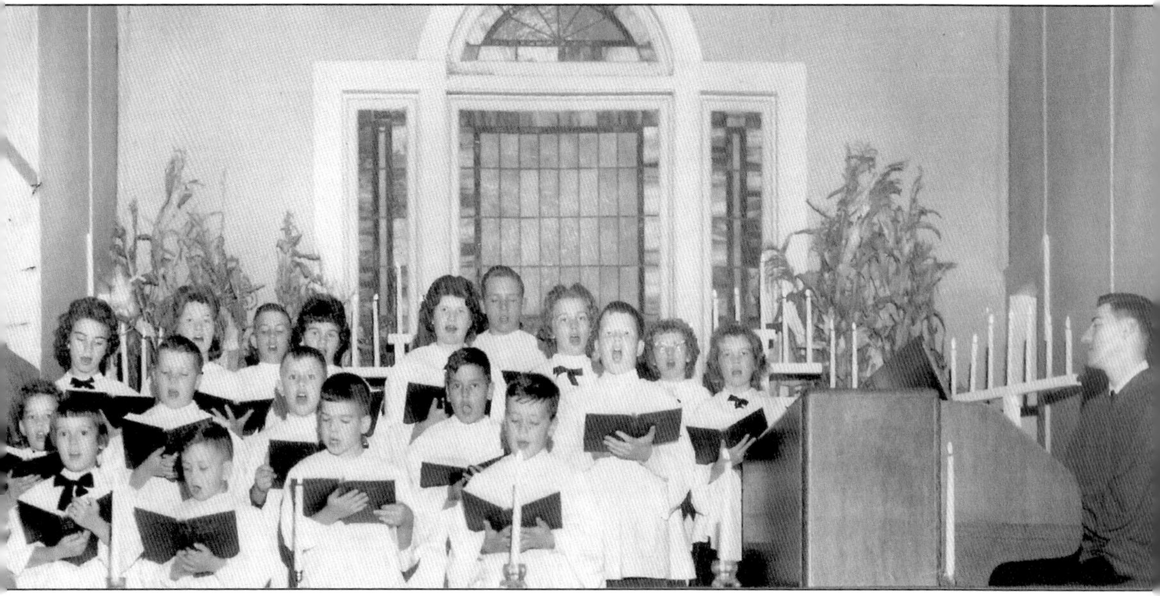

WOODSTOCK UNITED METHODIST CHURCH CHOIR, EARLY 1960S. Pictured from left to right are (first row) Debbie Brooks, Andy Sellers, Sonny Ramsay, and Tommy Alderman; (second row) Nancy Medley, Jerry Brooks, David Chambers, Woody Alderman, and Tommy Hampton; (third row) Barbara Parr, Carol Granger, Danny Brooks, Sandra Sellers, Lynn Hampton, Anthony Brooks, Gail Brooks, Sue Brooks, and Beverly Medley. The organist is Tip Ingram. (Courtesy of Sonya Brooks Dobbs.)

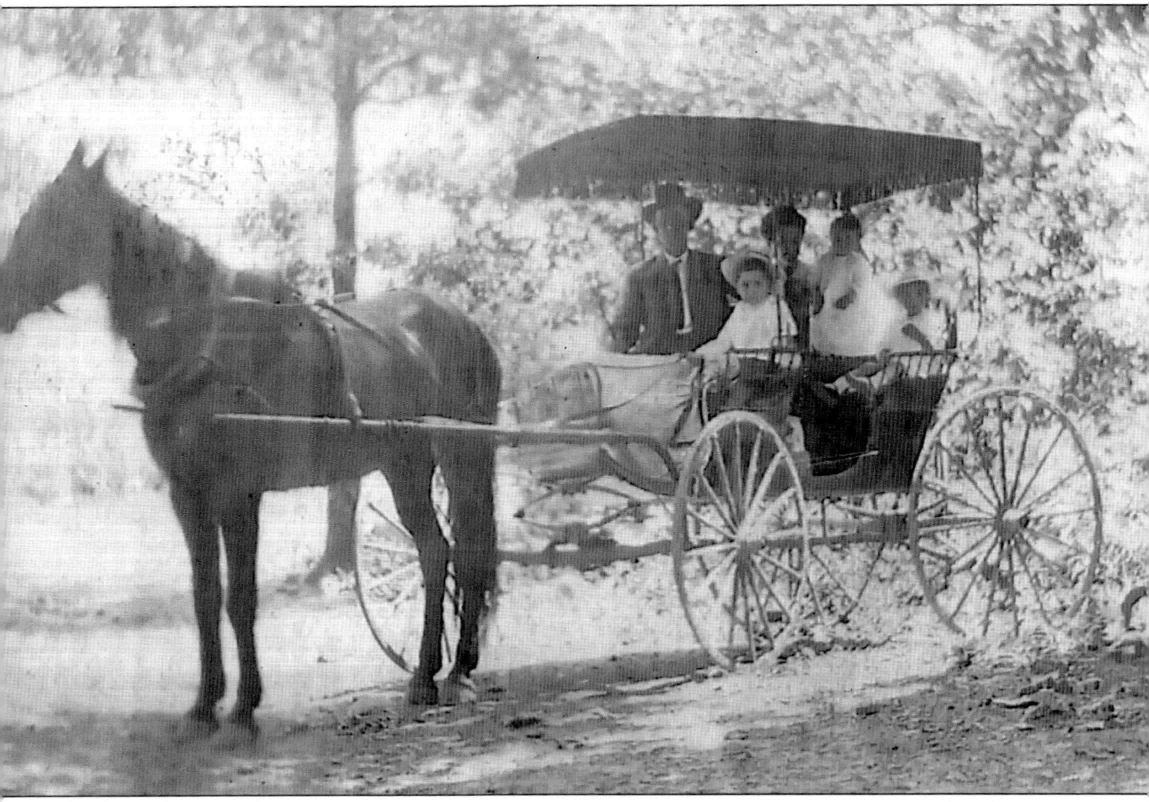

Riding to Sunday Services at Little River Methodist Church, Early 1900s. "Old Pat" pulls the Barnes family buggy to church. Pictured are, from left to right, Claud Barnes, father; James Newton Barnes (boy in front); Emma Barnes; Claud Barnes Jr. (baby); and Miller Davis Barnes (in back). Claud Barnes served as Sunday school superintendent. Early parishioners traveled by horse and wagon to services once a month. (Courtesy of Millicent Barnes Fox.)

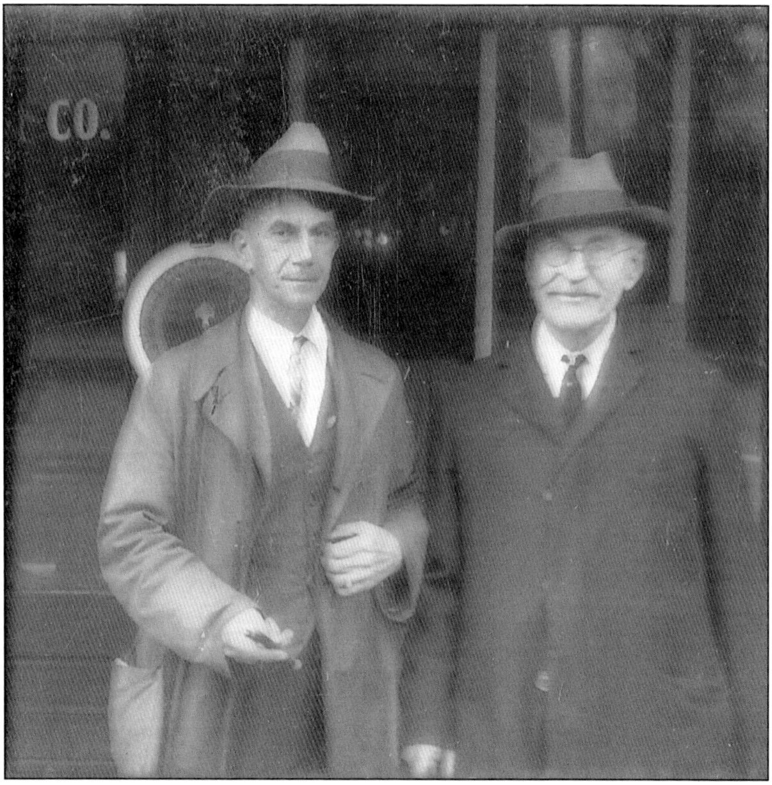

SAM DAWSON AND JOHN W. GOBER, 1930. Pictured are local businessman Sam Dawson (left) and preacher John W. Gober. The Woodstock Methodist parsonage was destroyed by a fire in 1921 and was rebuilt in 1922 by John Hillhouse and Sam Dawson. John W. Gober and A. P. Watkins were the preachers of the church at the time. (Courtesy of Preservation Woodstock, Inc.)

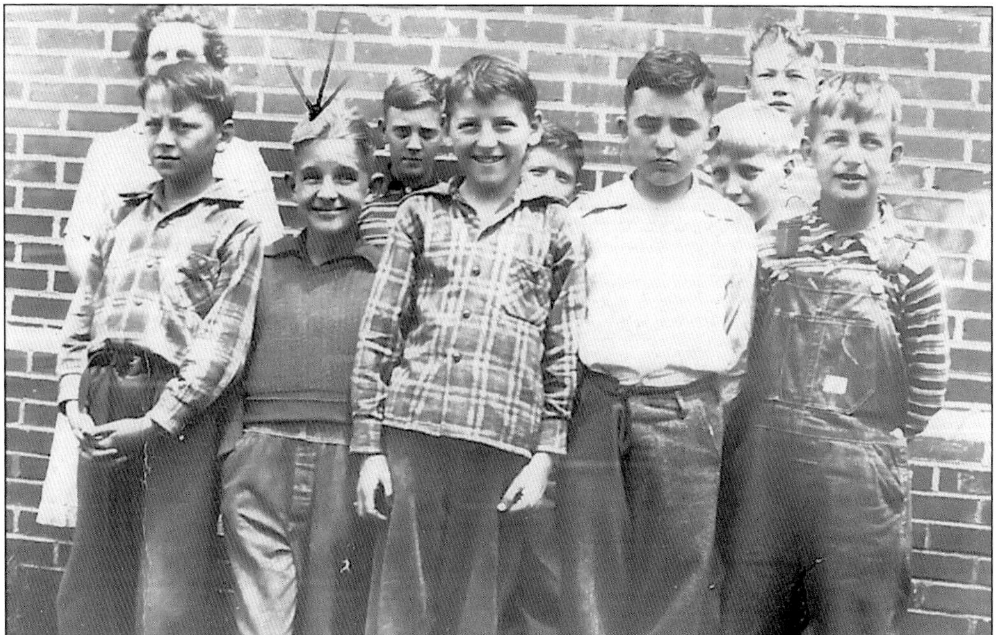

ROYAL AMBASSADORS LEADER GUYNELL FOWLER AND BOYS CHURCH GROUP, 1942. Pictured are, from left to right, Hunter Ingram, Herbert Fowler, Lonnell Hill, (hiding) Sonny Reeves, Tip Ingram, Bill Poor, Frederick McClure, William Johnston, and Tom Fowler. (Courtesy of Tom Fowler.)

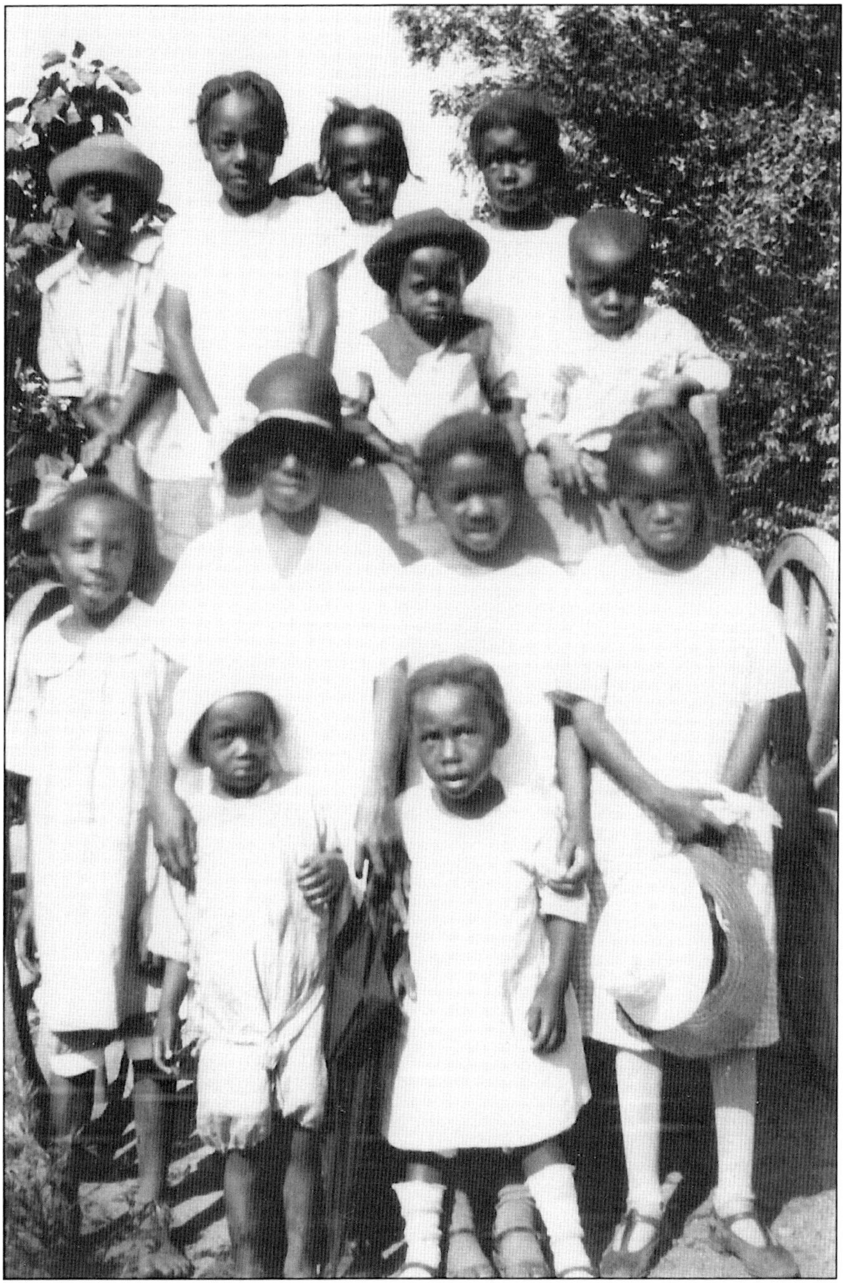

Sunday School at Mount Olive Baptist Church, 1930s. Before 1866, several African American Baptist Woodstock residents met and worshipped by a brush arbor on the east side of the present-day Mount Olive Baptist Church, located on Mill Street. G. Watson donated an acre of land so a church building could be constructed. In 1866, a small wooden church was built on that acre, and Rev. William Thomas was the church's first pastor. W. H. Dean and other Enon church members met with Reverend Thomas to help organize the church. H. A. Burge wrote the meeting minutes. As the congregation grew through the years, the church purchased more land and expanded the building. The present church building was erected in 1954. (Courtesy of Preservation Woodstock, Inc.)

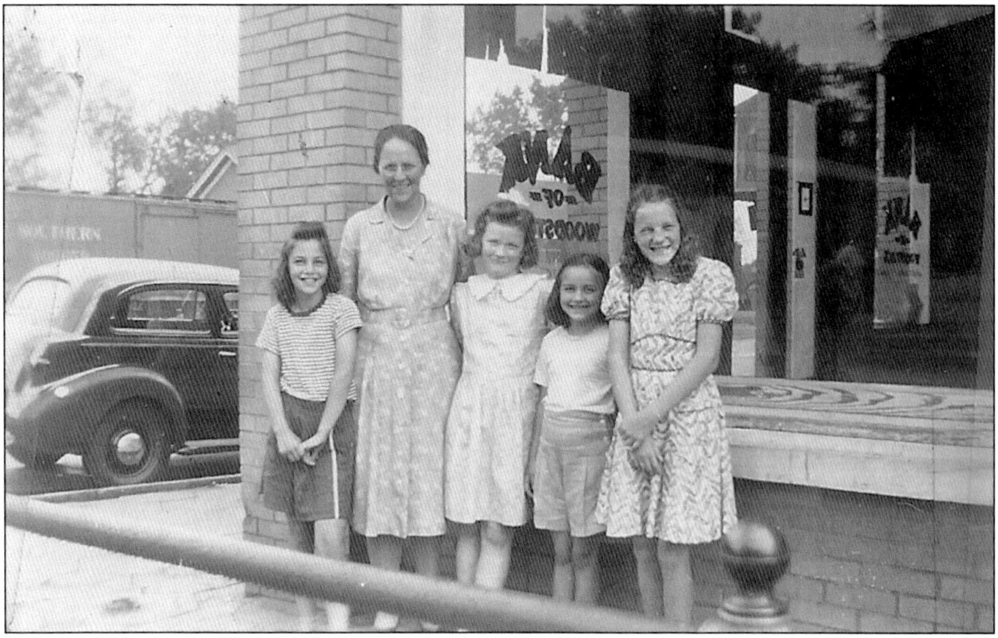

Girls Auxiliary of Woodstock Baptist, 1943. Standing at the side of the Bank of Woodstock, from left to right, are Sally Johnston, Mary Howell, Mabel Smith, Patricia Johnston, and Ernestine Rusk. Mary Howell served as director of the Women's Missionary Union at First Baptist, which oversaw the Girls Auxiliary. Girls Auxiliary provided opportunities for girls to participate in mission-oriented projects. (Courtesy of Jeanne Cosey.)

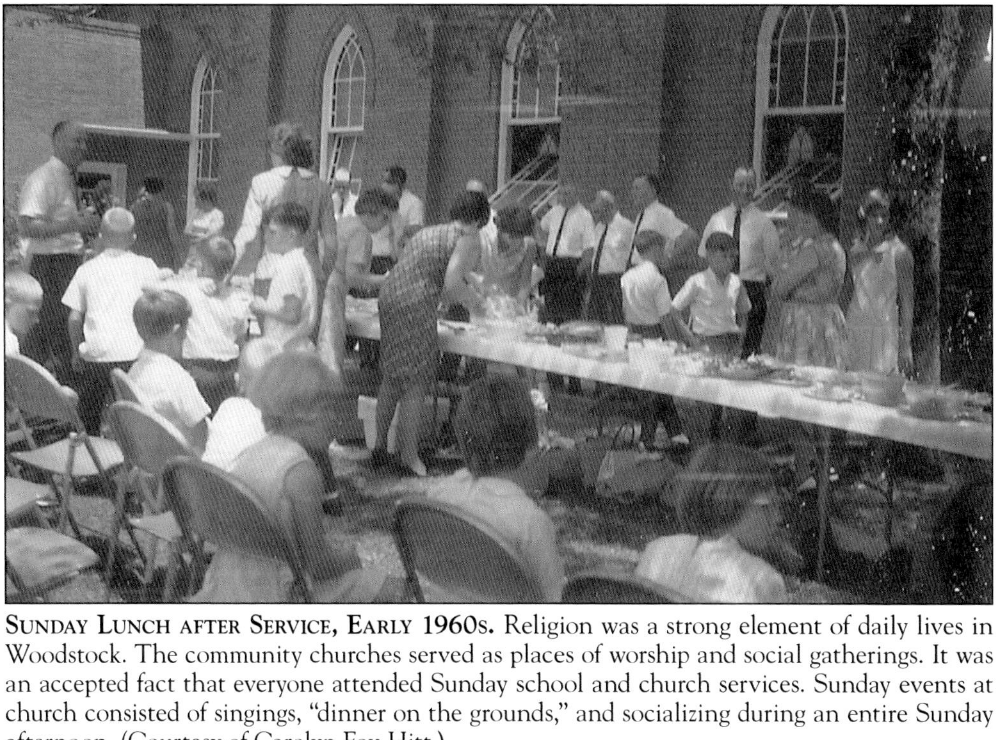

Sunday Lunch after Service, Early 1960s. Religion was a strong element of daily lives in Woodstock. The community churches served as places of worship and social gatherings. It was an accepted fact that everyone attended Sunday school and church services. Sunday events at church consisted of singings, "dinner on the grounds," and socializing during an entire Sunday afternoon. (Courtesy of Carolyn Fox Hitt.)

Eight

Education

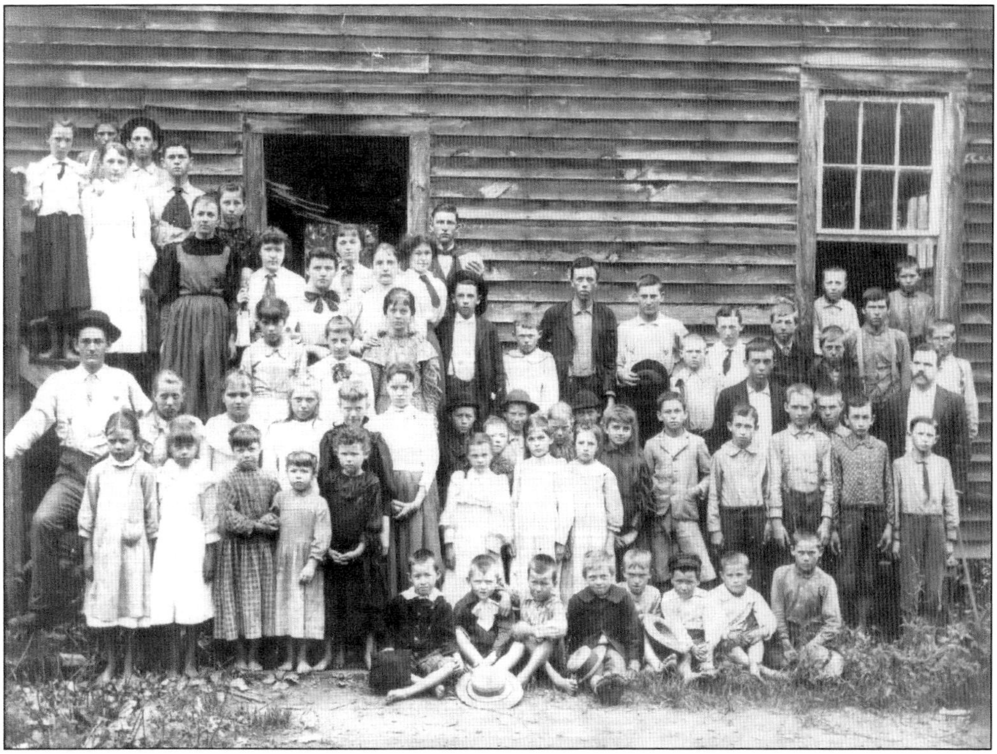

Little River Academy, 1894. Pictured are schoolmaster Robert Rusk (far right with moustache) and teacher William D. Rusk (far left with hat). Before the Civil War, students attended Little River Academy, a log cabin about 4 miles southeast of Woodstock, now the site of Little River Methodist Church. The school was known to be the largest rural school in Cherokee and Cobb Counties in the late 1800s. P. D. Wheelan, born in Dublin and educated for the priesthood, taught at the school in the 1860s. Perry Pinkney Dupree, after serving in the 2nd Reserves and guarding prisoners at Andersonville, became Wheelan's student. (Courtesy of Marilyn Dobbs Morrell.)

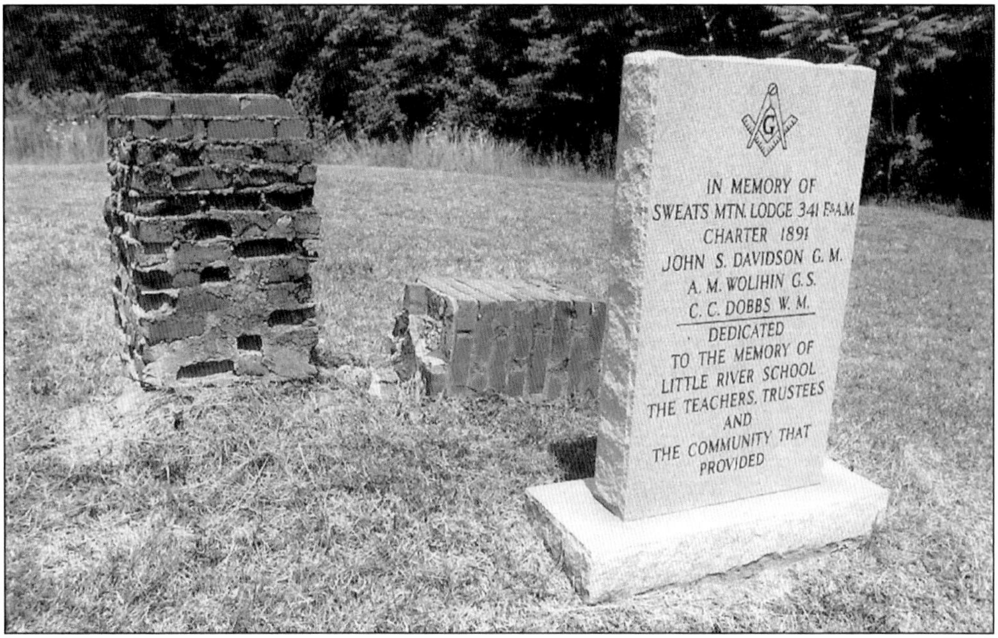

Little River Academy Remains. The original one-room school building burned in 1887. A new school was erected in 1891 as a spacious two-story frame building. The Masons met on the second floor and dubbed their meeting place "Sweats Mountain Lodge." The Masons continued to meet in the school until sometime after 1940, when Little River Academy merged with Woodstock School. (Courtesy of Felicia Whitmore.)

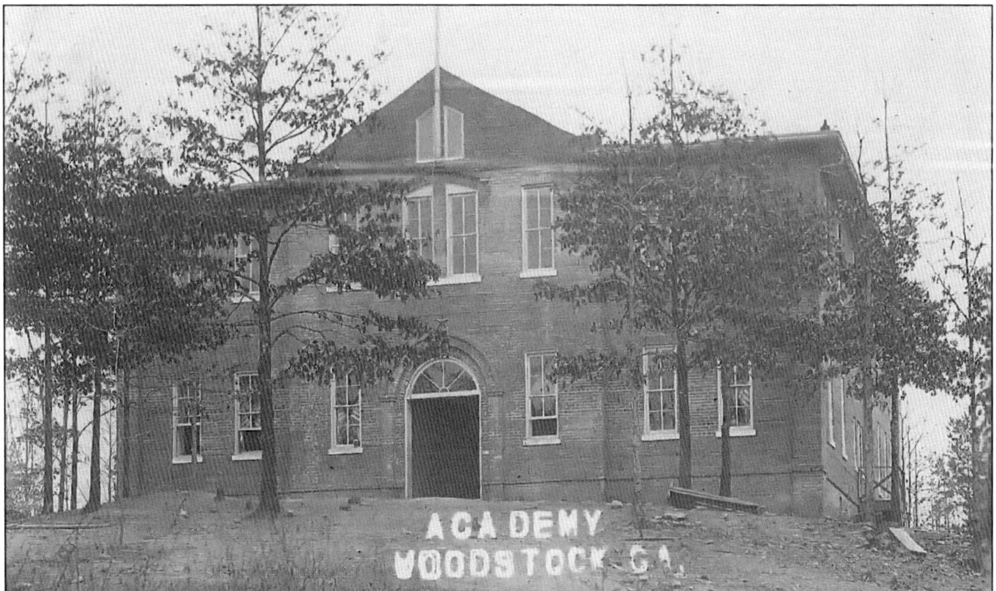

Woodstock Academy, Established 1870s. Built on land that was once W. H. Dean's cotton field, the school replaced the crowded wood-framed building located behind Woodstock Baptist Church. Before the late 1930s, students took turns carrying water from the well across the street. A bucket and dipper were placed in each classroom. Students brought their own drinking cups or made cups from folded pieces of tablet paper. (Courtesy of Harold Johnston.)

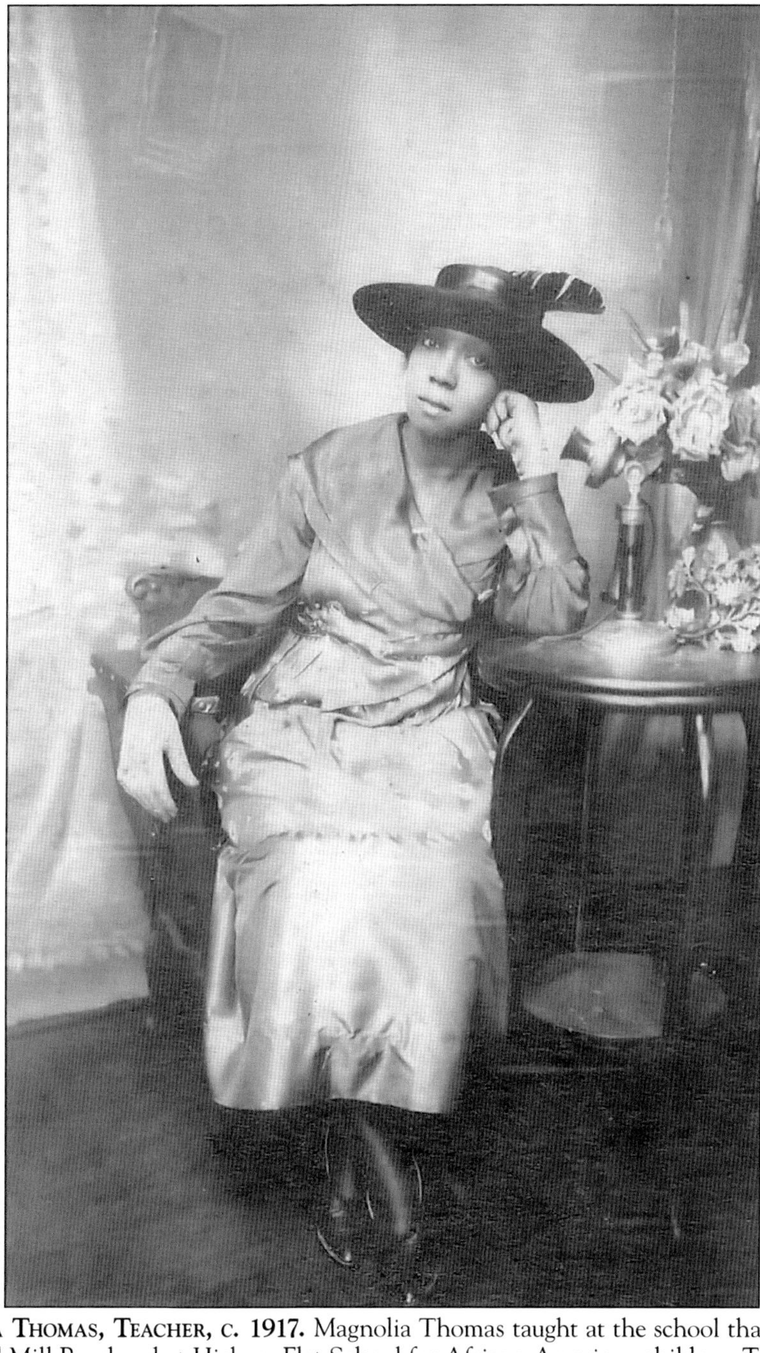

Magnolia Thomas, Teacher, c. 1917. Magnolia Thomas taught at the school that was once on Arnold Mill Road and at Hickory Flat School for African American children. Thomas was born in 1890 in Canton, Georgia. When she was a young woman, she and her mother moved to Woodstock to a house her brother Robert built for them. Magnolia Thomas graduated from Spelman in Atlanta in 1918. Well-educated and deeply religious, she was greatly respected as a teacher and resident in Woodstock. Everyone called her Miss Magnolia. Later in her life, she traveled, kept books for several of the churches in Woodstock, and remained devoted to her church, Mount Olive Baptist Church. She never married. (Courtesy of City of Woodstock.)

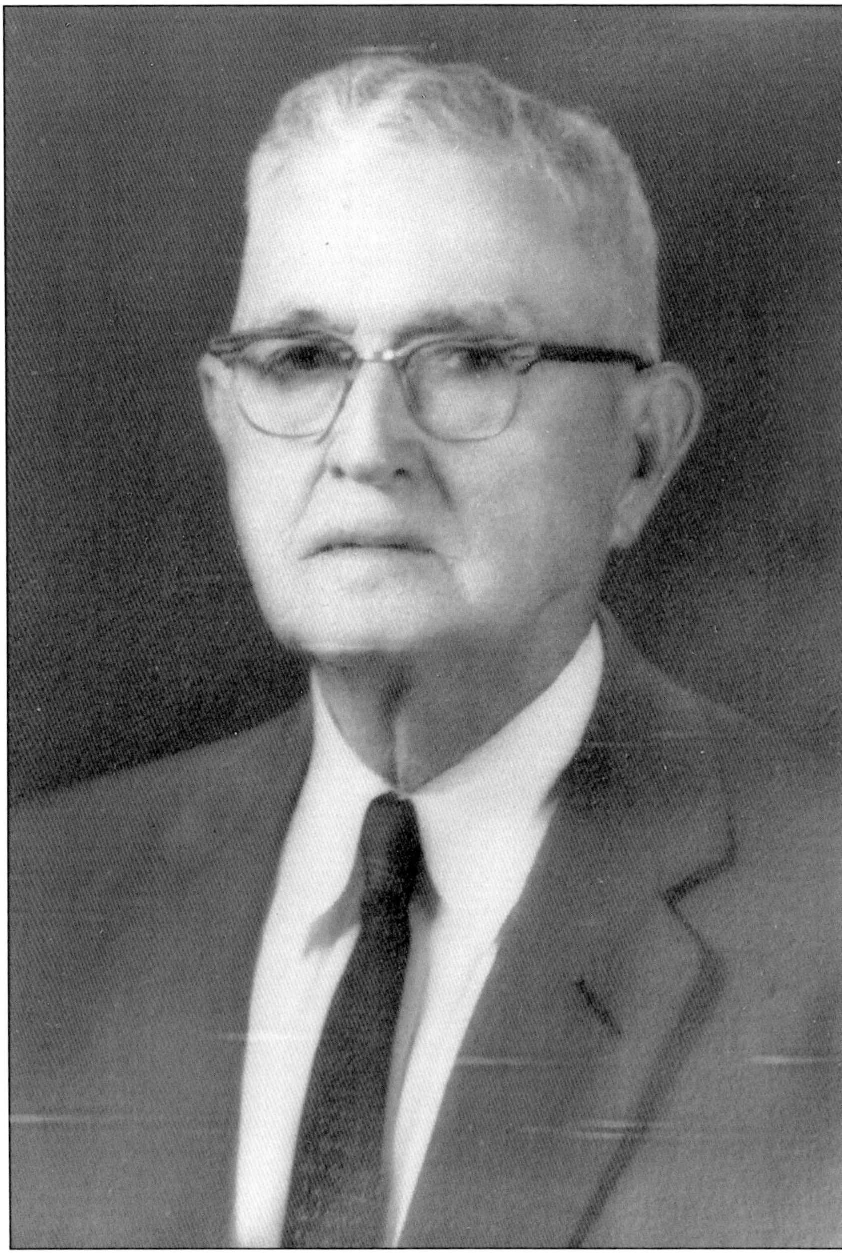

EUGENE T. BOOTH, TEACHER, PRINCIPAL, CHEROKEE COUNTY SCHOOL SUPERINTENDENT. Booth (1878–1972) taught and served as principal from 1913 to 1937 and as Cherokee County superintendent in 1937. He also served as Woodstock Baptist Church pastor from 1929 to 1948. He was educated at Mercer University and Southern Baptist Theological Seminary. Booth's father, William A. Booth, who served in the Civil War, also taught school. His mother, Caroline R. Carrie, was daughter of the owner of the Big Shanty Inn, where the Great Locomotive Chase began. Eugene Booth began his teaching career in 1902 at the age of 20. He married Lucy Gibson, one of his students, in 1907. They had four children: Harold, Eugene, William, and Christine. E. T. Booth Middle School is named after the elder Eugene. (Courtesy of Preservation Woodstock, Inc.)

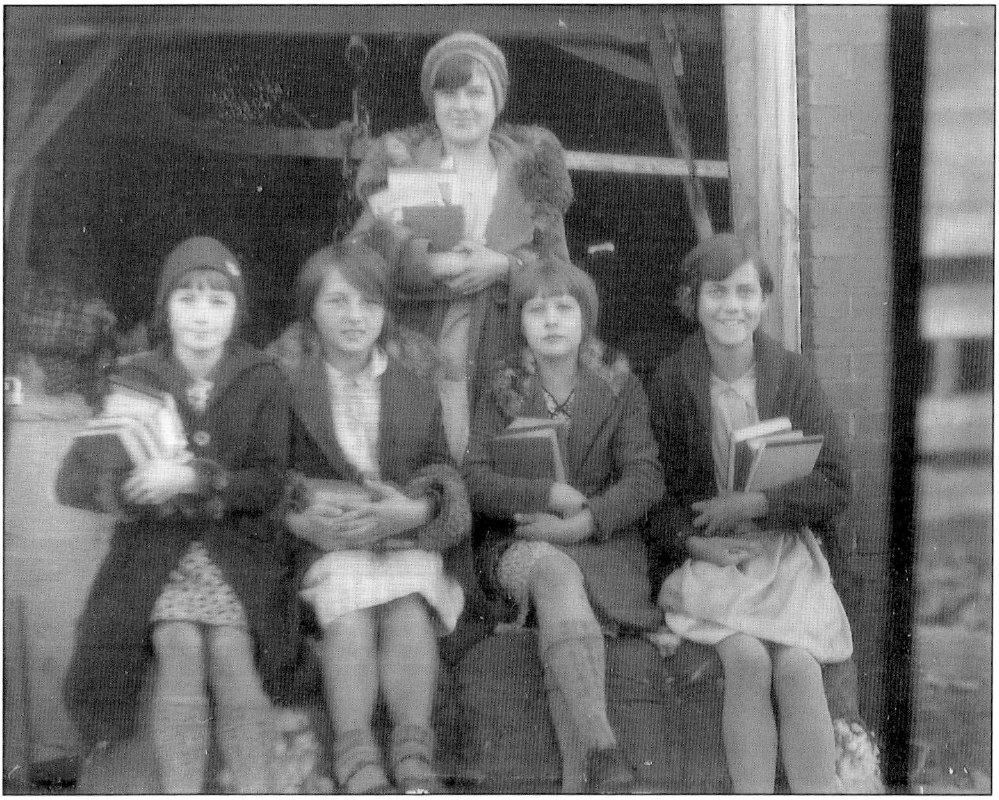

SCHOOLGIRLS OF WOODSTOCK SCHOOL, C. 1930. Students of Woodstock Elementary pose with their schoolbooks in front of a cotton warehouse. Sitting are, from left to right, Velma Dobbs, Iris Fain, Dee Freeman, and "Jinx" Wright; standing is Lucretia Rusk. (Courtesy of Preservation Woodstock, Inc.)

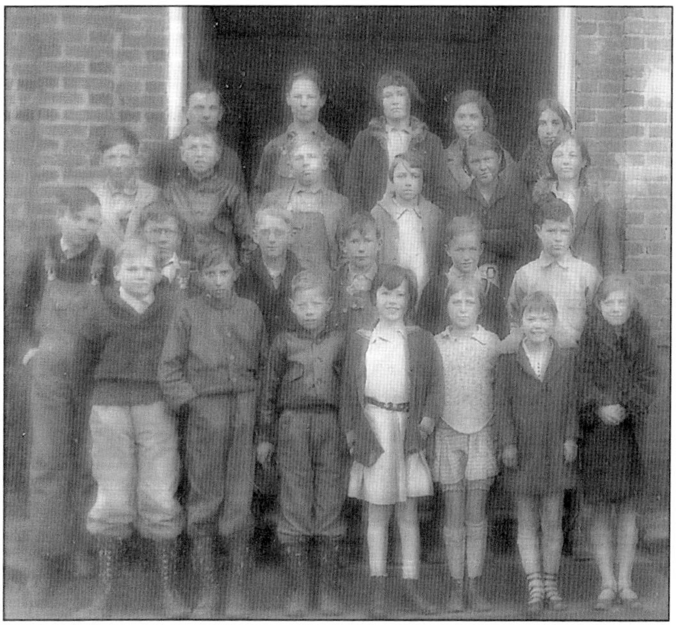

WOODSTOCK SCHOOL, FOURTH AND FIFTH GRADE, 1930. Pictured are, from left to right, (first row) Bernard ("Doodle") Robertson, Oscar Ghorley, Lewis Poor, Alice Dean, Juanita Hicks, Becky Medley, and Evelyn Whitmire; (second row) four unidentified, Harold Hames, and Tom Van Sant; (third row) unidentified, Herbert Priest, Homer Hubbard, and three unidentified; (fourth row) unidentified, Coy Mullinax, unidentified, Pearl Nelson, and Edna Ghorley. (Courtesy of Preservation Woodstock, Inc.)

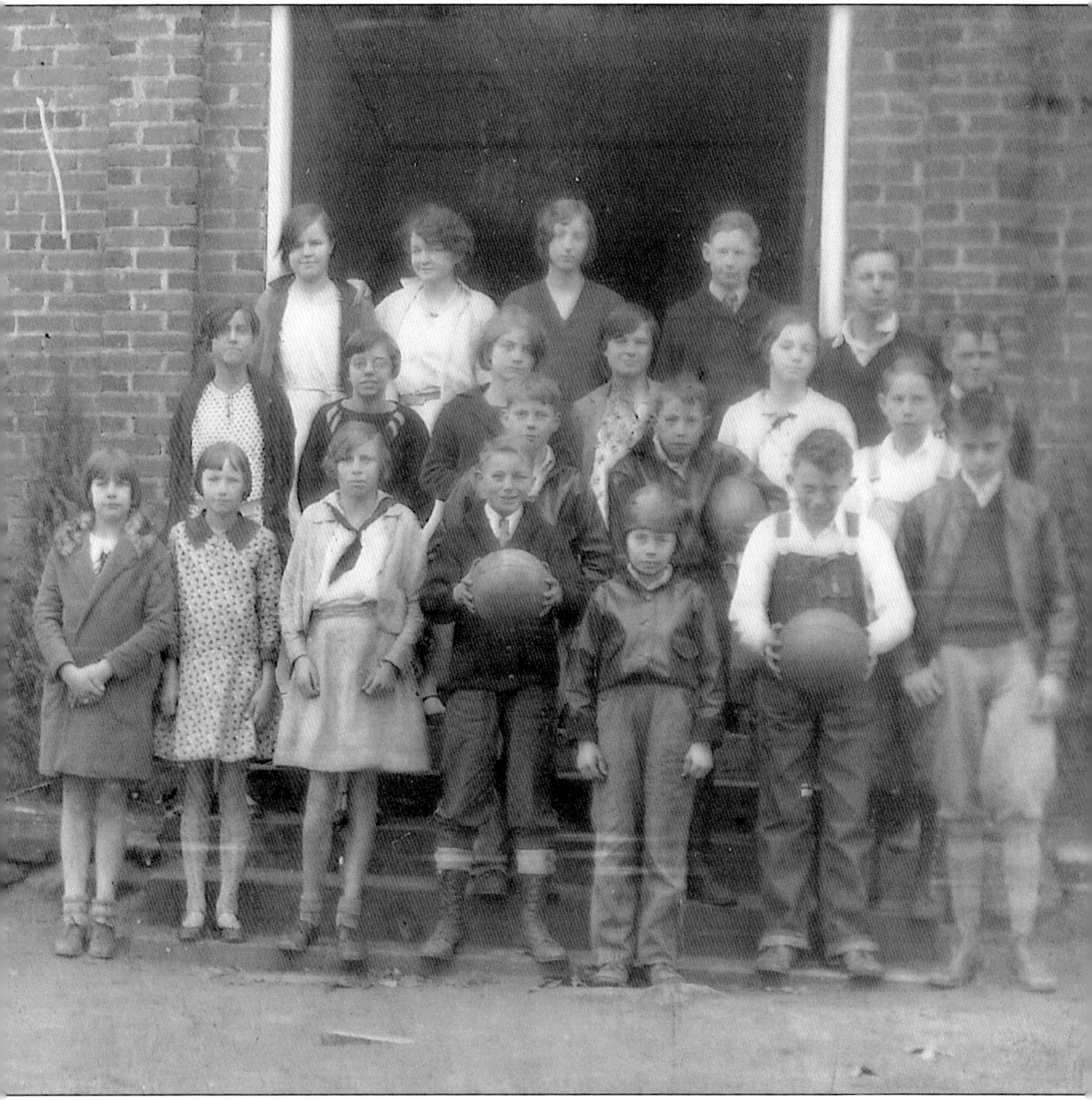

Woodstock School, Sixth Grade, 1930. Pictured are, from left to right, (first row) Dee Freeman, Velma Dobbs, two unidentified, Albert Poor, Smith Johnston Jr. (holding basketball), and Dean Power; (second row) Jake and John Haney; (third row) Jinx Wright, Ruby Lee McClure, unidentified, Lucretia Rusk, and three unidentified; (fourth row) unidentified, Beulah Biddy, unidentified, Carl Tarpley, and Ralph Holbert. (Courtesy of Preservation Woodstock, Inc.)

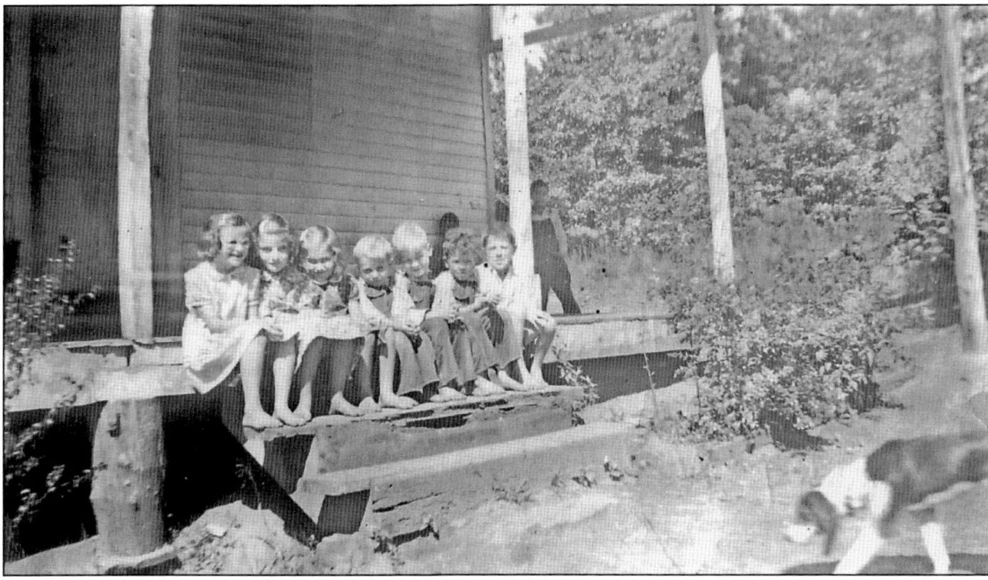

Mill Creek School, 1942. Pictured are, from left to right, Helen Martin, Ruby Jean Evans, Jeannette Parker, Louis Smith, Cecil Atkins, Morris Smith, Harry Nelson, and Frank Nelson (standing in background). Mill Creek Baptist Church organized a school in the original church building on East Cherokee Drive until 1918, when they decided to construct a new structure. The school existed until 1942, when the school consolidated with Woodstock Elementary. The school building was demolished in 1947 to create a church cemetery. (Courtesy of Mary Ann Parker Eubanks and Jeanette Parker McArthur.)

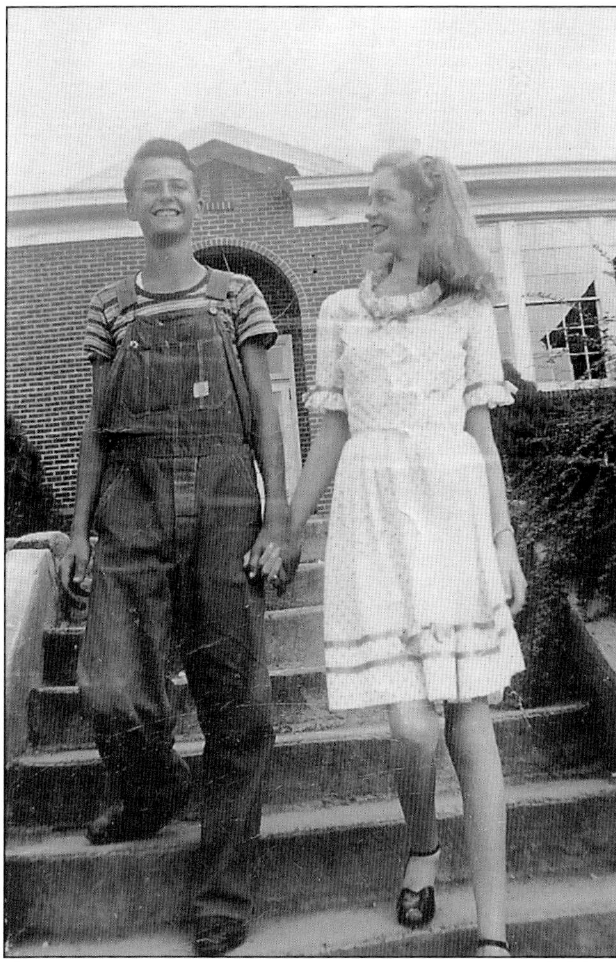

Clarence "Blackie" Edwards and Mary Lou Freeman, 1943. Edwards and Freeman hold hands in front of Woodstock School during the summer of 1943. (Courtesy of Mary Lou Freeman Reece.)

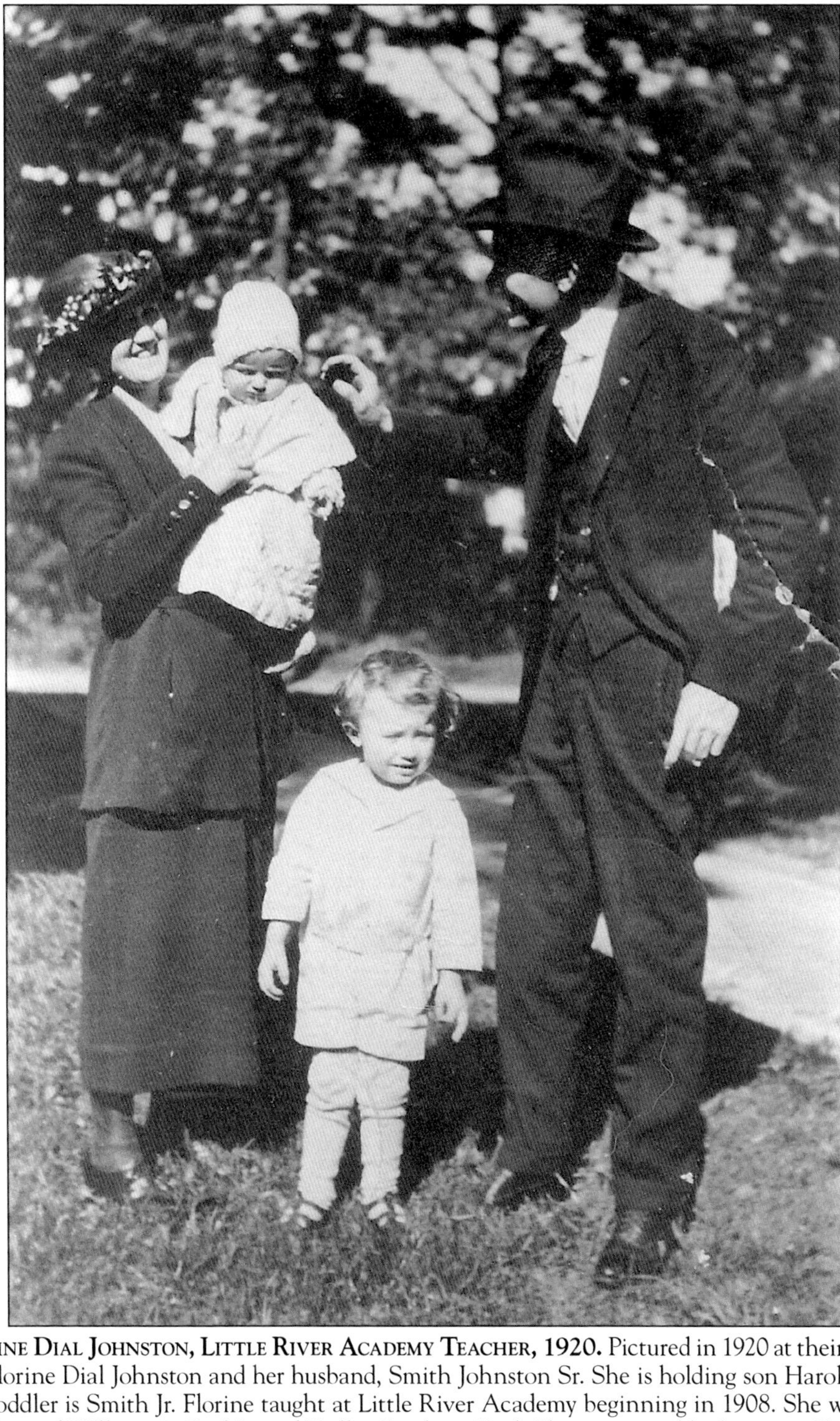

Florine Dial Johnston, Little River Academy Teacher, 1920. Pictured in 1920 at their home are Florine Dial Johnston and her husband, Smith Johnston Sr. She is holding son Harold, and the toddler is Smith Jr. Florine taught at Little River Academy beginning in 1908. She was the daughter of William C. Dial Jr. and Dollie Gresham Dial. She was raised by her aunt Elizabeth Lathem when her mother died when Florine was two years old. Elizabeth Dial Lathem operated a boardinghouse. (Courtesy of Harold Johnston.)

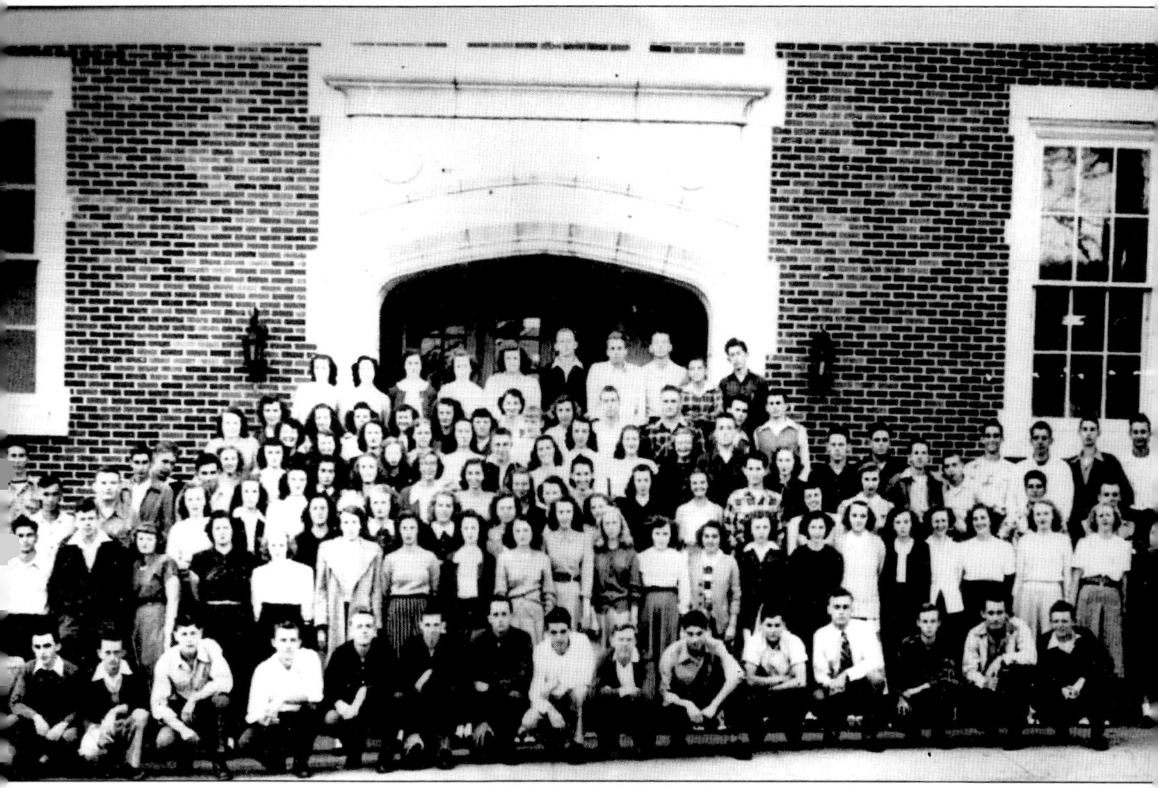

Canton High School Graduation Class, 1949. The first Woodstock school did not have an 11th grade and therefore did not have a graduating class until 1917, when Bonnie Bozeman and Mary Bates Kemp received diplomas. The 11th grade was discontinued the next school year, making this Woodstock's only high school graduating class. In the early 1930s, the 10th grade was discontinued. Woodstock students attended Canton High School, the only high school in Cherokee County. Woodstock opened its own high school in 1996. (Courtesy of William and Mary Johnston.)

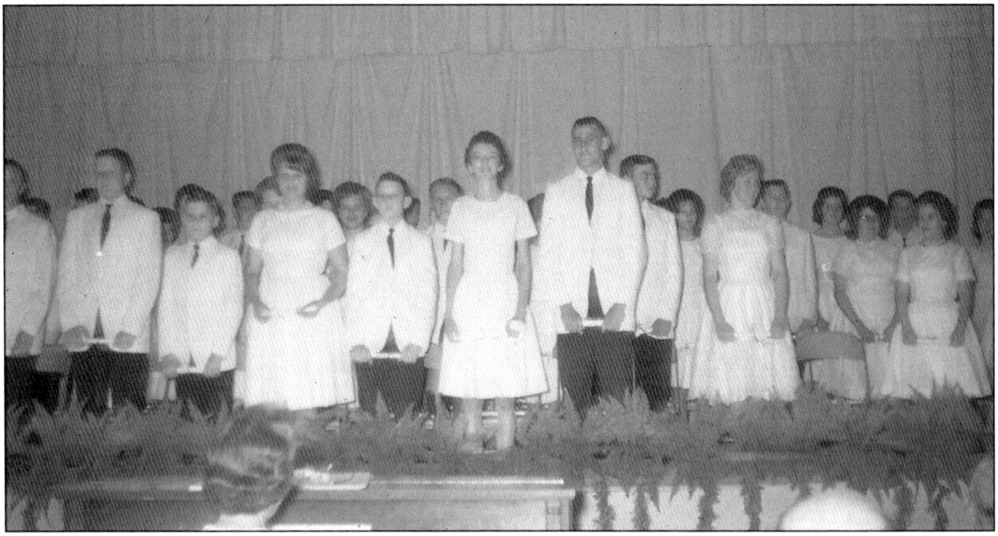

Woodstock School, Eighth-Grade Graduation, 1964. Because Woodstock did not have its own high school, eighth-grade graduation was an important event for the community. Pictured in the school auditorium are, from left to right, Tommy Hampton, Benny Hause, Dana Price, Allan Stenger, Elaine Hubbard, unidentified, James Cook, and the remaining are unidentified. (Courtesy of Elaine Hubbard.)

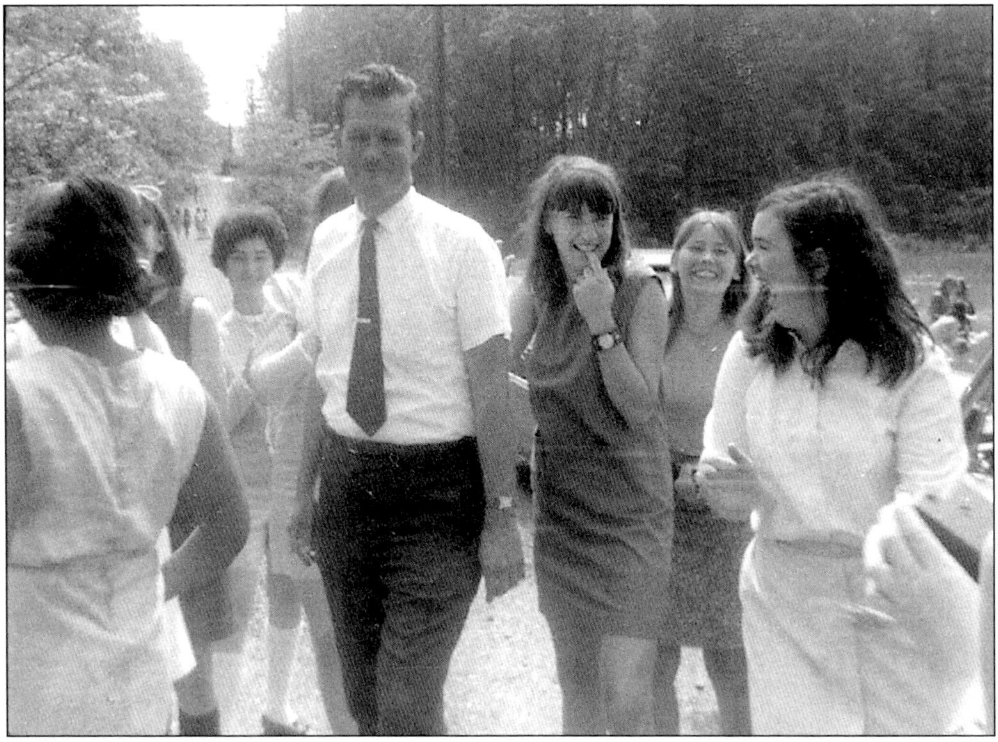

Recess at Woodstock School, 1969. Eighth-grade girls enjoy time at recess with teacher Lewis Peters. Peters became principal after William Booth retired. Pictured from left to right are Vicky Boddy, Lewis Peters, Phyllis Grimes, Sherry Turner, and DeDe Hayden. (Courtesy of Brenda Austin.)

Nine

Leisure and Civic Groups

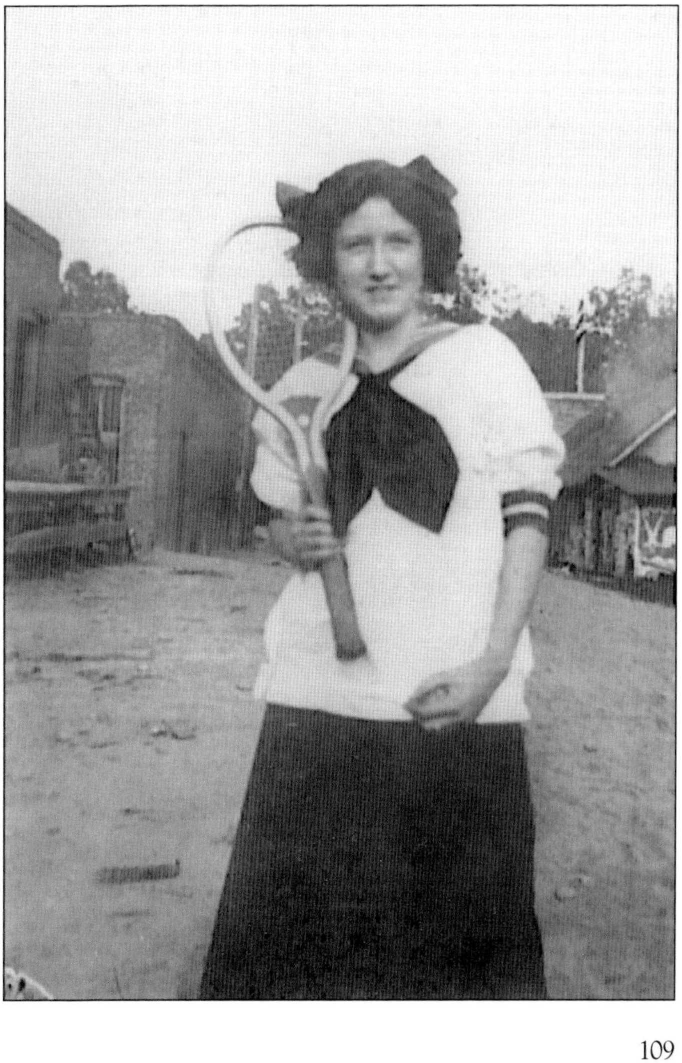

Villa Dean, 1913. Several tennis courts existed in town before the 1930s. Tennis became a favorite pastime for some residents. Public courts were located west of the Main Street business district and behind the Woodstock Methodist and Baptist Churches in 1915. (Courtesy of Alice Dean Felton.)

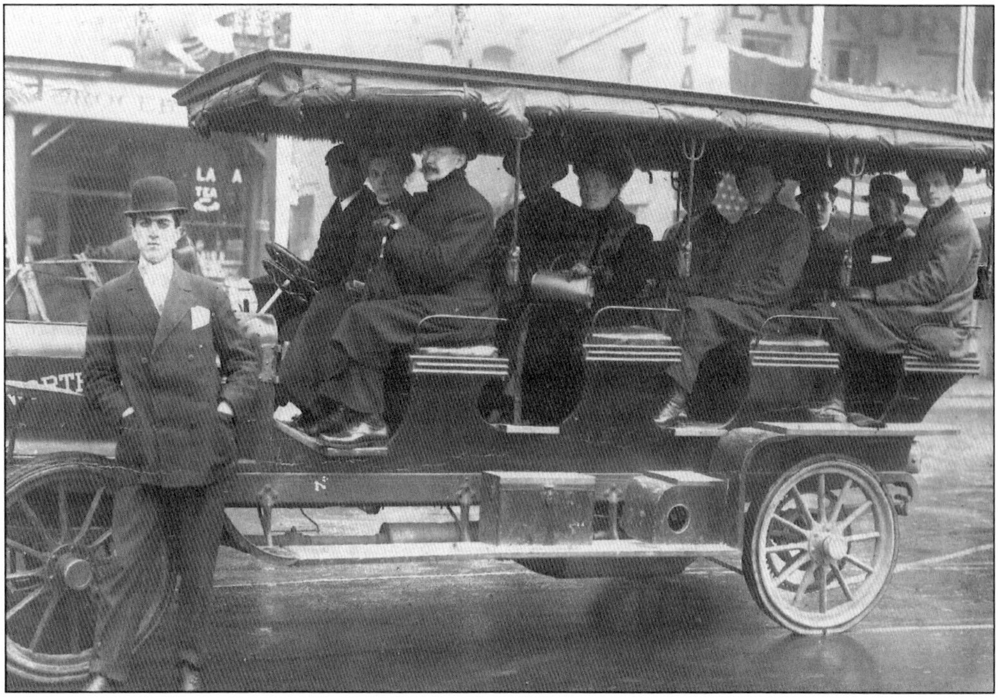

WOODSTOCK RESIDENTS AT PRESIDENT WILSON'S INAUGURATION, MARCH 4, 1913. In the rear of the sightseeing car are, from left to right, Oscar Perkinson, Dr. Jim Boring, and Smith L. Johnston Sr. Linton Dean is seated in front of them on the second to last row of seats. The driver made a wrong turn and got in front of the presidential inauguration parade and could not turn off the road because of exits filled with spectators. The four guys from Woodstock and other spectators in the car led the parade unexpectedly. (Courtesy of Harold Johnston.)

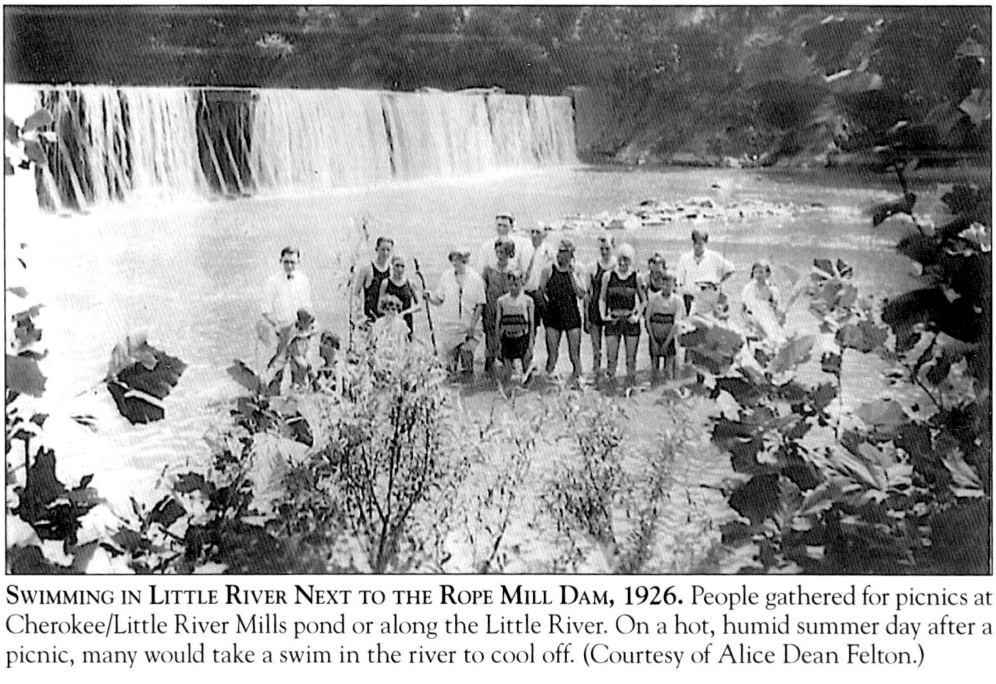

SWIMMING IN LITTLE RIVER NEXT TO THE ROPE MILL DAM, 1926. People gathered for picnics at Cherokee/Little River Mills pond or along the Little River. On a hot, humid summer day after a picnic, many would take a swim in the river to cool off. (Courtesy of Alice Dean Felton.)

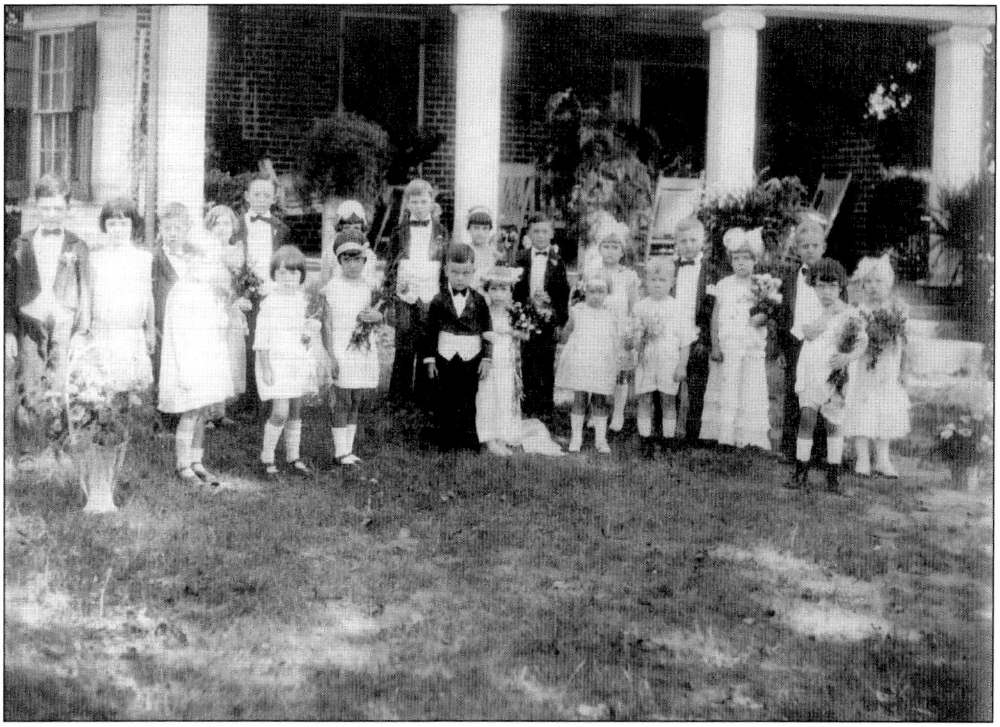

Tom Thumb Wedding Party, Dean Home, c. 1926. The wedding ceremony took place in the school auditorium. Pictured from left to right are (first row) Eunice Peek, Frances Mullinax, Frances Wright, Roy Thompson (groom), Jeanne Powers (bride), Mary Zell Robertson, Albert Beavers, and Avis Haney; (second row) Tom Van Sant, Alice Dean, Lewis Poor, Evelyn Whitmire, Richard Hillhouse, Jane Johnston, John Haney, Sara Frances Dial, Hugh Johnston Jr., Marie Kemp, Harold Johnston, Evelyn Beavers, Paul Herdon, and Sara Robertson. (Courtesy of Sara Frances Dial Ramsay.)

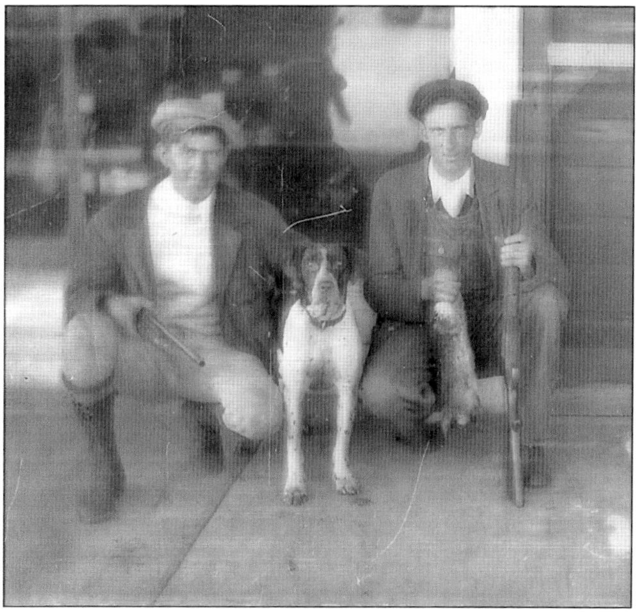

Jay Durham and Charlie Hillhouse after Hunting, 1930. Fox, squirrel, possum, and rabbit hunting were also popular pastimes. Some residents who owned hunting dogs spent weekends in the Thousand Acre Woods, now the Towne Lake community development. (Courtesy of Preservation Woodstock, Inc.)

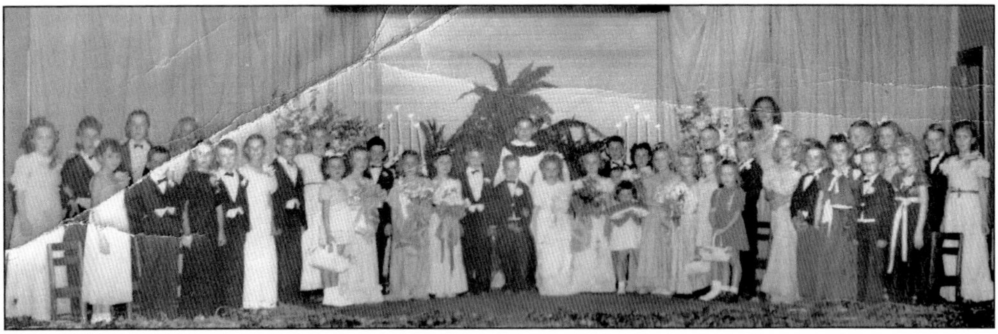

Tom Thumb Wedding, First-Grade Class, 1945. Shown are, from left to right, (first row, center section) Joyce Neese (holding basket), Shirley Wright, Mae Collum, Faye Crowe, Weyman Biddy, Jimmy Dobbs (groom), Joan Morris (bride), Michael Booth, Brenda Wood, Ann Anderson, Judy Carpenter, Patsy Hubbard, Barbara Wright, and Mary Frances Bryant; (second row) Shirley Reeves, Dan Cook, Shirley Chambers, Vernon Lingerfelt, Austine Cook, John Ragsdale, Nina Scott, Billy Paul Rusk, Tip Ingram (center, minister), Billy Wheeler, Mildred Booth, Lat Carpenter, Doyle Cook, Mildred McArthur, Lewis Smith, Kathryn Millwood, Glenn Dobbs, and Mary Ann Parker; (third row) Mary Lou Collins, Billy Millwood, Joe Reece, and Kansie Lee Castleberry; (third row, right section) Sally Johnston, Sarah Sue Collins, Jackie Danger, Laurell Dunn, Harold Collum, and Geraldine Scott. (Courtesy of Tom Fowler.)

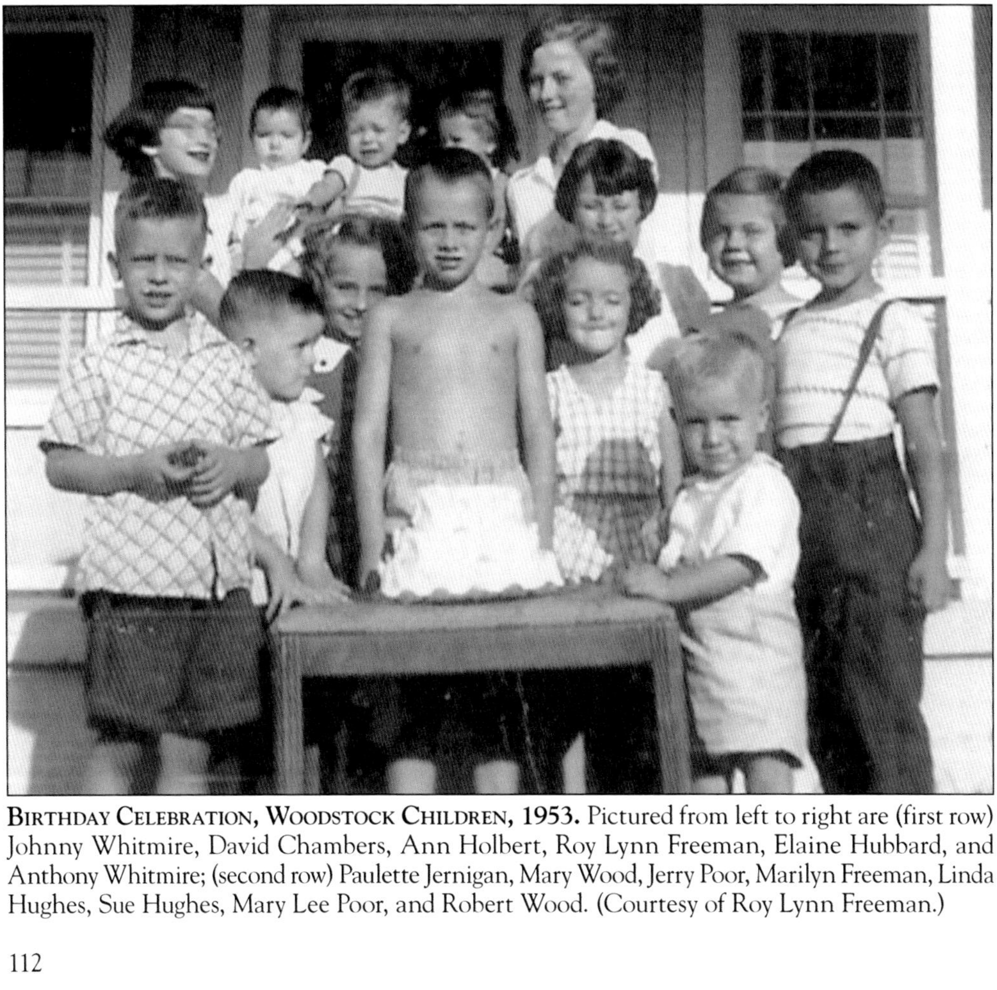

Birthday Celebration, Woodstock Children, 1953. Pictured from left to right are (first row) Johnny Whitmire, David Chambers, Ann Holbert, Roy Lynn Freeman, Elaine Hubbard, and Anthony Whitmire; (second row) Paulette Jernigan, Mary Wood, Jerry Poor, Marilyn Freeman, Linda Hughes, Sue Hughes, Mary Lee Poor, and Robert Wood. (Courtesy of Roy Lynn Freeman.)

TOM FOWLER, BASEBALL PLAYER, 1955. Fowler is pictured at spring training with the Red Sticks in Lutcher, Louisiana, in 1955. Fowler played baseball at North Georgia College in 1952, and the next year, he signed with the Atlanta Crackers. The Crackers were part of the Class AA Southern Association, and from 1907 until 1965, Ponce de Leon Ballpark became its home field. He later joined the minor-league Baton Rouge Red Sticks as part of the Evangeline Baseball League in Louisiana. (Courtesy of Tom Fowler.)

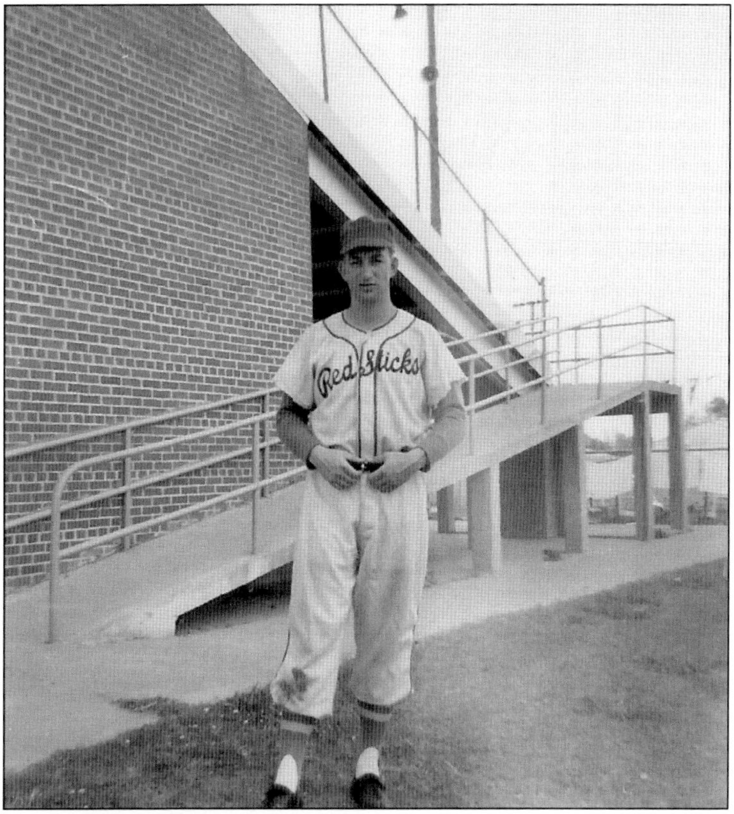

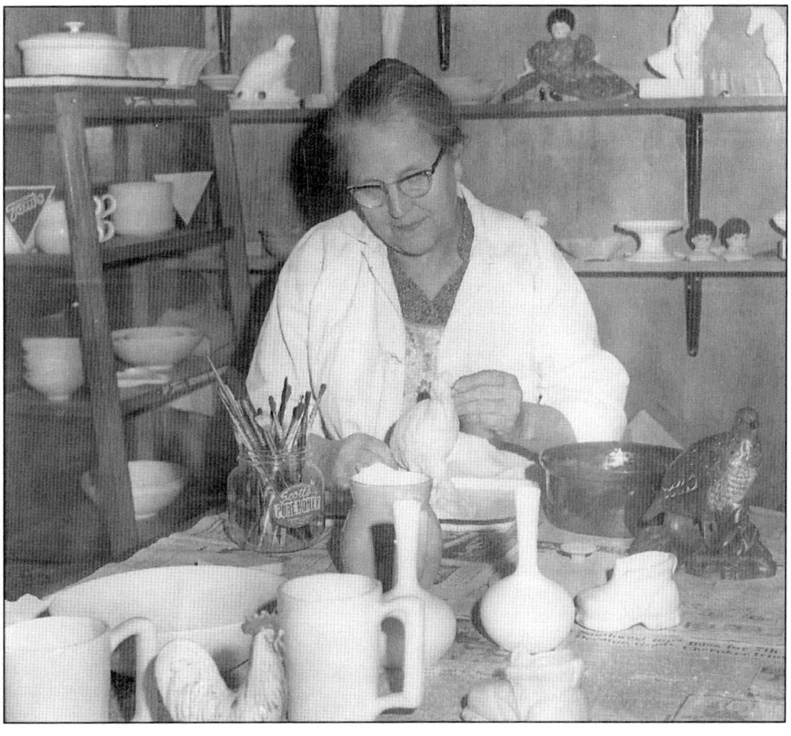

MARY SMITH HOWELL WITH HER CERAMICS, LATE 1950S. Mary Howell fired and painted ceramics in her workshop later in her life to stay active. She taught ceramic classes to children and adults. (Courtesy of Jeanne Cosey.)

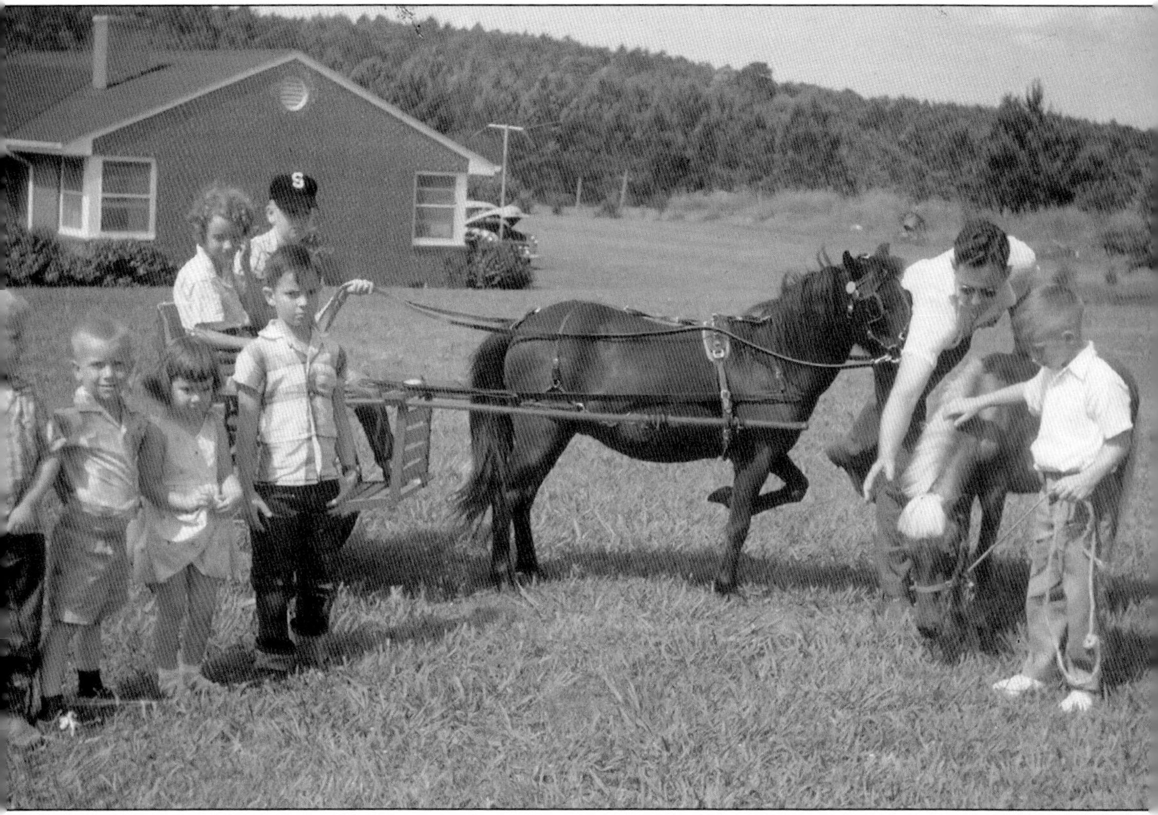

Woodstock Children and Ponies, Late 1950s. Small-town children had an advantage of playing away from traffic and other city obstructions. Several neighborhood children gathered at Ruby Lee Freeman's home to take turns riding the cart and pony. Pictured from left to right are (first row) David Chambers, Anthony Whitmire, Mary Wood, and Robert Wood; (seated in the cart) Elaine Hubbard and Roy Lynn Freeman; the adult is Bernard Pyle, whose ponies are also pictured, and Johnny Whitmire is petting the pony. (Courtesy of Elaine Hubbard.)

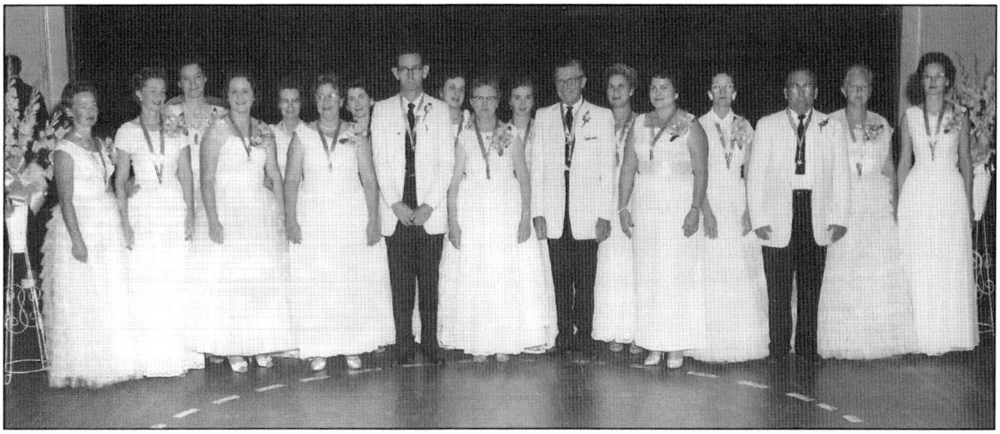

THE ORDER OF THE EASTERN STAR, 1959. James Calvin and Pearl Parker established an order in Woodstock in the 1950s. Female relatives of the Freemasons could join the order. The fraternal organization helped local charities and encouraged spiritual values. (Courtesy of Mary Ann Parker Eubanks and Jeanette Parker McArthur.)

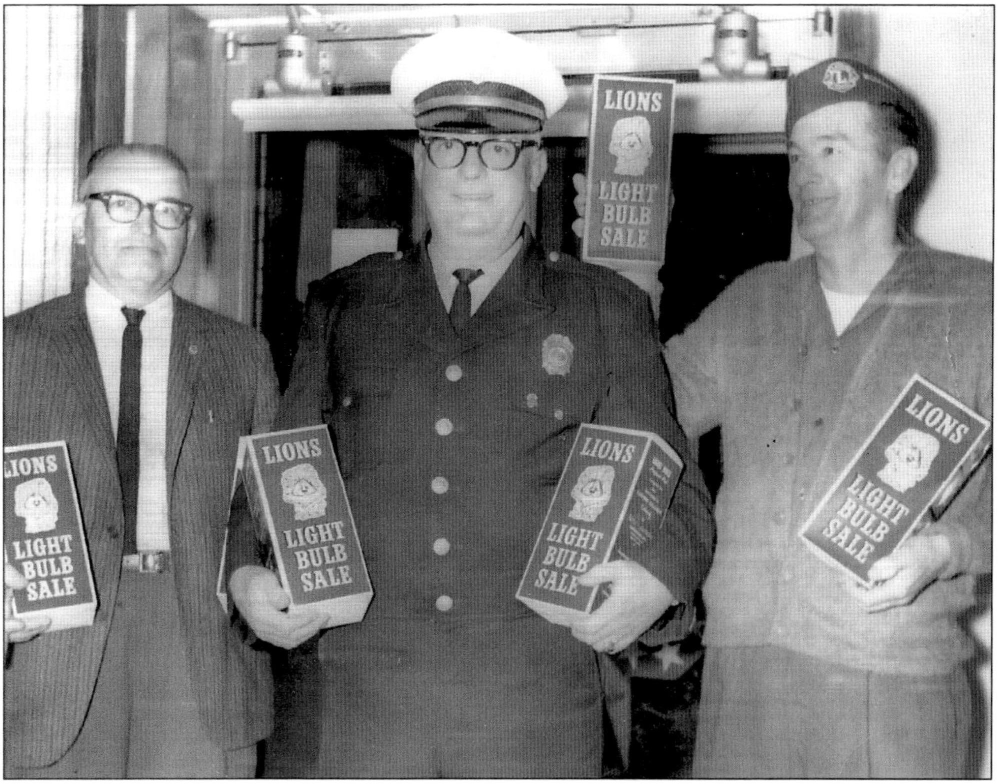

MILLER BARNES (LEFT), C. J. BOWLES (CENTER), AND JERRY POOLE (RIGHT), EARLY 1960S. The Woodstock chapter of the Lions Club was chartered in November 1961. Lions Club members organized projects and held events to raise money for the visually impaired. They also raised money to provide improvements to Woodstock, such as lights for the baseball field, furniture for the medical clinic, and Christmas lights for Main Street. The club donated money to the library, the nursing home, and a day care center and sponsored Christmas parties for the homeless. (Courtesy of Woodstock Public Library.)

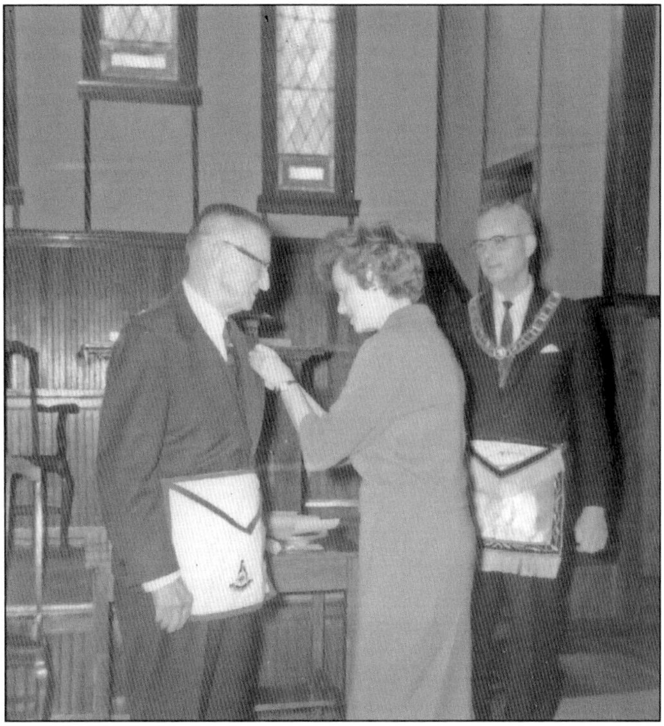

Masonic Apron Presentation, 1967. Pictured are, from left to right, Dean Power Jr., Power's sister Jean Johnston, and an unidentified man. The Sweats Mountain Masonic Lodge at Little River Methodist Church merged with the Woodstock Lodge in 1945. The upper floor of the Johnston Company served as the Masonic Lodge meeting room for decades. Power's father, W. D., had been Worshipful Master in 1928. Most Woodstock businessmen belonged to the Masonic Lodge. The Masons financially supported the community and local charities and encouraged spiritual values. (Courtesy Richard Johnston.)

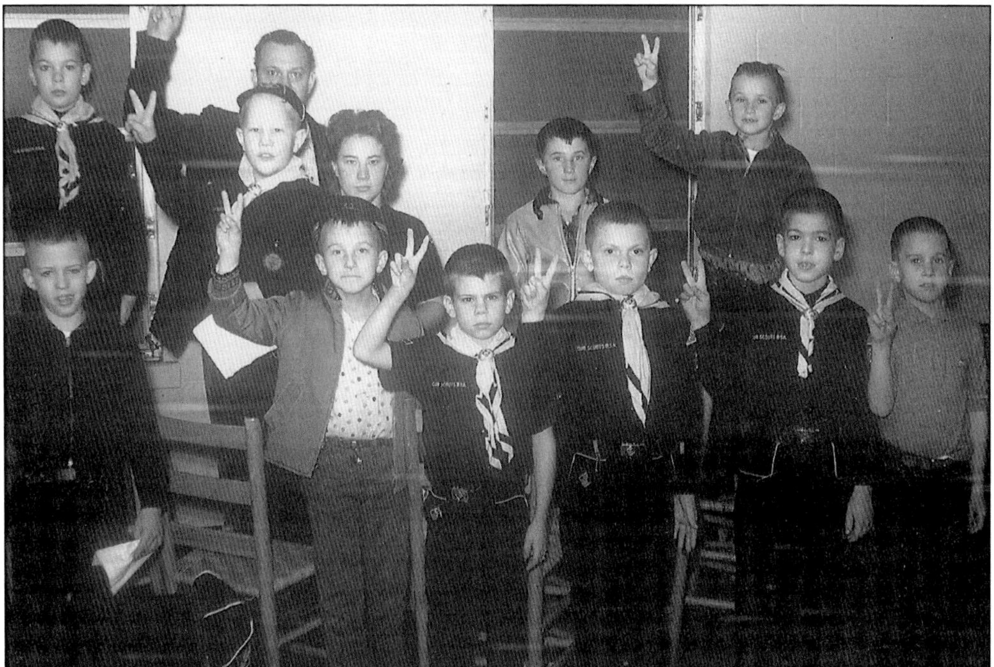

Cub Scouts Troop, Christmas 1962. The troop met at Woodstock Methodist Church for meetings. Pictured from left to right are (first row) Eddie Dawson, Smith Johnston III, Murl Burch, David Keenum, Joe James, and Sonny Ramsay; (second row) three unidentified, Sandra Newborn (leader), Chuck Newborn, and Lane Anderson. (Courtesy of Sara Frances Dial Ramsay.)

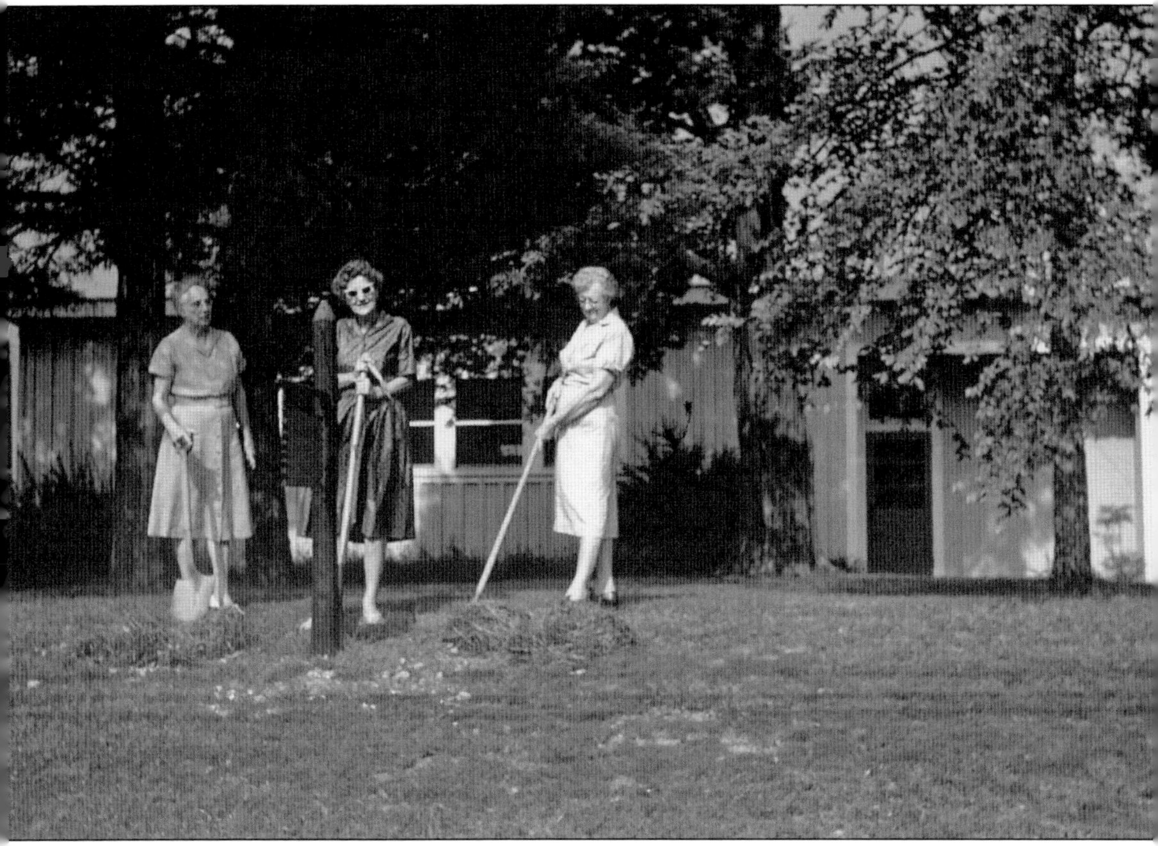

Garden Club, 1962. Woodstock Garden Club members are pictured in front of the Woodstock Community House in 1962. From left to right are Bertie Van Sant, Florine Johnston, and Lucy Booth. Twenty-three charter members organized the Woodstock Garden Club in August 1940. The club's mission was beautification of gardens, yards, and the entire community. The women decided that Woodstock needed a central building for community events. The Garden Club organized funding and planning of the Community House, which was completed in July 1961. The building was constructed on Main Street where a log house had once stood. The women kept a scrapbook of meeting minutes and mementos of their events from 1944 to 1989. (Courtesy of Russ Sims.)

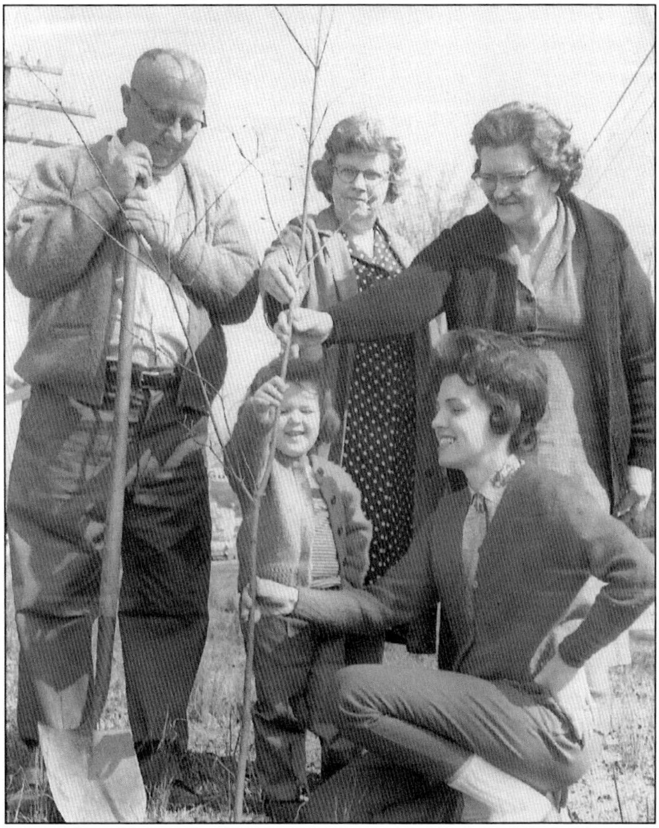

Woodstock Garden Club Members, 1964. From left to right, Hubert McAfee Jr. ("Bo"), Bertha McAfee Barnes, Willie Collins, Millicent Fox, and Carolyn Fox plant trees along the railroad track. (Courtesy of Carolyn Fox Hitt.)

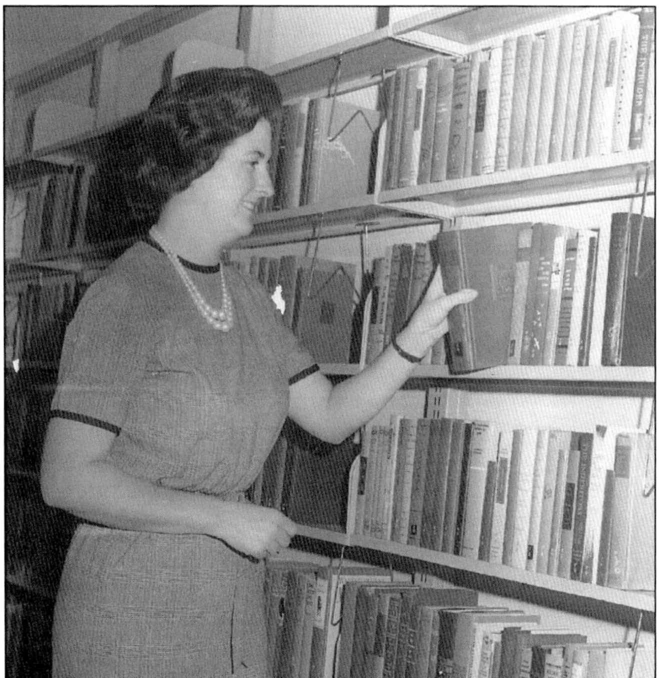

Woodstock Junior Woman's Club Member Sylvia Edwards, March 1964. Edwards shelves books in the new Woodstock Public Library. The city council appointed the first board of trustee members: Elizabeth Johnston, Barbara Ingram, and Sara Frances Ramsay. Because of limited funding, the library opened for only two afternoons and two evenings a week. The library occupied an area of the Johnston Building on the southwest corner of Main and Mill Streets. The library became a branch of the Sequoyah Regional Library System, comprised of Cherokee, Pickens, and Gilmer Counties. (Courtesy of Woodstock Public Library.)

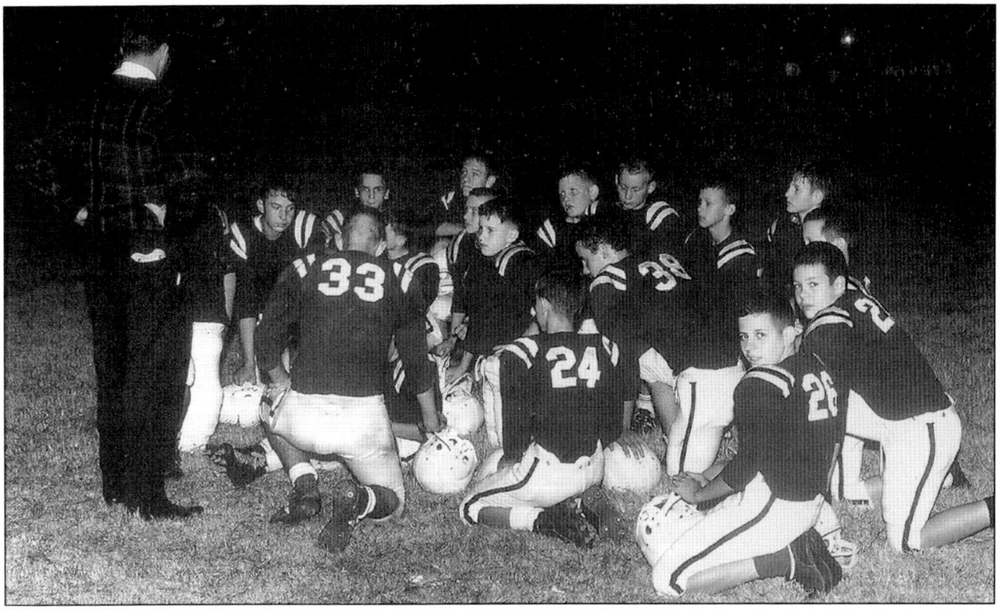

Woodstock Football Players, SCRA Park, 1964. Pictured are coach Young Smith, Bob Edgeworth, Lane Anderson, Joe James, Bobby Croft, Eldridge Bentley, and Marvin Grimes. Others are unidentified. The main goal for SCRA (South Cherokee Recreation Association) was to create a Little League ball field. SCRA became a community effort to create athletic programs for all ages. SCRA was established and incorporated as a nonprofit organization in May 1963, separate from the Cherokee County Parks and Recreation Department. During the 1960s, SCRA sponsored Arabian, English, and halter classes and Western horse shows on the fields. (Courtesy of Carolyn Fox Hitt.)

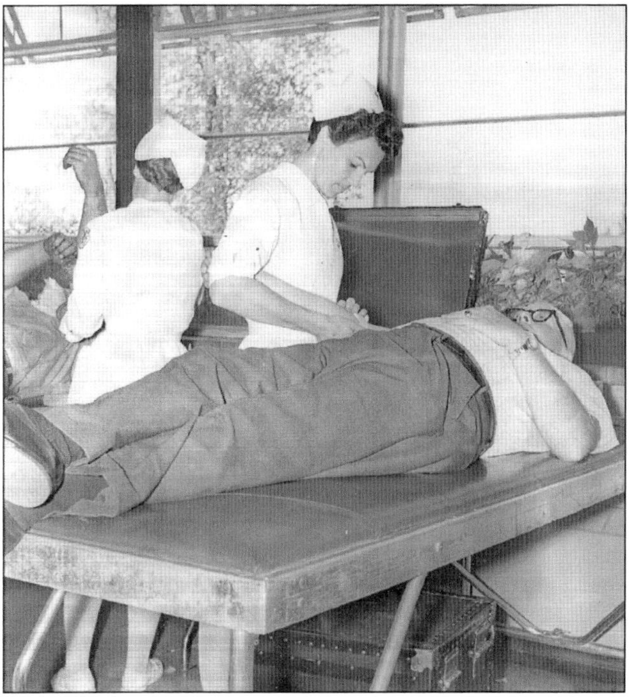

Blood Drive, Woodstock School, 1964. Police chief C. J. Bowles donates blood at Woodstock School cafeteria. He served as Woodstock's only policeman and later became chief of police. He ran for Cherokee County sheriff that same year. (Courtesy of Woodstock Public Library.)

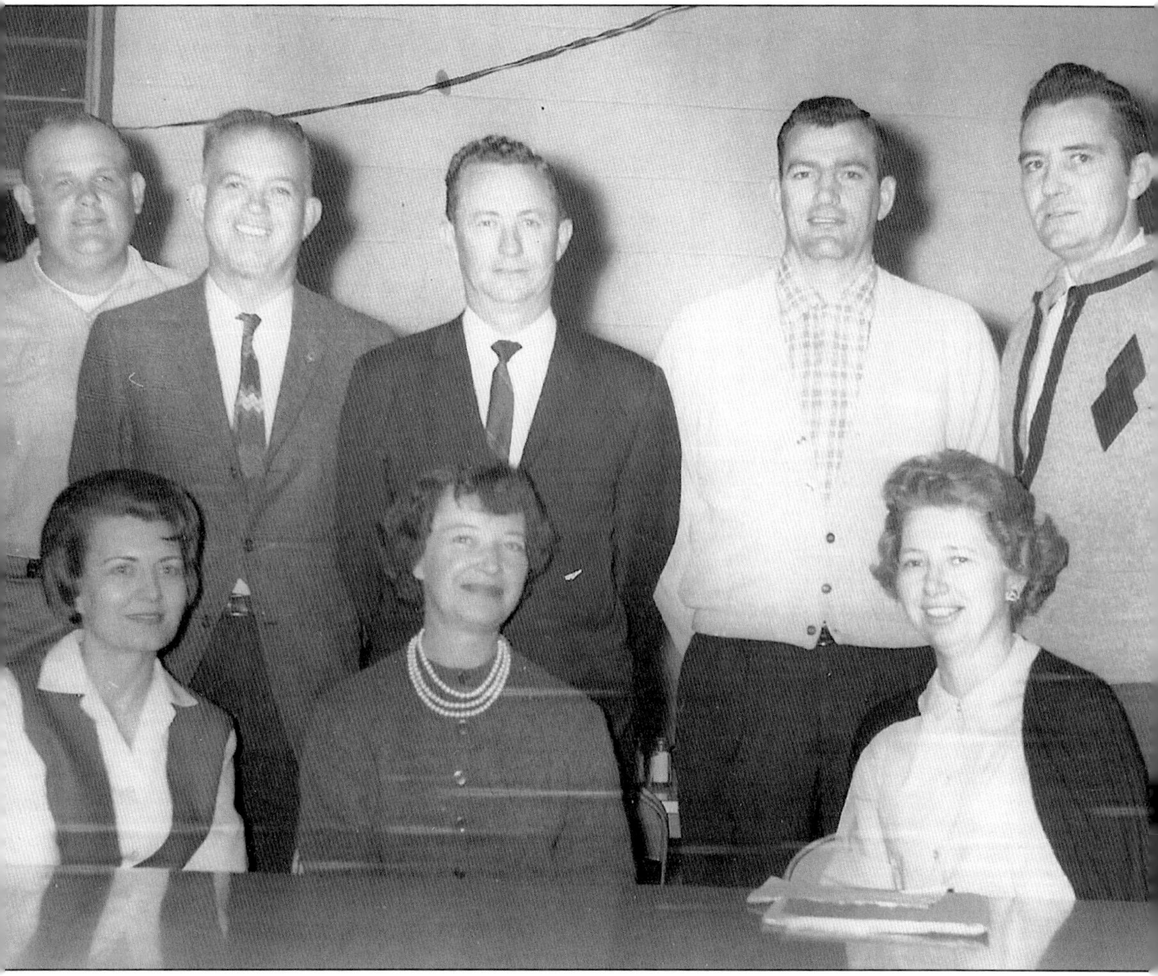

Founding SCRA Directors, 1965–1966. Pictured from left to right are (seated) Sara Poor, Reba Vaughan, and Elizabeth Johnston; (standing) B. E. Roberts, Bill Drinkard, Harold Hames, athletic director Young Smith, and Bob Lewis. Other directors who were not pictured were Howell Stenger and Tom Fowler. Young Smith, ex-paratrooper and teacher at Woodstock Elementary School, coached the football, basketball, and baseball teams. (Courtesy of Jeanne Cosey.)

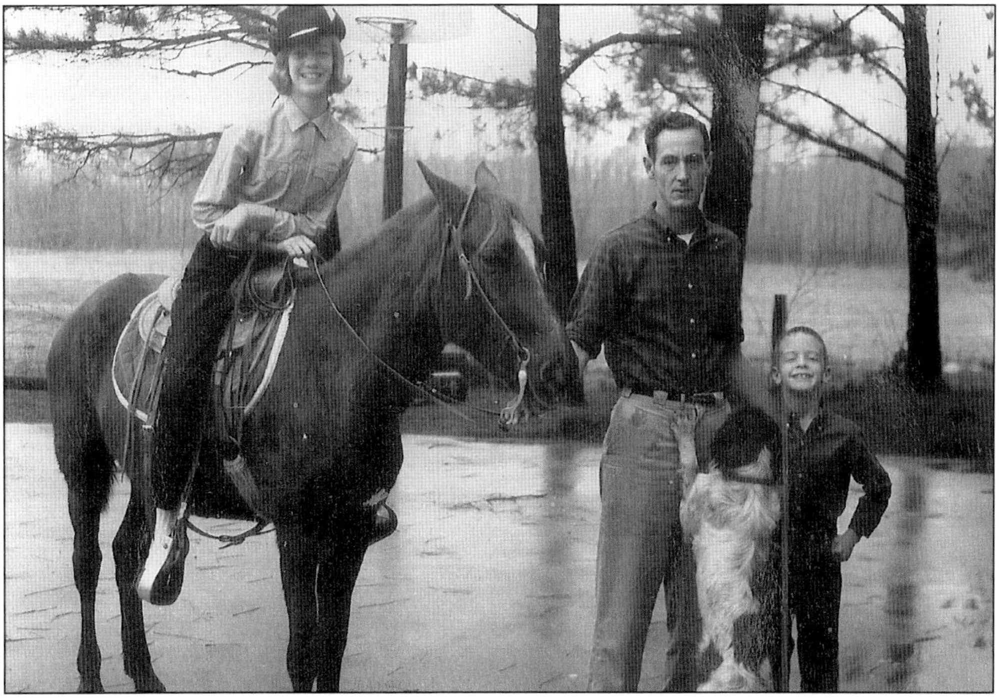

Horse Riding at the Reece Farm, 1965. Merritt Reece owned a cattle farm that was replaced by the Towne Lake/I-575 interchange in 1980. Pictured are, from left to right, Jannis, Merritt, and Dennis Reece with their dog. (Courtesy of Mary Lou Freeman Reece.)

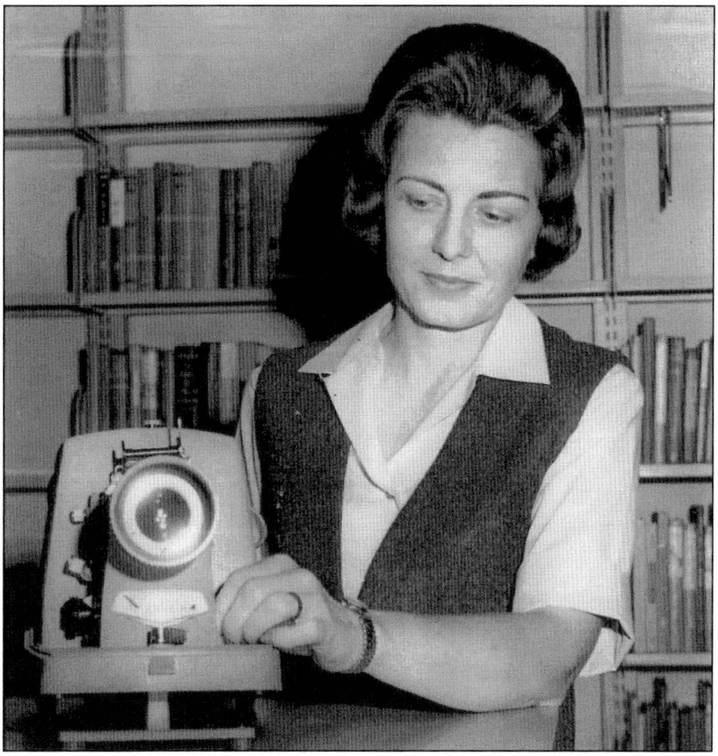

Librarian Sara Poor, 1966. Librarian Sara Poor tries out the library's first audio visual equipment. Poor served as librarian from the day the first library opened in the Johnston Building. The library occupied the Bank of Woodstock building from 1972 to 1989. (Courtesy of Preservation Woodstock, Inc.)

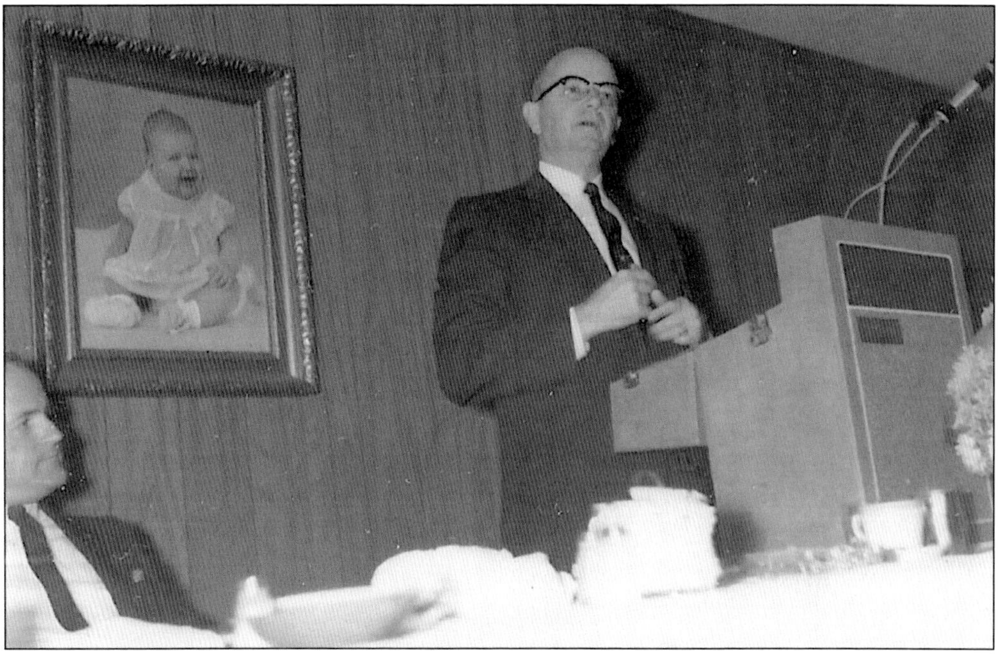

Georgia Governor Lester Maddox, Woodstock Lions Club Meeting, Pine Crest Restaurant, 1967. Maddox became an outspoken adversary of integration in the late 1940s and 1950s. Though opposed to integrating schools, it was the public accommodations provisions of the Civil Rights Act of 1964 that placed Maddox in the national limelight. Elected governor in 1966, Maddox surprisingly appointed many blacks to state boards and commissions and is remembered for regularly scheduling "People's Day" at the capitol so anyone could meet and talk with him. (Courtesy of Preservation Woodstock, Inc.)

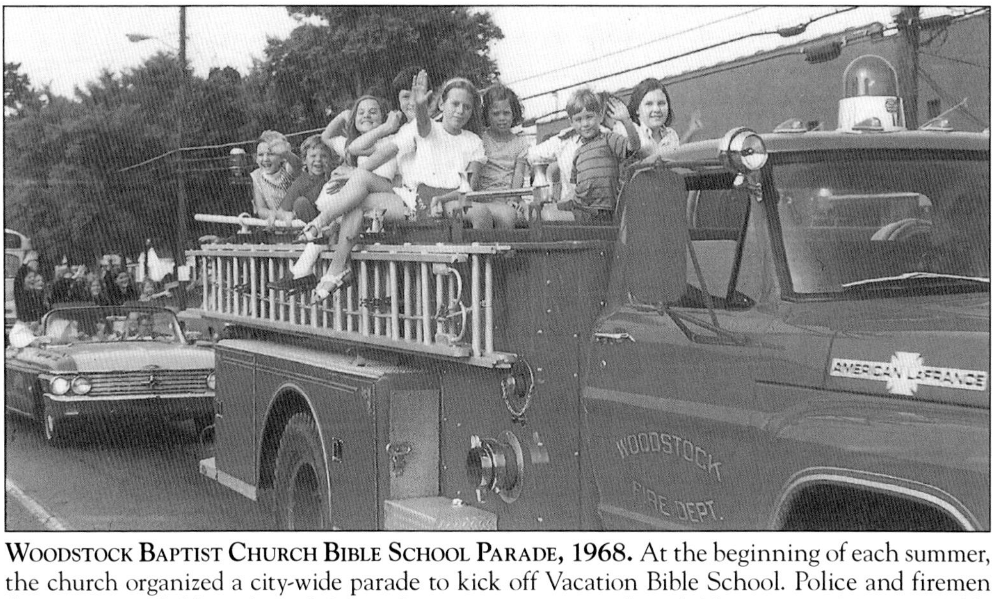

Woodstock Baptist Church Bible School Parade, 1968. At the beginning of each summer, the church organized a city-wide parade to kick off Vacation Bible School. Police and firemen drove waving children through Main Street to encourage other children to join Vacation Bible School. Most of Woodstock's children attended all of the Vacation Bible Schools offered by the community's churches. (Courtesy of Carolyn Fox Hitt.)

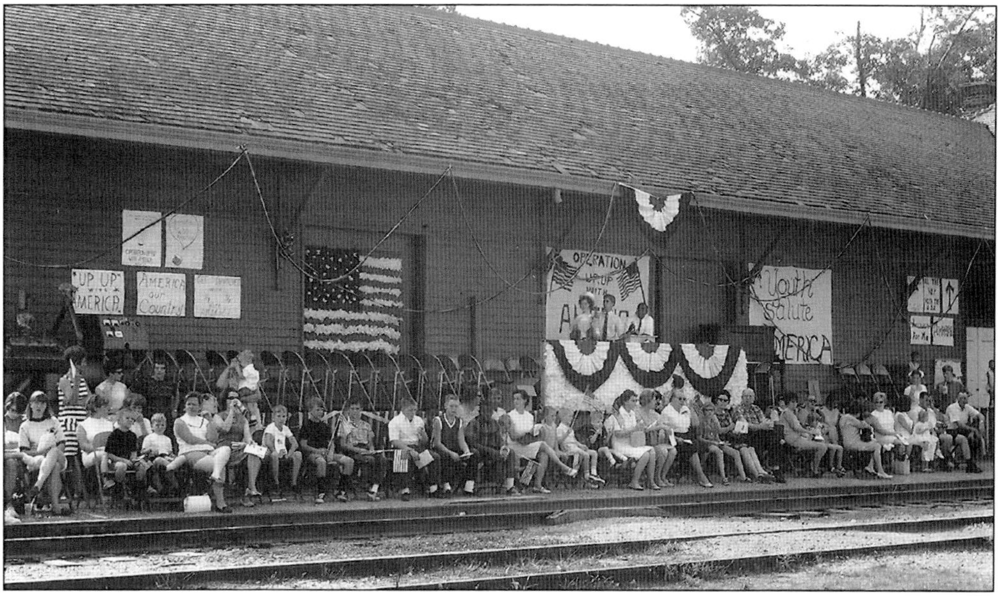

Up, Up With America, August 1968. During the turbulent 1960s, protests of disagreement took place across the country. But in Woodstock, a group of teenagers organized a demonstration to promote America called "Up, Up With America Day" on August 24, 1968. A parade, demonstration, testimonies, marching bands, and a picnic were held in Woodstock. Several political figures, such as Congressman Phil Landrum, and Atlanta television celebrities participated in a parade and rally. The event received media coverage from all the Atlanta television stations as well as coverage in the newspapers. In the photograph below, the boys standing in the truck are David Cleghorn, Frank Poor, and Jeff Cleghorn. Also pictured are, from left to right, Judy Reeves, Millicent Barnes Fox, Carolyn Fox (with hat), Tom Cleghorn (in stroller), Mary Lou Holbert (on knees), Amanda Reece (holding flag), and Sarah Sue Cleghorn. (Both courtesy of Carolyn Fox Hitt.)

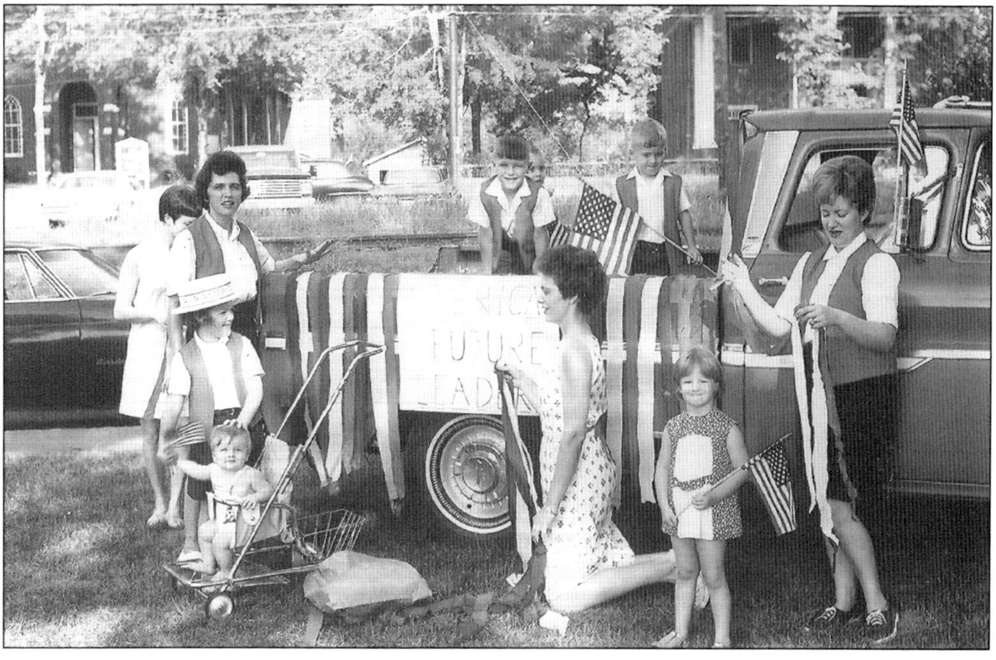

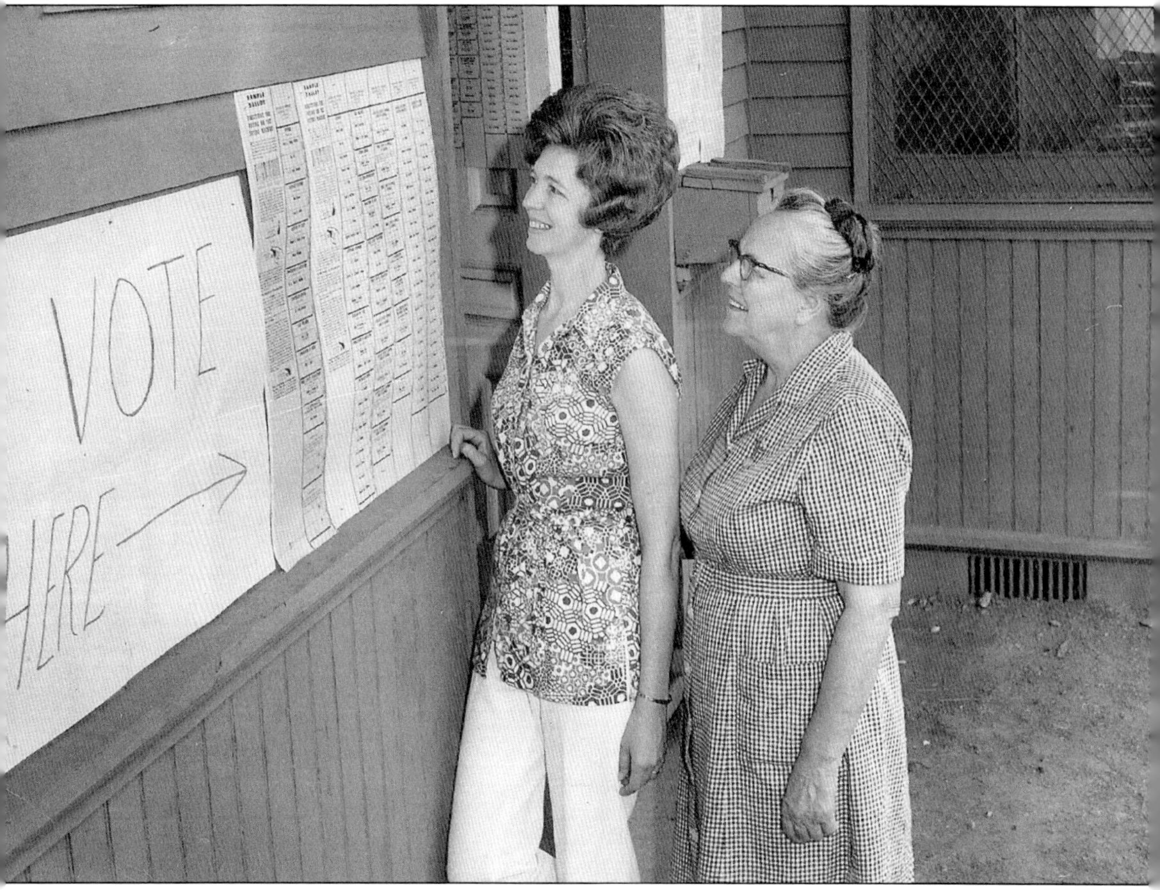

Mary Lou Reece and Mary Howell Review the Voting Ballot for the 1970 Election. Not only did the depot serve as the telegraph station and mail, passenger, and supply stop, it served as the official polling site until the late 1990s. The 1970 election was the first election that voters cast their votes by machine. Jimmy Carter was elected governor in the 1970 election, beating Republican Hal Suit. Carter later became the country's president in 1976. (Courtesy of Mary Lou Freeman Reece.)

Ten

Woodstock's Famous

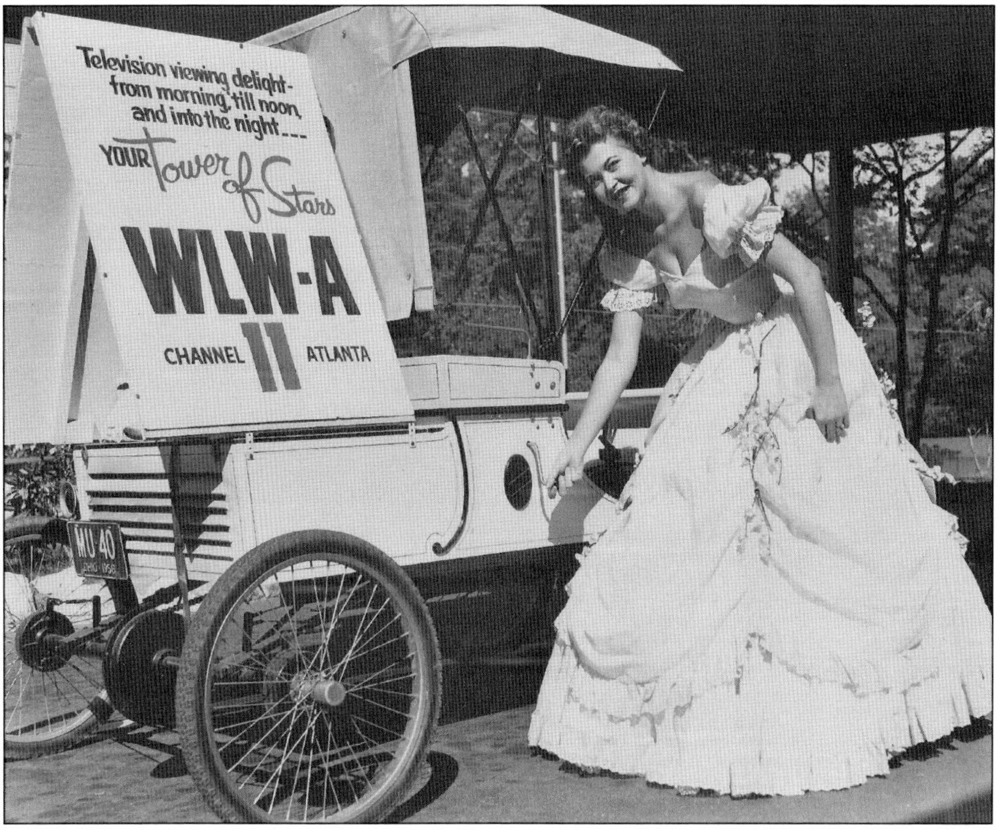

Jeanine Parris, Miss Georgia, 1955. At age 22, Jeanine Parris of the Canton/Woodstock area finished in the top 10 at the Miss America Pageant in 1955. She won 30 other beauty titles and later attended modeling school and worked in radio, television, and newspaper. Her mother created her pageant gowns. She resided in Woodstock until her death in the 1990s. (Courtesy of Karen Smithwick.)

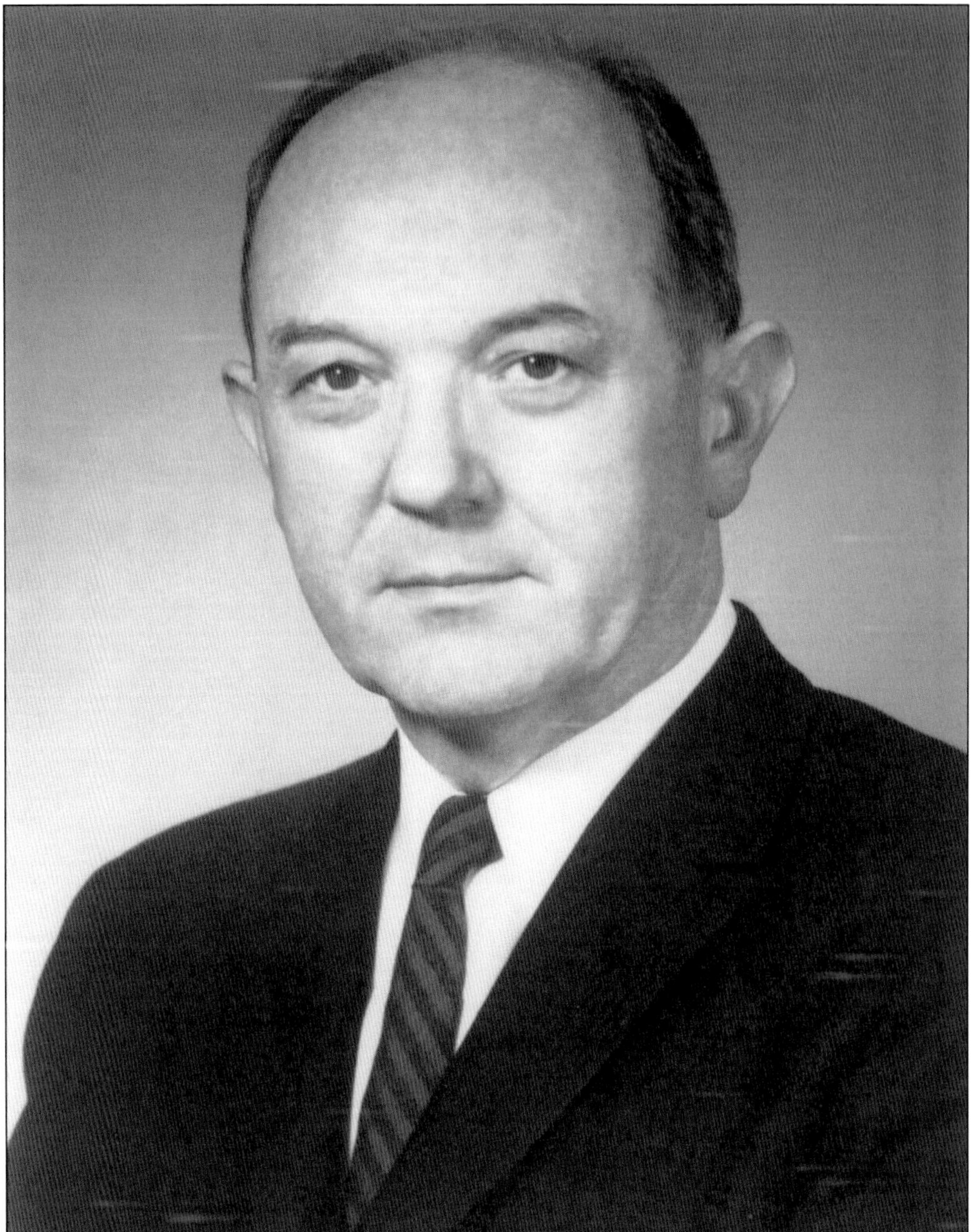

Dean Rusk, Former Secretary of State, 1961 to 1969. Born on a cotton farm near Little River in 1909, Rusk rose to become secretary of state during the Kennedy and Johnson administrations. He attended St. John's College in Oxford as a Rhodes Scholar and received the Cecil Peace Prize in 1933. Rusk's grandfather Col. James Edward Rusk served in the Confederate army and settled on a farm east of Woodstock. Colonel Rusk also served as a state senator 1886 to 1887. As secretary of state, Dean Rusk was involved with policies surrounding the Bay of Pigs, the Cuban Missile Crisis, and the cold war. He was the second longest serving secretary of state. The current Dean Rusk Middle School is named in his honor. (Courtesy of Marilyn Dobbs Morrell.)

Eugene T. Booth Jr., Rhodes Scholar and Scientist. Son of E. T. Booth, Eugene Jr. attended Oxford, University of Georgia, and Columbia University. While teaching at Columbia, he worked on splitting the atom. He later worked on the Manhattan Project, which led to the development of the atomic bomb. He set up research in Italy for submarine work with NATO and then conducted research for American Optical Company. He worked with Leon M. Lederman, Nobel Prize winner in physics, on a project in 1948 when Booth was a professor and director of the cyclotron project. Some of Booth's writings are stored at the Smithsonian Institution Archives. (Courtesy of Preservation Woodstock, Inc.)

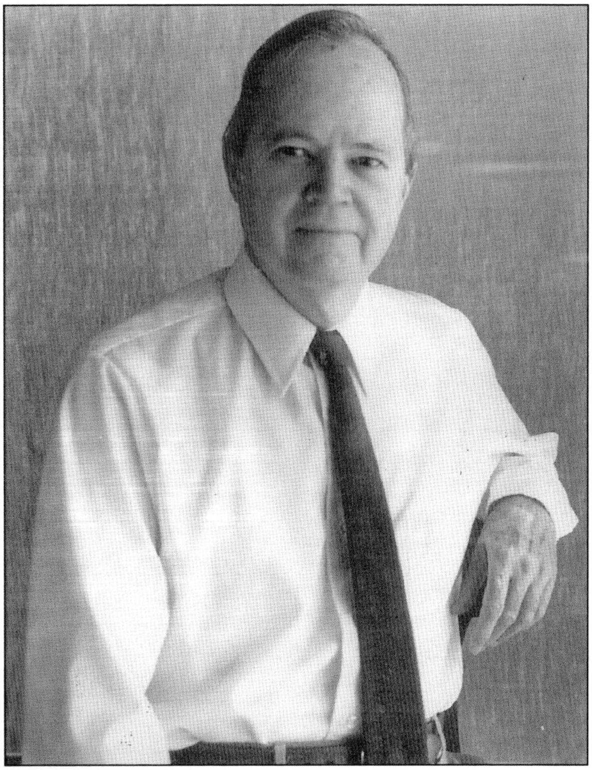

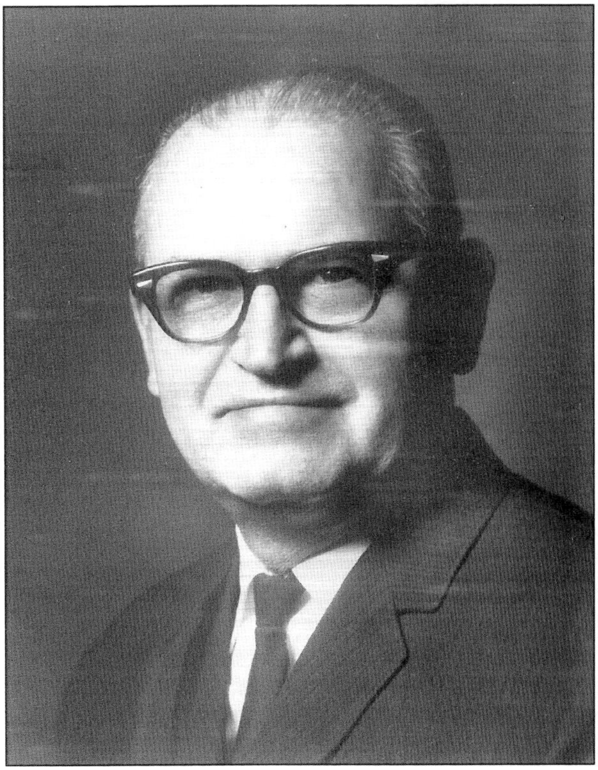

Miller D. Barnes, Architect, 1965. Graduate of Georgia Tech in 1932 with a bachelor of science degree in architecture, Barnes practiced architecture in Atlanta for 30 years. He helped design many landmark buildings that mark the skyline of Atlanta, such as the Atlanta/Fulton County Stadium. Barnes served as Woodstock's mayor in 1959 and designed the Woodstock Community Center. (Courtesy of Millicent Barnes Fox.)

Consistent with our mission to preserve history on a local level, this book was printed in South Carolina on American-made paper and manufactured entirely in the United States. Products carrying the accredited Forest Stewardship Council (FSC) label are printed on 100 percent FSC-certified paper.

MADE IN THE USA